Prairie
Justice

Prairie Justice

A History of Illinois Courts under French, English & American Law

Roger L. Severns

Edited by John A. Lupton

Southern Illinois University Press
Carbondale

18 17 16 15   4 3 2 1

The publication of this book has been made possible through a generous donation from the Illinois Supreme Court Legal History Society.

Jacket illustrations: five new justices, all Democrats, added to the Illinois Supreme Court when the Democratic-controlled legislature expanded the court from four to nine members, including (*from left*) Sidney Breese, Thomas Ford, Samuel H. Treat, Walter B. Scates, and Stephen A. Douglas. Illinois Supreme Court Historic Preservation Commission. *Background*, page from *Registre des Insinuations des Donations*, 1750, cropped. Perrin Collection, Illinois State Archives.

Library of Congress Cataloging-in-Publication Data
Severns, Roger L., 1906–1961, author.
Prairie justice : a history of Illinois courts under French, English, and American law / Roger L. Severns ; edited by John A Lupton ; foreword by Dennis Rendleman.
pages cm
Includes bibliographical references and index.
ISBN 978-0-8093-3369-1 (hardback)—ISBN 0-8093-3369-4 (cloth)—ISBN 978-8093-3370-7 (ebook) 1. Courts—Illinois—History. I. Lupton, John A., 1966– editor. II. Title.
KFI1278.S48 2015
347.773'0109—dc23   2014017074

Printed on recycled paper. ♻

The paper used in this publication meets the minimum requirements of American National Standard for Information Sciences—Permanence of Paper for Printed Library Materials, ANSI Z39.48-1992. ∞

Contents

List of Illustrations   vii

Foreword   ix
Dennis A. Rendleman

Editor's Introduction   xv

Illustrations

Foreword
Dennis A. Rendleman

ON THURSDAY, APRIL 29, 1959, the *Chicago Daily Law Bulletin* announced on page one: "'Prairie Justice'—an intriguing account of the development of law in Illinois from its earliest days—will be published in serial form in the Chicago Daily Law Bulletin, starting with a special introduction in the Bulletin's Law Day issue on Thursday, April 30."[1]

Not long after I became associated with the Illinois Supreme Court Legal Historical Society in the early 1990s, I was presented with a loose-leaf binder, filled with yellowing newspaper clippings from a colleague at the Illinois State Bar Association (ISBA). Karen Davidson, who had worked at ISBA since she was a teenager, thought I might be interested in these articles. They had been published in the paper when she worked in the ISBA publication department in the 1950s. She had saved the clippings but didn't know anything else about the articles.

To say I was interested was an understatement. At the same time, I was also baffled that the newspaper articles had never resulted in publication as a book. And thus began a long—not quite historic—process of researching both the origins of the manuscript and the life of the author, as well as the effort to publish and distribute the manuscript. Similarly, this dual mission to research the origin and publish the manuscript tracks the simple life span of several good ideas that never fully matured on their own, but, now, after long fermentation, have finally come to fruition.

The History of the Lost History

In March 1990, Richard E. Friedman announced the newly formed corporate entity called the Illinois Supreme Court Legal Historical Society. Original officers were Richard E. Friedman, Olive Foster, Cheryl Niro, Carolyn Taitt, and Dennis Rendleman. The Society was established to promote and encourage educational research of Illinois legal historical matters as a 501(c)(3) not-for-profit organization. The group began funding with a grant from the Philip H. Corboy Foundation, which was followed by limited fundraising from 52 individuals that federal tax law required. Subsequently, the Illinois Bar Foundation made a grant to help fund preparation and publication of the *Prairie Justice* manuscript.[2]

However, this was the early 1990s at the height of the Lincoln Legal Papers Project (now Papers of Abraham Lincoln), and the focus of legal history in Illinois was firmly centered on the monumental task of looking for courthouse documents connected to Abraham Lincoln. This extraordinary and important Lincoln project tended to suck the air out of other legal historical efforts. Consequently, the Illinois Supreme Court Legal Historical Society never found its footing. Now, fortunately, the Illinois Supreme Court Historic Preservation Commission has come into existence. Established under the Illinois Supreme Court Historic Preservation Act in 2007 by the Illinois General Assembly, there is, at long last, a formal legal mandate to preserve the judicial history of Illinois. In the Commission there is a focused effort to assist and advise the Supreme Court in this mission.[3] As its last, best act, the Society is collaborating with the Commission in the publication of *Prairie Justice: A History of Illinois Courts under French, English, and American Law.*

The history of the manuscript is almost as interesting as the history told by the manuscript. And the research on the manuscript's history continues. Recently discovered articles in the *Chicago Daily Law Bulletin* have disclosed that *Prairie Justice* began as a project of the Illinois State Bar Association. According to an introduction to the serial version of the manuscript published in the 1950s, the ISBA assigned its Committee on History to undertake the writing of a history of the Illinois Supreme Court ... in 1933![4]

To support the saying that "a camel is a horse designed by a committee," no evidence has been found of the work product of the august team, which, over time, included a former governor, former justices, and other legal dignitaries.[5]

However, the connection between ISBA, the *Law Bulletin*, and Roger Severns was mysterious. The answer arrived through the discovery of a 1955 roster for the Illinois State Bar Association Committee on Legal History and Biography showing Roger L. Severns as a member. Further, a biographic statement prepared in 1959 provided by his son William states that the manuscript was prepared "under contract with Illinois State Bar Association."[6] Thus the connection between ISBA and Severns is established but not fully explained.

We have not discovered the reason for the project's publication in the *Chicago Daily Law Bulletin* and lack of publication in book form. There is also a curious statement in the Editor's Note to the Introduction in the *Law Bulletin* stating that the ISBA Committee on Legal History and Biography was disbanded in 1956 "when its work was completed." Is this intended to mean that Severns completed *Prairie Justice* in 1956?

It should be noted as well that edited excerpts from the manuscript were published in the *Illinois Bar Journal* in January and March 1968, as an Illinois Sesquicentennial Feature titled "Illinois Courts Prior to Statehood."[7] It is exciting finally to bring this manuscript to book form.

Roger L. Severns

The formal biography of Roger Severns, which I prepared to accompany the manuscript and which was approved by his son William in 2000, reads thus:

Roger L. Severns is the author of a volume on the history of law and the legal system in Illinois and the northwest, which he prepared under a contract with the Illinois State Bar Association.

Mr. Severns dedicated hours of laborious research in producing *Prairie Justice*. He traveled to courthouses across the state to review archives, old files, family papers, or anything he heard about that could be of value . . . most of this information seemed to be housed in out-of-the-way or obscure places. He often took his family with him on his research trips. His son, William, remembers his parents discussing their stay in a "seedy hotel somewhere in the area of Kaskaskia . . . while dad was gathering material from ancient repositories . . . we looked down through a heat vent to see some men playing cards, one of whom was twirling a revolver around his finger. Those were not the days of interstates and Super 8s."

Roger L. Severns was born in Centralia, Illinois, on January 20, 1906, and moved to Chicago in 1908. He received his Bachelor of Arts degree in 1927 from Beloit College; attended Chicago Kent College of Law from 1929 through 1933, receiving his Bachelor of Laws Degree in 1932 and his Master of Laws Degree in 1933. He then attended the University of Chicago Law School and received his Juris Doctor Degree, cum laude, in 1938.

In 1933, Severns accepted a position as Assistant Professor of Law at Chicago Kent and in 1934 became Associate Professor of Law at Kent where he taught Conflict of Laws, Constitutional Law, Trusts, Equity, and graduate seminars on legal philosophy and administrative law. He continued teaching at Chicago Kent and in 1944 he became associated with the law firm of Isham, Lincoln & Beale. He left Isham, Lincoln & Beale in 1956 to form Parkhill, Severns and Stansell. He continued to practice law and teach at Kent until he became ill with cancer in the fall of 1960. He died on June 16, 1961, in Chicago and is buried in Oak Woods Cemetery.

Mr. Severns's many community activities included work with the Hyde Park Neighborhood Club, a charitable organization working with children and teens who lack recreational and educational facilities.

Mr. Severns was married to Margaret L. Lauritzen in 1932 had two sons, Roger L. Severns Jr., and William L. Severns.

I have subsequently discovered that Severns was also an author of other scholarly publications. In 1940, he published "Equity and 'Fusion' in Illinois" in the *Chicago-Kent Law Review*.[8] This, too, was historical in nature in that it covered the merger of law and equity from their prior existence as two separate legal systems into one civil system with two separate divisions. This was a major development in jurisprudence and had been ongoing in the United States since the mid-nineteenth century. In Illinois, this "fusion" did not finally occur until 1934. Severns also wrote several other law review articles discussing equity and equitable jurisdiction.

Finally, we know that Severns was appointed to the Metropolitan Sanitary District of Greater Chicago in 1958, but was not reelected. He was an unsuccessful Republican candidate for Probate Judge of Cook County in 1954 and for Circuit Judge of Cook County in 1958.

Conclusion

Prairie Justice is a remarkable discovery. It provides us with a concise history of the Illinois law and courts from the first white settlers to the beginning of the twentieth century. Second, it provides us with a snapshot of the mid-twentieth century through Roger Severns's scholarship. Third, *Prairie*

Justice is a thought-provoking read. It encourages the reader to dig more into the characters and events that created Illinois' legal history.

And, it is a happy ending. Publication of *Prairie Justice* fulfills the mission of the Illinois Supreme Court Legal Historical Society and, as William Severns said in his letter to me in 2000, "I am glad to hear there is a possibility of a republication. . . . I was concerned that all the years of work that my father put into it would be wasted."[9]

Alas, the *cri de coeur* of every historian.

Editor's Introduction

ONE PIECE OF LITERATURE missing from the vast and interesting history of Illinois is a concise narrative of the judicial branch. Several histories of Illinois touch on legal and judicial aspects but never as the constant thread throughout the work.[1] Legal history in general and court histories, specifically, are a burgeoning sub-discipline with several state court histories and federal court histories published in recent years.[2] Surprisingly, there has been no narrative of Illinois' legal history.[3] As a growing state in the antebellum period, Illinois established itself as an important part of the Union. From its early days in the French colonial period to its unique situation among the Midwestern states, Illinois influenced the law in many other states. Its rich agricultural economy combined with unprecedented urban growth created many legal issues that the Illinois judiciary had to resolve, creating a blueprint for other states to follow.

Roger L. Severns's work is part traditional "bench and bar" and part innovative historical interpretation. Nearly all county histories produced in the late nineteenth and early twentieth century contained a chapter giving a short history of the courthouses, providing short biographies of prominent lawyers and judges, and including some of the more interesting cases that had occurred in that county. The best example is former governor John M. Palmer's *Bench and Bar of Illinois*, which presented chapters on nearly every county in Illinois in two large volumes to give an overview of the early lawyers and judges in the state.[4] Severns retains this simple formula but goes beyond it to include narrative that blends discussion of the leaders of the

Illinois judiciary with deeper analysis of the evolution and importance of the Illinois legal system. The end product is an engaging examination of the development of law in Illinois from the French colonial period through the end of the nineteenth century.

The book begins in the French settlements along the Mississippi River in the early eighteenth century and examines several cases that occurred under the Custom of Paris, the body of laws that migrated from France to the New World. After the Seven Years' War ended in 1763, the legal landscape of the Illinois region was thrown into turmoil as the British had little interest in cultivating a legal culture in a distant and sparsely populated area. After the Revolutionary War, Virginia possessed the area as a county but ceded its claims when the new United States passed the Northwest Ordinance in 1787. The Northwest Ordinance established the legal principles of the states from the old Northwest and beyond, introducing American law to the frontier. The Illinois country became a part of the Indiana Territory and then the Illinois Territory. Many new lawyers moved into the area; some stayed, some moved on. Once Illinois became a state in 1818, the Illinois Supreme Court began its work as one of three branches of government. Political factions grew from strong personalities in the 1820s as the state wrestled with important questions of slavery and economic development. Early Supreme Court cases reflected the legal issues of the day. Many of these cases concerned economic uncertainty, but a few had larger implications. By the 1850s, the Supreme Court had begun to establish itself as a co-equal branch of government after a new constitution removed the election process from the legislature to the voting public. In the post–Civil War period, the Supreme Court matured with capable jurists establishing important legal doctrine in a rapidly changing economy and social order.

Severns performed substantial research in Illinois court records in old county courthouses, the Illinois State Archives, and manuscript collections. The result is one of the first major legal history works to use lower court records to create an interpretive narrative for the French and territorial periods in Illinois history. In the statehood period, however, Severns relies on the Illinois Supreme Court Reports, a published collection of decisions by the Court, to illustrate trends in the Illinois judiciary. An examination of circuit court records may have shown a different view of the depth and breadth of the great majority of cases in Illinois. While the book roughly ends at 1900, the last major cases Severns noted were the 1873 case *Munn v. Illinois*, one of the Granger cases that gave the state regulation powers over private businesses with public interests, and the 1887 case *Spies v. People*, the Haymarket case that upheld the death sentence for convicted anarchists. Severns failed to note a number of other important cases from the late nineteenth century that prove his point of an independent and influential judiciary with cases that resonated well beyond the Illinois borders.[5]

Despite these omissions, as readers, we should not judge Severns too harshly and constantly remind ourselves that we are reading a book that was written in the 1950s. Severns should be commended for his laborious research, his well-written narrative, and for creating an excellent contribution to the legal/historical literature. In the 1950s, authors were not discussing the legal problems of women on the frontier, the simple debt cases between merchants and farmers, or the legal system's response to the social and economic issues of antebellum Illinois, except for those few cases that appeared on the appellate level.

Severns's book, written in the 1950s, places it in a different interpretive paradigm than legal history works of today. Only in the 1950s did the sub-discipline of legal history begin to emerge with the scholarship of J. Willard Hurst. Hurst rejected the study of legal doctrine and encouraged the study of the law as an additional component in a larger society. Severns cites Hurst's earlier, but lesser-known, *Growth of the American Law*,[6] but we do not know if he was aware of Hurst's groundbreaking *Law and the Conditions of Freedom*, published in 1956, as Severns did not cite it. The Hurst school of thought, stated in *Law and the Conditions of Freedom*, is that the law served to "release economic energies" to benefit men in all fields.[7] Severns gives credit to the legislatures for creating the body of the law, but his emphasis is on the power and growth of the courts, citing Hurst to show the tension between the two branches of government.

Equally as important, Hurst reminded readers that most, if not all, legal history written prior to the 1950s was East Coast oriented and that the law that worked in Massachusetts and Virginia did not necessarily translate to the Midwest and beyond.[8] Severns presents a legal history of arguably the most important Midwestern state and how its law was certainly the offspring of the European, Upland South, and East Coast body of law, but because of its geography and diversity, that it developed a new and geographic-specific body of law. Illinois is merely a stop on the progression of law from the East to the West.[9]

Severns subscribes to Hurst's ideology but not entirely to his methodology. In discussing the maturation of the Illinois Supreme Court, Severns agrees with Hurst that the law gave order to the chaos that society and the economy presented with land cases and railroad cases in both urban and rural environments. Severns mostly examined, however, Illinois Supreme Court cases and the doctrines they established. In ways, the book that Severns wrote fits perfectly with the context of the time in which he wrote it, but in other ways, Severns was ahead of his time. While Severns examines slavery-related cases, gender and women's rights, labor and class, and economy and wealth, those topics are not the central focus of his book. What Severns created is a hybrid of the bench and bar, social history, and political history of Illinois' legal system that fits, yet does not fit, with the school of thought that Hurst posited in the 1950s.

If Severns is ahead of his time in some respects, does *Prairie Justice* fit with the ideas of legal scholars that came after him: Morton Horwitz, Kermit Hall, and Peter Karsten? Morton Horwitz argued that the nineteenth-century legal system had been manipulated to favor economic growth of corporations and capitalism—a Marxist view of American legal history that became prevalent in the 1960s and 1970s. As social history also became more prevalent during that same period, Kermit Hall synthesized social history with legal history to explain the law as both proactive and reactive to the needs of the population at large. After the fall of the Soviet Union and Communism, an expected counter to Horwitz began to occur, culminating in the publication of Peter Karsten's *Heart versus Head*, which argued that "[c]ontinuity, not change" best describes the work of nineteenth-century jurists who applied rules to real people and not to altering doctrine for the benefit of the moneyed classes.[10]

Severns's ideas can be found in some of these later works. He certainly examines social history issues when discussing the French period in Illinois' legal history and reaches his conclusions by examining original French records. While the records do not follow typical lawsuits that would arrive with English-speaking pioneers, Severns is able to weave an excellent story and interpretation from the scant documentation. Marxist theory is nowhere to be found in Severns's book. There are no collusions to improve the wealthy at the expense of the poor. Severns appears to support best Karsten's ideas regarding judges and their treatment of the law to real-world problems that faced Illinoisans. Karsten particularly focused his research on Midwestern and Southern courts—and Illinois, as perhaps the most typical Midwestern state, enjoys a large share of Karsten's attention.

There has been a wealth of legal history published since 1959, and the audience needs to be aware of it as it pertains to Illinois' legal history. Legal history has blossomed because historians now have easier access to original trial court records. The Illinois Regional Archives Depository system of the Illinois State Archives is an excellent avenue to court records. Docket books and case files are stored in proper archival conditions, and indexes allow easier access to a great variety of cases to give researchers that very important window into life in any given period of time. This avenue did not exist in the 1950s when Severns researched.

The publication of Abraham Lincoln's legal papers is an excellent example of the creation of a body of original legal source material that spawned new research.[11] Since the original publication of the DVD edition of Lincoln's law practice in 2000, there have been at least seven books published on some aspect of Lincoln's legal career. Most of the books have Abraham Lincoln as the principal subject, but Daniel W. Stowell's *In Tender Consideration* has Lincoln in the background while the contributors examine women in the courtroom, inheritance issues, and children in court proceedings.[12] In addition to the great value of learning more about our sixteenth president, researchers of the Lincoln Legal Papers archive can better understand what life was like for farmers, merchants, women, and children of the antebellum Illinois period.

In addition to the publication of seminal works by Hurst, Horwitz, Hall, and Karsten, authors began to look more closely at trial court proceedings and specific areas of law, such as women's experiences, the profession of law generally, and individual cases.[13] Placing Severns's book into a continuum that exists after he wrote it perhaps is a slight disservice to him and the contribution he makes. Severns was one of the first—if not the first—author to examine the history of state's judicial system. This groundbreaking work, if published at the time, certainly would have inspired future work. Severns, of course, only scratched the surface of Illinois legal history. There are millions of stories to be told about the social, economic, and legal history of Illinois.

Editorial Method

When Dennis Rendleman presented me this manuscript, I read through it and was immediately interested, recognizing the lack of a legal history of the Prairie State. Rendleman and Donna Schechter took great pains in the 1990s to transcribe the original *Chicago Daily Law Bulletin* serial publication and to compile it into a single manuscript document. Fortunately, thanks to Rendleman, I did not have to re-transcribe the original articles nor use OCR technology to capture the words. To make sure that all words were captured from the original transcription process, I performed a visual collation of the original *Law Bulletin* articles with the Rendleman manuscript.

In the 1990s, Rendleman made significant effort to have the manuscript published, and he assembled photographs of judges, courthouses, and maps.

While the manuscript did not need additional historical research, it lacked a connection with modern historiography. My role as the editor was to alert the reader to more modern books and articles that Severns could have used had he written this book today. To bring the *Prairie Justice* manuscript to a modern audience, the editor added more recent secondary source material in the endnotes. In updating notes, the editor did not delete any of Severns's original footnotes but simply added books and articles published after 1959 to give the reader direction to more recent historical literature and to place the manuscript within a more modern historiography. The editor did not distinguish between the original and the additional notes, but the reader, by simple publication dates, will be able to determine the new material. The editor also employed consistent treatment to the style of the original footnotes, in many cases having to locate the book or article used by the author and converting the notes from a 1950s legal style to a modern *Chicago Manual* style.

The order of the original manuscript remains as Severns published it in the *Law Bulletin*. The only major deviation was to combine his chapters 2 and 3 into one chapter since both of his chapters were fairly small and were easily combined into the singular topic of the development, or lack thereof, of law from the end of the Seven Years' War to the Territorial period.

My most important role as editor was not to rewrite Severns's ideas but to make the words stronger and more readable. The editor strengthened the manuscript by improving Severns's writing style and by modernizing some archaic language that was commonplace in the 1950s. The great majority of writing style changes included the elimination of a good number of compound sentences in favor of simpler, more direct sentences and the elimination of many, but not all, instances of passive voice in favor of active voice. The resulting manuscript is stronger with Severns's assertions more prominent than before.

The work, the research, and the credit belong to Roger Severns. Dennis Rendleman and I are simply conduits through which the publication could take place. My role as editor was not to reinterpret Roger Severns's claims, not to rewrite completely Roger Severns's language, and not to redo Roger Severns's work. As editor, my role was simply to take an excellent piece of legal history, to tweak it for better readability, and to update the historical literature. Severns devoted a significant amount of time to creating this work. Rendleman devoted a significant amount of time compiling this work, and I am happy to have spent a significant amount of time to present it to legal scholars, students, lawyers, judges, and interested people of Illinois history.

Prairie
Justice

1. *"Whose Home Is in the Wilderness"*

"WILL YOU PROMISE, before God, to speak the truth concerning the matters I shall ask you about?" Michel Chassin, member of the Provincial Council, looked up from the documents before him to ask the question of the Black prisoner who faced him nervously on the other side of the table. Even before he finished speaking, the quill pen in the hand of Perillau, the *greffier*[1] or clerk-recorder, seated at the desk nearby, scratched as he began to record the question. The sentry on guard just inside the door of the room shifted uncomfortably in the afternoon heat of late August. Outside, the shadows lengthened across the parade ground enclosed by the earthen walls of Fort Chartres. Beyond the walls was the wilderness, the dark forests, and wild prairies of the Illinois country. A hundred yards west of the fort flowed the wide Mississippi, the yellow water reflecting the brilliance of the afternoon sun.[2]

It was the year 1725. Chassin and Perillau administered justice in the name of the King of France and of Navarre at Fort Chartres, seat of government in the Illinois district of the Province of Louisianne. Justice was being administered according to rules of law through the forms of the French inquisitorial procedure.

Fort Chartres was a lonely post. A few scattered houses clustered near its walls in the parish of Ste. Anne. Some thirty miles to the south was the town of Kaskaskia. Fortune would soon make it a capital city under three flags. North along the Great River[3] a little farther away, was the village of Cahokia, destined one day to stand alone against anarchy. The river was the highway that joined these wilderness villages to the French colonial empire.

Two thousand miles north and east, over the portages and through the Great Lakes was Quebec on its high rock, then at the peak of its brilliance as the capital of New France. A thousand miles south through the wide valley of the Mississippi was New Orleans, the seat of government of the Province of Louisianne. These were twin capitals, exemplifying the divided authority that in future days contributed largely to the fall of France in America.

To the east and to the west of the river was the wilderness, full of mystery and danger. Kaskaskia and Cahokia were truly villages beyond the frontier. The line of settlement advancing steadily from the eastern ocean would not reach them for many years.

The loneliness of his situation was not concealed by the humor in Michel Chassin's letter to Pontchartrain, the King's Minister of the Marine far away in Paris, when he wrote of his need for feminine companionship:

> You see, Monseigneur, that nothing is wanting now to make a solid
> settlement in Louisiana but a certain piece of furniture which one
> often repents having got, and with which I shall dispense, like the rest,
> till the Company sends us girls who have at least some show of virtue.
> If there happens to be any young woman of your acquaintance who
> wants to make the voyage for love of me, I should be much obliged to
> her, and would do my best to show her my gratitude.[4]

More than two centuries have passed since Chassin wrote his wistful letter. And it is more than two hundred years since justice was administered according to law in the first permanent settlements in the mid-continent.[5]

The story of how law is established in a new country, how it develops, and who and what are the people who make and mold it, is an important part of that country's history. Law must be imperfect, being a human endeavor. But law will reflect through changing times the ideals and aspirations of a people.

This is the story of how law came to the mid-continent wilderness called the country of the Illinois. It is the story of a legal system fashioned from many elements, some transplanted, some native, and it is a story of the judges, the lawyers, and the politicians who influenced the direction of its growth.

Before the frontier had pushed beyond the eastern mountains, the adventurers and the priests came to the Illinois country and left their French names in the history books. After these, along the game trails came the fur hunters and traders, the *coureurs de bois*. Later, when villages grew around the missions that had been built in the wilderness from faith by the priests, these runners-of-the-forest created some of the first problems for the administration of justice. The casualness with which they took native wives and their love of roistering and strong drink troubled the priests. The noise of their brawling and the ribaldry of their songs continued to disturb the quietness of village life as long as the fur trade lasted.

Close on the heels of the *coureurs de bois* came the *habitants*, or farmers, whose type may still be seen in towns along the Mississippi. Some of these people made the long voyage south from Quebec through the Great Lakes, across the portages, following the rivers southwestward to the Great River. Others came north from New Orleans, pulling hard on the oars with the *voyageurs*, or boatmen, to force the bateaux (a light-weight, flat-bottomed riverboat) against the surging current.

The *habitants* built their homes in the wilderness where the Jesuits and the priests of the seminary had built the missions. The scattered group of villages, some with French and some with Indian names, that they established in the broad bottomlands along the eastern bank of the Mississippi, developed a legal system based almost entirely on French and local influences. The starting point was the knowledge of and experience with French law that the villagers brought with them from Quebec and from New Orleans.

Just when and where in the midlands justice first came to be administered according to law is a matter of conjecture. The books say that the Mission of the Holy Family at Cahokia was established in 1699, and that the Mission of the Immaculate Conception, first founded in 1674 by Father Jacques Marquette near the site of modern Utica, was established at Kaskaskia a year later.[6] Tradition says of the two villages that grew up around these missions that Kaskaskia is the older. But it is probable that the beginnings of actual settlement in each date from the establishment of the missions.[7]

Earlier than these, in 1682, the French explorer Rene-Robert Cavelier, Sieur de LaSalle had built Fort St. Louis on the height now called Starved Rock and there is some evidence that there was a village near the fort. In 1690 or 1691, Henri de Tonti, the Italian-born soldier and explorer, built a new Fort St. Louis on "Lake Peoria" and a small number of French hunters and traders soon established homes near the fort. In addition to these there may have been other small settlements along the Illinois River before the eighteenth century began. Yet no records remain that indicate the existence of courts and the administration of legal rules in such settlements as may have existed.

There is written evidence that the rule of law by settlers in the mid-continent had its beginning in Kaskaskia, Cahokia, and the others of the little

3

cluster of French villages. These villages grew in the wide and fertile bottom-lands along the eastern bank of the Mississippi River where the river turns in a southeasterly direction to meet the Ohio River. Little remains of these villages to call to mind the time when the French dreamed of possessing all of the new world.

Today, Kaskaskia lies beneath the yellow waters of the Mississippi. St. Phillippe, Prairie du Pont, Nouvelle Chartres, and Grand Ruisseau are gone. Cahokia is a roadside sign, an old Catholic church, and a rebuilt courthouse with a legend.[8] Only Prairie du Rocher, drowsing at the foot of the limestone bluffs in the bottomland, lives to bear witness to the days when the Illinois country was claimed for the King of France.

The French villages in the Illinois were no mere trading posts. There was a time when Kaskaskia displayed some of the elegance of Quebec. There were homes in Cahokia and the other villages maintained in a style not generally associated with wilderness settlements in America.[9]

Politically, Kaskaskia became the most important French town between Detroit and New Orleans. It was built on the flat lands between the Kaskaskia and the Mississippi Rivers, a few miles above the site of the modern city of Chester, Illinois. At the high point of France's fortunes in America, more than a thousand people made their homes there. In size it was scarcely rivaled by Cahokia, situated about fifty miles to the north on the Mississippi near the limits of what is now the city of East St. Louis.

Mild climate, deep alluvial soil, and proximity to the Great River were the factors that attracted the French to these locations. Broad prairies where crops could be planted without first clearing away the forest drew them as a lodestone. Surrounding the prairies were the tangled woodlands of the bottom, where wild fruits and nuts grew in profusion. Above all, there was the Great River, the highway home to Quebec or south to New Orleans.

Thus attracted, they built their homes in the wilderness, the blue-ker-chiefed, laughter-loving *habitants* and *voyageurs*. They worshipped their God in the old way of their Catholic faith and laid out their villages around the churches that the zeal of their priests had raised beyond the frontier. On the village streets could be heard the *patois*, or dialect, of the *coureurs de bois*, the gutterals and tone speech of the native peoples, and French as good as that spoken in Quebec.

There were different conditions of people in these villages. Some few were members of noble families and were entitled as of right to the "Sieur" of formal French courtesy. Others could write "Ecuyer" after their names, just

4

Summer evening in a French village in Illinois. Abraham Lincoln Presidential Library and Museum.

as Englishmen in the seaboard towns could write "Gentleman" after theirs. Among the ranks of plain men were the *habitants* and *voyageurs*. The former were the peasants, the tillers of the soil, who went to dances and to church with equal enthusiasm. The latter were the boatmen, the restless ones, who sang the songs learned on the long days and nights in the bateaux on the journeys to Quebec and New Orleans. Along the streets passed the fur hunters, the *coureurs de bois*, with their preferences for liquor, riot, and native Indian women, as wild and unpredictable as the wilderness itself.

Life was reasonably kind to these people. The hot summers made the thick, black soil productive almost beyond belief. When came the long autumns, the loveliest time of year in Illinois, there were abundant harvests, and the lazy southward migration of wild geese and ducks offered food aplenty to be obtained almost without effort. The winters were usually not confining, and game was plentiful.

Even when sometimes in the spring or fall the Mississippi rolled yellow and turbulent through the streets of the villages and swept away possessions, it was still the Great River joining them with France as it was established in America. Now and then, there was famine or disease, and there were winters when the wilderness seemed about to reclaim the land. But the lives of the people were mostly happy. And they knew, as did no other settlers in America, how to live at peace with the native people whose villages sometimes almost joined their own.

It was characteristic of these peace-loving French that one of their earliest communal wants should be for an authoritative means of settling the disputes that inevitably arose whenever people lived together. Quarrels that backwoods Virginians would have settled with their fists were taken by the French to the priest or military commandant for decision. This comparison may partially explain the fate of French law in Illinois in later days. The priest was probably the first to exercise the function of settling disputes. The church was the most important institution in the life of the village community. Meetings were held before the church door and notices were posted there, sure to be seen by all.[10]

As the French villages grew and prospered a need developed for a division of the functions of government, and an old process was repeated. After a few years these villages developed the first judicial tribunals in existence anywhere in the vast area that eventually became the Territory Northwest of the River Ohio.[11] It is now impossible to determine when that decisional function was separated from the general administrative functions of military and religious officials, but it is definitely established that courts were in operation before the end of the first quarter of the eighteenth century.[12]

It is strange that John Law and the "Mississippi Bubble" were directly connected with the formal establishment of a system of law for the French in the Illinois. Law's Company of the West, which brought tragedy to France, was chartered in 1717. The charter granted to the company practically guaranteed a complete monopoly of trade and of governmental functions in the Province of Louisianne. One provision in it required recognition of the Custom of Paris as the basic law.[13] On September 27, 1717, an ordinance formally attached the Illinois country to Louisianne.

The "Mississippi Bubble" burst in 1720, but the Company of the Indies, which inherited the rights of the Company of the West, retained control of the province until 1731. Thus the royal charter, the regulations established by the companies, and the Custom of Paris together formed the law in force in the Illinois country during the early period of French dominion.

The Mississippi turns eastward for a brief distance below Ste. Genevieve, a French village in the time before Spain took its turn at governing the western wilderness. There it moves through what was once a channel of the Kaskaskia River. In the 1880s, the Great River dredged that channel to fit its own vast

6

proportions and whatever inhabited the banks was engulfed by the yellow water. Kaskaskia was swept away as the water washed over its foundations.

By great good fortune many of Kaskaskia's documents and records dating from 1714 were saved from the flood and from the dangers of negligence.[14] Along with equally valuable material from Cahokia,[15] they are available to the historian. From these documents and records it is possible to reconstruct the beginning of law in a wilderness community.

From the brittle pages of handmade paper, the law-in-action at Fort Chartres in 1725 comes to life as Chassin questioned the Black prisoner who stood before him that August afternoon:

> And thereafter, we summoned the said Pirrobe, negro accused by the said Perico of having aided him in the robbery of the warehouse, of whom we have demanded if he was resolved to speak the truth, causing him to take the necessary oath before the examination.
> He answered that he would not tell any falsehood.
> We asked him whether he knew the named Perico.
> He answered that he knew him but that he had never been associated with him.
> We asked him whether he had gone to the Indian Village with him.
> He answered [that he had] not.
> We asked him if he did not have knowledge that the said Perico had decided to rob the warehouse.
> He answered [that he had] not.
> We asked him if the said Perico had not proposed to him that he go with him.
> He answered that he had never spoken to him concerning this.[16]

A certified copy of a conveyance of land to "Messieurs the Missionaries of Cahokia and Tamarois" was executed by Pierre Dugué de Boisbriant, Knight of the Military Order of St. Louis, first Lieutenant of the King in the Province of Louisianne, Commandant of the Illinois, and by Marc Antoine des Ursins, manager of the Royal Company of the Indies. Dated June 20, 1722, this document helps fix the approximate date of the establishment of the first court ever to administer law and justice in the woods and prairies of the Midwest. The copy recited that a certain Bertlor Barrois, in his capacity as notary, certified that he compared the document with the Register of the Provincial Council of the Illinois.

Boisbriant, a French officer representing the crown in dealing with the affairs in Illinois of the Company of the Indies, built Fort Chartres about 1720 not far from the site of the present ruin. From his headquarters at the fort he conducted most of the affairs of government in the district. In 1722, he appointed from among his officers a Provincial Council or court (the French word is *conseil*) of seven members that had jurisdiction over criminal and civil affairs throughout the district.[17] This was almost certainly the first formally organized court ever to sit in the Illinois country.

A substantial part of the records of this Council have been preserved among the Kaskaskia manuscripts.[18] Until 1731, when the crown assumed control of Louisianne from the Company of the West, the Council functioned as the principal judicial body in the Illinois. Its duties were not exclusively judicial, however, for it also legislated extensively as established by the large number of proclamations among its records. It also proclaimed the Royal Ordinances, issuing them in the name of "Louis, by the grace of God, King of France and of Navarre." The Council also ordered grants of land and probably performed other important administrative duties, but it was the chief organ for the administration of justice and appears to have gone about the business of judging in an orderly and conscientious manner.

It heard both civil and criminal cases. One of its earliest cases concerned the enticement and ravishment of the daughter of a citizen of Kaskaskia. The decision of the Provincial Council ordering reparation to the outraged parent was appealed to the principal officers for Louisianne at New Orleans. These officers issued a directive in the name of the King to the Provincial Council ordering the enforcement of its decision and the issuance of an order requiring the offender to cease molesting the girl.

A consideration of the records of the Council indicates that the law it administered in cases not covered by specific ordinances was largely a rude equity, reflecting the standards of fairness of the day and the place, rather than the rules of the Custom of Paris, which the charter required. The procedure before the Council strongly resembled the procedure before the chancellor in the beginning of English equity. Aggrieved parties brought matters before it by petition much in the way that poor suitors in England in the fifteenth century sought the aid of the King's conscience through his council or his chancellor. "Mekely beseecheth" said importunate petitioners to the Curia Regis. "Supplie humblement," pleaded the *habitants* in search of justice in the Illinois in the 1720s. Frequently they concluded their petitions with "*Votre tres humble et tres obeissant serviteur*" ("Your very humble and very obedient servant"). A member of the Council endorsed its decisions directly on the petitions, and the *greffier* recorded the decisions in a book called the *Registre du Counceil Provinciall des Illinois*.[19]

In almost all cases, the testimony of witnesses was reduced to writing in the form of depositions taken by the *greffier* before a single member of the Council. In criminal cases, the Council used the inquisitorial form of procedure, as in the case of Pirrobe. A *procureur*, or attorney, represented the King, but the records do not indicate that the accused was given the privilege of counsel. Frequently, the magistrate conducting the inquisition was in fact the representative of both sides. Professional advocates would not make their appearance for many years.

Though the Council was the principal court, it is possible that there were single judges in the villages who determined small cases. In France, the *greffier* had certain judicial powers in the trial of less important cases, and he possibly exercised these powers in the Illinois.

As has been stated, officers directly representing the French crown assumed the functions of government in the Province of Louisianne in 1731. They continued to exercise control until the conclusion of the Treaty of Paris in 1763 and for a short time thereafter. French colonial policy was extraordinarily bad. The jealousies and machinations of officials in Paris and the general attitude of parsimony toward the American possessions hastened the end of French rule. Yet during the greater part of the period from 1731 to 1763, there existed in the French wilderness villages a legal system superior in development and more successful in operation than any that would follow for many years.

To form some picture of the administration of justice according to law under French control, it is necessary briefly to consider the system of government that France established in the Province. French colonies in America were subject to the authority of the Minister of the Marine, who was a member of the Council of State and responsible to the King. Louisianne was a royal province and to govern it, the King appointed two officials of equal rank. Of these, the governor was nominally in charge of the defense and general administration of the Province. The intendant shared the general administration with the governor and had independent jurisdiction over the police, finances, and administration of justice.[20]

Louisianne was divided into nine parts or districts, three of which—New Orleans, Mobile, and the Illinois—were of principal importance. The Illinois district was bounded by the Ohio River on the south, the Missouri and Illinois Rivers on the north, and extended an indefinite distance east and west of the

Mississippi. In the Illinois, the commandant acted as deputy governor and an officer called the *ecrivain principal* (principal scrivener or clerk) represented the intendant and had jurisdiction over legal matters.

The Superior Council, appointed by the King, assisted the governor and the intendant at New Orleans. Its chief function was to act as a court, and it had jurisdiction to hear appeals from any part of the province. The *ecrivain principal* became the principal judge in the Illinois and appeals from his decisions were sometimes taken to the Superior Council at New Orleans.[21]

There appears to have been a royal judge for the Illinois at Kaskaskia throughout most of the period from 1731 to 1754.[22] It is also possible that local courts consisting of judges popularly selected adjudicated minor civil and criminal affairs in each of the other villages, but no records of the proceedings of such courts appear to have survived.

The French villages in the Illinois prospered for more than two decades after 1731. As their population increased and their social organization became more complex, the influence of law upon the lives of the inhabitants became stronger. Justice was administered according to rules of law. In time the Custom of Paris became the basic system of secondary law that was applied when ordinances and proclamations did not cover specific cases. The crown, the royal officials at New Orleans, the commandant at Fort Chartres, and to some extent, the villagers themselves exercised legislative functions (the making of ordinances and proclamations). In this period, householders received strips of land adjoining the village commons, and the community exercised in public meetings considerable control over the kind of crops that each should plant.

Bertlor Barrois, *greffier royale*, was a faithful civil servant of the King of France for twenty years. One day in the Record Office of the Royale Jurisdiction of the Illinois, Province of Louisianne, he opened a new book of blank white paper and made an entry which began: *"Aujourd'huj quinze Janvier milsept cente trente sept . . ."*

The entry he made on that January day in 1737 at Kaskaskia related that Louis Norman Labriere had brought his marriage contract with Catherine Clement to be inscribed in the public records and that the relatives of the bride had been reasonably generous in providing her dowry. It was no primitive legal system that required such a contract to be committed to writing by a royal notary and to be inscribed in a record whose title, *Registre des Insinuations des Donations,*[23] employed the technical language of the civil law.

The book that Barrois began on January 15, 1737, was the clerk-recorder's minute book of certain types of voluntary transfers of property, called "donations" by the French law. Regularly each year for twenty years Barrois took the *Registre* in the early part of January or February to the principal judge in the Illinois. This judge inspected and closed the register, writing a certificate in the book that it conformed to the requirements of the law. Internal evidence established beyond question that such a record was kept as early as 1731. As *greffier*, Barrois kept other record books, such as the *Registre des Audiences*, or record of court hearings, a fragment of which still exists.[24]

The *Registre des Insinuations des Donations*, over which Barrois labored, furnishes a yearly record of the names and titles of the royal judges in the Illinois for twenty years. The seventh entry in the book reads in translation as follows:

> Today the twenty-third day of February one thousand seven hundred thirty-eight we, Louis Auguste de LaLoere Flancour, Esquire, Ecrivain Principal of the Marine, subdelegate of M. de Salmon, Intendant, and holding the seat of Justice in the Illinois, having found the present Register to conform to the regulations relating to inscriptions, and especially to the declaration of the King of the seventeenth of February, one thousand seven hundred thirty-one, after having ended and paraphed it, have closed it [the Register], returning it to Bertlor Barrois in his capacity of greffier of the jurisdiction of this seat of justice, to be by him communicated to all persons who have an interest in it, the whole according to the intent of the aforesaid declaration, and I have signed
>
> de Laloere Flancour

Flancour made such annual entries until January 16, 1747. On that date Joseph Buchet, describing himself as *garde des magasins* (royal warehouse keeper), attorney for vacant property, and guardian of the royal jurisdiction, stated that the seat of justice was vacant. Flancour had died. In later entries Buchet wrote "King's attorney" and "Principal Judge of the Illinois" among his titles.

The records show that the seat of royal justice was at Kaskaskia from 1737 to 1754. In about 1750 the French commandant with the Irish name, Makarty, had commenced the reconstruction in stone of old Fort Chartres on a site eighteen miles above Kaskaskia. The fort, while never completely finished, was probably ready for occupancy about 1754. That year the *Registre* contains only two entries. Barrois and Buchet moved the seat of justice to Nouvelle

trente trois

charge d'entretenir les lieux et bâtimens de toutes
ses reparations viageres, et rendre le tout en bon etat
lorsque ladit[e] constitué par ladite donation viagere
finira, Ladite presente donation faite à la charge qu'il n'y
ait aucun enfant nez, ou à naistre dudit mariage, auquel
cas d'enfant ladite donation viagere demeurera nulle
et comme non faite, comme il est porté audit contrat
de mariage ce requerant leurs ff franç, valleé, insinuation
... ... en par nous Greffier soussigné ledit contrat de mariage
et apres lecture faite en notre greffe d'icelui, l'avons
insinué et registré sur les registres des insinuations
de ce siege suivant l'ordonnance, pour lui servir et
valoir de ce que raison sont acte, ... fait aux ...
en notre greffe les jour es an que dessus   BARROIS

Greffier

Extrait des registres des insinuations de la
Jurisdiction Royale des Illinois
Aujourd'huy quatorzieme jour de Septembre
mil Sept cents cinquante un, est comparu par devant
le Greffier soussigné en son Greffe Sr François Baptiste
habitant de la prairie du Rocher y demeurant ...
Sainte anne de present en cette ville porteur du
Testament solennel de feu Jean Baptiste Tollet ...
Reçu par Mr Nicolas Laurent Prestre missionnaire
apostolique, vicaire de M^r ... aussi Prestre et
missionnaire apostolique aux Illinois, aumonier pour
le Roy au fort de Chartres et curé de la paroisse
Sainte anne, le Dixieme jour de Decembre mil sept
cents quarante six, portant quand il aura plu à Dieu
de retirer son ame de ce monde, veut et ordonne
que son corps soit Inhumé au cimetiere de la
chapelle St Joseph de la susdite prairie et le
jour de son deces le lendemain ou le premier jour
qu'il se pourra apres son enterrement il soit dit
et celebré un service. Ledit testateur donne

A page from the *Registre des Insinuations des Donations* with signature
of *greffier* Bertlor Barrois, 1750. Perrin Collection, Illinois State Archives.

Chartres, the village that grew up under the guns of the most pretentious military structure in all French America. There it probably remained until French sovereignty in the Illinois passed into history.

On January 12, 1757, Monsieur Buchet certified the *Registre* for the last time. He noted that he returned it to Barrois, "to allow it to be communicated without removal, to all persons who have any interest in it, the whole according to the intent of the said Declaration of February 17, 1731. Done at Nouvelle Chartres the day and year above written." On that same day Barrois, older by twenty years than when he wrote the first page, made the last entry he was ever to make in the *Registre*. Two months later a new *greffier* signed "Labuxiere" to an entry concerning a will.

The decline of French royal power in the new world can be clearly followed in the *Registre*. Labuxiere carried forward, carefully at first, the record of his predecessor. Once he inadvertently left part of a page blank and drew a wavering line down the middle, writing "*Passé par erreur*" (passed by mistake). But for some reason, only once thereafter does the *Registre* bear the inscription of a royal judge. At the end of a page after an entry dated November 20, 1763, Lefebvre, then acting judge, wrote "*Arreté Le Present journal ce Dix Fbre 1764*" (Closed the Present record this 10th of February 1764).

After 1758, the entries became much briefer and carelessly made. There were four entries in 1763, the year in which the Treaty of Paris was signed. There was only a single entry in 1764, relating to a marriage contract, the parties to which resided in St. Louis. Then the record stops, to be briefly resumed in 1768. In that year Labuxiere, still styling himself *greffier royale*, stated that the *Greffe* or Record Office was then at St. Louis. Two entries were made in 1769, and then the *Registre des Insinuations des Donations de La Jurisdiction des Illinois* was closed forever. Gone too from the Illinois was the power of his Majesty, the King of France. What remained, and would remain for more than a century, was the sound of French speech on the streets of Kaskaskia, Cahokia, and Prairie du Rocher. The basic secondary system of law established by the French judges remained too, for a time.

The charter of the "Company of the West" had imposed upon the company the duty of recognizing the *Coutume de Paris* (Custom of Paris) as the basic law of Louisianne. Historians asserted that this particular form of French common law prevailed throughout the Illinois but offered no proof save the provision of the royal charter.[25] Much more convincing was the testimony of Barrois, carrying out his duties according to the King's *ordonnance* at the Record Office in Kaskaskia.

Today the twenty-eighth of May, 1753, there appeared in the Record Office of this jurisdiction, before the Clerk-Recorder undersigned, Bonaventure Bertlot, volunteer in this country dwelling in this village, bearer of the act of mutual donation between Jen. Baptis. Guilbert, called Laframboise, and Anne Dudevoir, his wife, executed before M. De Saint Ange, Captain Commandant at Post Vincennes, formerly of this jurisdiction. These presents bearing witness that Sr. Jean Baptiste Guilbert, called Laframboise and Dame Anne Dudevoir, his wife, by him authorized according to the effect of these presents the spouses stipulating for themselves and each other, in the presence of their parent and friends hereafter named, to wit Monsieur Boulanger, officer of the King at the said post and the Sr. Toussaints Guilbert called Laframboise, citizen at said post. The said spouses have declared and represented that they have contracted between themselves their marriage, before and under the License of our Mother the Holy Church represented by a Recolet missionary priest, journeying to a post of the Miamis. And finding [that] no person appears and says anything against it [the marriage] they may declare mutually and reciprocally their wills with terms and conditions agreeable to themselves. They have returned today to establish an authentic act as their will at once and forever to have between them a community of property, movable and immovable and a present and future acquisition following the Custom of Paris, obligating themselves reciprocally for debts and pledges made and created before the said marriage, the said wife, Anne Dudevoir, not having asked any dower other than that which is assigned and acquired according to the said Custom of Paris . . .

This entry and others leave little doubt that the Custom of Paris was the basic system of law according to the rules by which most civil affairs were transacted.

"In the south of France is the written law, in the north of France are the Customs." French customary or common law varied from province to province. Theoretically, the validity of its rules rested upon their establishment by continued usage. A single judicial decision could not, as in the English Common Law, establish a rule, but precedent must be piled upon precedent. Nor were the Customs in any except a historical sense unwritten laws.

The Custom of Paris was the established law in the part of France that included the Royal Domain. As Louisianne was a royal province it was logical to select the Custom of Paris for the basic system of law. The Custom had been compiled or committed to writing in 1510 and had been revised in 1580.[26] It was the law that had certain fundamental similarities to the other Customs of northern France and was in its general operation not unfamiliar to most of the inhabitants of the Illinois. It was rather easily adapted to the requirements of a new country.

There would be little evidence as to the manner in which the Custom of Paris applied in the Illinois were it not for the chance that saved the *Registre des Donations* from destruction. The most typical and probably the most important civil transactions were recorded in it. The diligent Barrois inscribed them down to the smallest detail, obeying to the letter the Royal Ordinance of 1731 concerning notaries.

There are in all 120 entries in the *Registre*, excluding the certifications. About one-half of them relate to marriage contracts. Others concern donations (voluntary transfers) of various kinds and wills. The lawyer trained in the Common Law who reads Barrois's abstracts is struck at once by the truth of the statement that the civil law was a law of contract. Most transactions of legal validity were accomplished by agreement between the parties. Indeed the Royal Ordinance of 1731 required acceptance by the donee in person or by an attorney as essential to the validity of most donations.

Marriage was first an agreement and secondarily a relationship. The records indicated that marriages accomplished by contract were valid, even though religious sanction was not obtained until later. Marriage contracts in the Illinois were frequently drawn by the royal notary and executed before him, but they might be drawn by others and inscribed by the notary at a later date. They were often joined in by the bride's relatives who provided her dowry. Very often they established a *communauté* or community of the property of both spouses owned at marriage and a *conquet* or joint ownership of property acquired during the marriage. The device of community property was almost the rule. The characteristic feature was that these things were established by agreement of the principals.

That curious historical accident, the doctrine of consideration in contracts, was, of course, unknown to the simple inhabitants of the French villages in the Illinois. One who wished to make a gift had simply to manifest that intention in writing before a notary or witnesses, and the donee could register the document with the *greffier* and enforce it against the donor. Delivery of the property actual or symbolic was not required.

The donations recorded in the *Registre* are of many interesting kinds. There are the *donations mutuelle et reciproquall* whereby a husband and wife established a *communauté des biens* (property) *meuble et immeuble* (movable and immovable). There were donations by relatives for the good fortune of a marriage. Others were conditional donations that created something very like the Common Law equitable charge upon property.

One entry describes such a donation by an old couple of all their property to persons outside the family in return for support because the children of the couple were wayward. In another, an aged couple disposed of their property in return for support, adding quaintly, "finally, that they should have no other cares than those of praying to God, drinking, eating, and promenading if good to them that seems."

Wills and testaments were executed by both men and women and distributed movable and immovable property. Some of the wills were executed before the royal notary and some were witnessed wills. Others were nuncupative—oral declarations of persons who believed they were about to die. In the latter cases, it was to the priests that the testamentary directions were given *in extremis*.

Remnants of the feudal system can be observed in this early law but they were fast disappearing. Women enjoyed a considerable amount of freedom in the matter of legal transactions and could acquire and dispose of property. After marriage, of course, a wife's property was subject to the husband's control unless otherwise agreed. A woman who had established a *communauté* of property with her husband could have relief if he deserted her. After obtaining the consent of the judge, an act of renunciation could be executed and registered, which would enable the wife to recover her own property and pay family debts from the husband's share.

The system of law that the French judges applied in the district of the Illinois was a well-developed system. By comparison with the law that the Virginians established, the French law seems almost too highly developed for these settlements beyond the frontier. Unlike the Common Law, the theory of its administration was paternalistic in that its formalities were in the care of civil servants like Barrois.[27] The faithfulness and intelligence of these men were the factors that rendered the system workable among the people, most of whom certainly had no knowledge of its subtleties.

Where the Common Law attached consequences to the acts of individuals, *ex post facto*, the French law attached consequences to those acts done under the guidance of public officials. A taught submissiveness to authority was characteristic of the French *habitants*, who were the principal element of the population. Both church and state had contributed to this result. It is clear that the French law was an important factor in the happiness and well-being of the people and provided adequate means for the settlement of their disputes.

When the French *fleur-de-lis* on the shield above the great gate at Fort Chartres represented the sovereign authority in Illinois, there existed a legal system basically different in fundamental theory and in administration from that which was later established. This older system did not long survive a change in government, although some of its rules probably continued in effect for a long time.

The transition to a new system was hard. Even before French power in the Mississippi valley yielded to British supremacy, new kinds of settlers came to make their homes in the French villages. These had other ideas of the relation of law to life. Perhaps both groups shared the ideal that justice should be administered according to law. But the legal experience of the newcomers was with a system fundamentally different from the one that had served the French so well. As had happened in the old world, so in the new, Common Law and Civil Law contested for supremacy.

2. Law and Anarchy,
Virginia County, Federal Territory

THE SEVEN YEARS' WAR was over, and the French dream of magnificence
through colonial possessions in the new world ended in the cession of all
the northwest to Britain. The Treaty of Paris in 1763 marked the beginning
of a period during which the existence of law as a body of rules was all but
destroyed by the disintegration of civil government.[1]

The people of the French villages on the Mississippi received the news
of the cession of the Illinois country to Britain with consternation. To many
of them the future seemed dark and uncertain if they remained in their wilderness homes. They had justification for their misgivings concerning the
British. Many British civil and military officials had not been chosen for their
tolerance and understanding of alien customs and ideals.

Moreover, British policy in dealing with the native people did not give
confidence to the people of the Illinois that they would be able to continue in
peace with the tribes who were their close neighbors. The wave of religious
fanaticism and the messiah-craze among the tribes in the area around the
Great Lakes had begun to make the Indians of the Illinois country uneasy.
The madness that was infecting them was anti-British in aspect. The genius
of Pontiac was welding the tribes into a confederacy, the object of which was
to resist British advance.[2]

It is no wonder, then, that laughter was out of turn in Kaskaskia and the
other villages along the Mississippi. Heads of families, many of them among
the most influential citizens in the Illinois, gathered their possessions and
crossed the Great River into what would soon become Spanish territory.[3]

Some stopped at Ste. Genevieve or at New Madrid, others continued to St. Louis, the new trading center then rising in the wilderness.

The exodus continued during 1764 and 1765. The French commandant in the Illinois in 1764 was the kindly Louis St. Ange de Bellerive, who had been summoned from Post Vincennes to succeed de Villers. He was gallant and just, but without the spark of leadership that might have inspired his countrymen in their dark hour. Even had St. Ange possessed the ability to maintain among the French a sense of loyalty to their communities, he could not have persuaded the people to stay without the assistance of their spiritual leaders, and it appeared that the priests would not remain under British rule.[4]

Thus a major catastrophe overtook the French in the Illinois, who had established the rule of law beyond the frontier. Although the Treaty of Paris had been signed in 1763, the year 1765 saw the French authorities still in control. The country to the north was troubled by the Indian uprising that Pontiac had led, and the Illinois country was cut off from Canada and the northern posts. Finally, on October 9 in that year, Captain Thomas Stirling with about a hundred troops of the Black Watch Regiment reached Fort Chartres.[5] On the following day the banner of St. George and St. Andrew became the symbol of government in the Illinois.[6]

The next two decades were among the unhappiest in all the history of the Illinois country. A sorry consequence of the breakdown of civil government that characterized this period was the almost complete absence of legal development. Obedience to the authority of a few officials had been a striking feature of the French regime, but the British entered upon the occupation of this new territory without even a plan for its government. The administration of justice was left in the hands of the military commanders, most of whom were more interested only in personal gain.[7]

Captain Stirling remained in the Illinois only about two months. After consultation with the principal citizens, he appointed a certain Jean Baptiste Lagrange[8] to decide all disputes. Nothing is known concerning the judicial acts of this person. Major Robert Farmar,[9] Lieutenant Colonel John Reed, and Captain Hugh Forbes, each in turn became commandant, and none of them contributed anything toward the establishment of civil government for the demoralized people of the Illinois.

The notorious Lieutenant Colonel John Wilkins took charge in 1768. Wilkins commissioned six judges who were "authorized to form a Civil Court of Judicatory," with powers expressed in their commission to "Hear and Try in a Summary way all Causes of Debt and Property that should be brought before them and to give their judgment thereon according to the laws of England to the best of their Judgment and understanding."[10]

Wilkins's purpose in creating this court, which held alternate sessions at Fort Chartres and Kaskaskia, was to aid the British merchants in collecting their debts.[11] The French, in the absence of any courts for the settlement of disputes, had resorted to arbitration, which the French law permitted. French law dictated the decisions of the arbitrators, and the commandant enforced those decisions.[12]

In 1770, the court was given jurisdiction over criminal cases. Wilkins's proclamation offered a justification: "[T]he present Establishment of the Country does not admit the Tryals of Juries on account of its small number of inhabitants as Well as their Want of Knowledge of the Laws and Customs of England." Wilkins's cupidity soon drew him into disagreement with the court, and he apparently abolished it in 1770.[13]

Law and the administration of justice, always regarded by the French as especially important, were in a sorry plight. In 1771, the distracted inhabitants sent emissaries to New York to beg for relief from General Thomas Gage. This effort brought no immediate results and matters went from bad to worse.

At last, in 1774 Parliament passed the Quebec Act, which attached the Illinois country to Canada and contemplated the establishment of courts and civil government. But the plan was not placed in operation at once, and the outbreak of hostilities between the eastern colonies and the mother country ended the matter forever.

Meanwhile, matters continued to drift in the French towns on the Mississippi. Numbers of French, dismayed by the lack of any prospect for the reestablishment of order, continued to cross to the Spanish side of the Great River. But new faces began to appear. Restless backwoodsmen and shrewd traders from the east moved in increasing numbers to Kaskaskia and Cahokia. The days of British supremacy in the Illinois were numbered.

The records of the British period that have survived are few and badly kept. Handmade paper was occasionally watermarked with lions rampant instead of the fleur-de-lis. Most legal records from this period are records of arbitration, and they indicate clearly what had occurred in the administration of civil justice. French law permitted arbitration as an alternative to litigation. Each party to a dispute could name one arbitrator. The two so chosen would name a third.[14] When civil courts ceased to function, arbitrators took their places. A principal weakness of the system was its dependence upon the military commandant for enforcement of decisions.

Military tribunals or the commandant himself dispensed criminal justice during this period except during the short existence of Wilkins's "Court of Judicatory." It is certainly possible that the villages may each have elected a magistrate and that these dispensed justice in the old way, but the records do not establish it.

Wilkins finally resigned in disgrace; Major Isaac Hamilton, who partially destroyed Fort Chartres, succeeded him. Hamilton departed for Fort Pitt in 1772, leaving Captain Hugh Lord as representative of the crown at Kaskaskia. Captain Lord was a kindly man who was able in some manner to quiet the discontent without inaugurating any substantial changes. When he left for Detroit in 1776, he chose Phillipe Francois de Rastel, Chevalier de Rocheblave, to represent British authority in his stead.

Rocheblave soon came to occupy a difficult position. He had no more than assumed control when intrigues began. His countrymen, the *voyageurs* and *habitants*, largely supported him, for they were accustomed to acceptance of regularly constituted authority. But the American traders, such as the Murrays and Thomas Bentley, had begun to exert a powerful influence in the Illinois and worked actively against him and British interests. Rocheblave asked for troops but without result. His position was too uncertain to permit him to do very much for the organization of civil government. He fretted away his time in Kaskaskia until the July night in 1778 when George Rogers Clark's men took him prisoner in his French cap and nightgown.[15] The coming of Clark, the American frontiersman and Revolutionary hero, marked a second great change in the affairs of the Illinois villages. The frontier was overtaking them. Rallied under the rattlesnake flag of Virginia, Clark's men were the advance guard of the frontiersmen, "the tall, lank visitors, brown as snuff, with their long, straight squirrel rifles" who brought new attitudes and new problems for law to the Illinois country.

The American Revolution in the west had established a new sovereignty. Clark took possession of the Illinois in the name of the Republic of Virginia and set about the job of consolidating his position. Once again the distressed cry for a civil government arose. Clark wrote:

> I inquired particularly into the manner the people had been governed heretofore and found, much to my satisfaction, that the government had generally been as severe as though under martial law. I resolved to make capital of this, and took every step in my power to cause the people to appreciate the blessings enjoyed by an American citizen. This enabled

me, as I soon discovered, to support by their own choice almost supreme authority over them. I caused a court of civil judicature, elected by the people, to be established at Cahokia. Major Bowman, to the surprise of the people, held an election for the magistracy, and was himself elected judge of the court. His policy in holding an election can easily be perceived. After this similar courts were established at Kaskaskia and Vincennes. There was an appeal to myself in certain classes of cases, and I believe no people ever had their business done more to their satisfaction than these had for a considerable time by means of this regulation.[16]

Thus began in the midlands the American policy of an elective magistracy. Some few records of Clark's courts for the years 1778 and 1779 remain. From them we discern that the administration of justice according to law was being reestablished. The records were written in French and they show that for a time, at least, there was a renewed vitality in the rules of French law. There exist records of sales of goods at public auction in satisfaction of debts, a petition of a minor who had married for a share in the estate of a deceased parent, and a petition of a minor for emancipation according to the Custom of Paris. The old method of transferring land by a ceremony in the presence of witnesses was also in evidence. All indicate the application of rules that were well known.

While the French law recovered a position of supremacy, its recovery was incomplete and temporary. Many of the ablest of the French citizens had left the Illinois forever. Some with ability who remained were convinced that more was to be gained by adopting American ways than in preserving the cultural isolation of the French population. In particular, the traders, the frontier's men of business, held this viewpoint.

Never again in the Illinois would records in the French language be kept with the diligence and care which Bertlor Barrois bestowed before the fall of France. The wounds caused by the destruction of civil government during the British period had weakened the established law and only the most basic rules remained. The majority of the French population in 1778 could not write, and the people seem to have had little feeling for the legal significance of the written document. Although the French law returned for a while, it was diluted in administration with the same rude equity that had been applied when Fort Chartres was young.

"Be it enacted by the General Assembly, That all the citizens of this commonwealth who are already settled, or shall hereafter settle, on the western side of Ohio aforesaid, shall be included in a distinct county, which shall be called Illinois county."[17] In Williamsburg, capital city of Virginia, on December 12, 1778, Governor Patrick Henry turned from a reading of the statute that had been enacted by the legislature three days before, to begin a letter: "John Todd, Esqr: By virtue of the act of Genl Assembly which established the County of Illinoies, you are appointed County Liut. or Commandt there, and for the genrall tennour of your Conduct I refur you to the law." The letter was filled with much of the wise counsel that the great governor could put into words.[18]

News of Clark's victories in the Illinois had reached Virginia in mid-October. The General Assembly introduced a bill providing for the government of the newly won territory on November 30 and passed it on December 9. In the flush of its military success, Virginia made an effort to aid the people in the villages along the Mississippi. The act established a civil government and permitted the inhabitants to choose the officials who were to serve under the county lieutenant.[19]

Concerning the kind of law that was to be administered in the courts, the language of the statute was short but significant: "[S]aid civil officers ... shall exercise their several jurisdictions, and conduct themselves agreeable to the laws which the present settlers are now accustomed to."[20] Thus the Virginia legislature recognized the wisdom of allowing the people of a newly acquired territory to retain their established laws.

The Virginia period in Illinois history began with high promise for the return of orderly government. The choice of John Todd as county lieutenant was a wise one. Todd was a lawyer turned soldier. He had received some formal education in Virginia and had studied law with an uncle, practicing for a short while in Botetourt and Bedford counties. In 1776, he was established near Lexington in the Kentucky country, which he represented in the Virginia Legislature. He was public spirited and capable, with some experience in the art of government. Moreover, he had served with Clark in the conquest of the Illinois. A sentence from Governor Henry's letter to Todd truly expressed the spirit in which the new regime was established: "Considering, therefore, that early Prejudices are so hard to weare Out, you will Take Care to Cultivate and conciliate the affections of the French and Indians." The high promise, however, was never realized.

John Todd returned to the Illinois in May 1779. He proceeded at once to the organization of the civil government, creating three districts, one for each of the three principal villages. The Kaskaskia district included Prairie du Rocher, Nouvelle Chartres, and St. Philippe. The Cahokia district included

During the Revolutionary War, George Rogers Clark helped to secure the Illinois country for the new United States. Abraham Lincoln Presidential Library and Museum.

Prairie du Pont and the French settlement at Peoria. All the Wabash country was included in the Vincennes district. Each district had one court to consist of six judges from the principal village and representatives from the others. The first election was held in Kaskaskia on May 12, 1779. Jean Gabriel Cerré, the most prominent French citizen in the district, headed the court chosen on that day.[21]

The courts created under this plan, which George Rogers Clark and John Todd presented to the people who assembled before the church door in Kaskaskia in the Illinois springtime, administered the law under Virginia authority only until 1782. The original act of the Virginia Legislature expired by its terms twelve months after enactment at the close of the legislature's session. The legislature prolonged its life by renewal in 1780, but it came to an end two years later.[22] At its close, the Illinois country was again in chaos, to which the lack of a colonial policy and the cupidity of British commandants had reduced it such a short time before.

A brief examination of the story of the courts of Kaskaskia and Cahokia during the Virginia period is important to an understanding of legal developments in the Illinois.[23] Kaskaskia was a center of intense political activity from its early prominence in the 1720s until it went quietly to sleep in 1819 when the Illinois capital moved elsewhere. In 1780, a series of intrigues began that lead to the downfall of the newly organized civil government. The frontiersmen from across the mountains—independent, restless, and ready to fight at a careless word—came in numbers to the Illinois after Clark's military success. They and the traders disturbed the even tenor of French ways.

Kaskaskia soon was prey to all the evils that grew out of the mutual mistrust of widely different elements in its population, which lacked even the common bond of language. The seriousness of the situation increased as it became apparent that the coming of the American frontiersmen likely meant an end to the long peace with the Indians.

The court at Kaskaskia became involved in the intrigues to such an extent that it ceased functioning for periods of time. At Cahokia, however, the court continued to function without material interruption. In large part the absence at Cahokia of antagonistic elements in the population continually contending for supremacy accounted for this difference with Kaskaskia.[24]

The court records kept at Cahokia in the years 1778 to 1782 revealed that French law, with its basis in the Custom of Paris, was still the underlying law. A decade before, British arrogance directed Wilkins's Court of Judicatory to decide cases according to the law of England.[25] With better judgment, the Virginians allowed the French to retain their law. Yet here and there in the records can be discerned the beginning of Common Law influences, which manifested first in procedural matters. For example, the Cahokia court used the process of execution in enforcing an order, instead of directing specific restitution in the French way.[26]

But in the main, the older law prevailed. The same concepts of property that the faithful Barrois so carefully described in the days of the vigor of French law still governed the holding of property under Virginia. Opposing parties sometimes examined the records of the *greffier royale* to establish certain interests. In a case in 1782, one Langlois, who called himself simply *notaire*, wrote a certificate after a copy of a marriage contract that had been inscribed by Barrois.[27] The copy contained gaps that Langlois, with conscious or unconscious humor, in good French, explained in his certificate: "I certify that the present copy conforms to the original which I have copied word for word although the mice have eaten it almost to ribbons and the lines which are found in blank are the fault of the departed mice. I have drawn up the present copy at Kaskaskia the 26 of December, 1782."

The Virginia Act under which civil government began so bravely in 1779 expired in 1782. Near anarchy again overtook the villages in the Illinois, and law entered another period in which it developed imperceptibly or not at all. Kaskaskia was the scene of a bitter struggle for power made more complex by increased activity in land speculation. The courts continued to function to some extent, at least at Cahokia. Elected magistrates served from time to time, and there was some effort at regularity in sessions of court. The Cahokia court designated one of its number to hold weekly sessions, while the whole court met once a month.

The catastrophe to civil government that accompanied the end of external authority is evidenced by a 1785 document. By means of this document, Antoine Girardin, newly elected magistrate of the Cahokia court, endeavored to secure obedience to the court as a condition of his taking office. In translation it reads, in part:

> To Messieurs the magistrates holding court of justice at the Cohos and Messieurs the inhabitants comprising the village and community of inhabitants.
>
> Gentlemen:
>
> Antoine Girardin having been elected magistrate of this court the twelfth of this month cannot exempt himself from making to you, gentlemen, these representations before taking possession of the trust with which it has pleased you to elect him.
>
> Which representations lead only to the welfare of the community, to render and discharge to each and all an equitable justice and avoid as much as it shall be possible the Costs thereof:
>
> 1. I ask that the Court shall consist of seven magistrates including the president and shall convene only every three months upon a certain indicated day for the purpose of judging all cases which shall present themselves, and in the event there be appeal, the appellant shall have recourse to the gentlemen of the jury, for their definite verdict;

2. That the court shall appoint one of the magistrates, the most enlightened among the seven, to be the Judge of the week.

. . .

6. That in the event of any rebellion or hindrance to our sentences where the commandant shall be obliged to lend main force, there shall always be four pairs of irons and four pairs of handcuffs deposited with the bailiff in case of need for those revolting to our sentences or the criminals and seditious gentry or insubordinates.

. . .

8. That those who shall be put in irons shall before leaving give *one piastre* to the bailiff or blacksmith who shall have put them there and [who shall] uniron them and shall procure their own food, or it will be furnished to them upon payment, according to the custom of prisoners, and they shall be guarded by two militiamen who shall be paid by the prisoner.

. . .

These are my just representations, except as I am better advised, and in default of acceptance I declare that I renounce all offices of magistry in order not to appear any more in Court

At the Cohos, June 14, 1785

Antoine Girard

The document indicates that the inhabitants signed (most of them by mark) to indicate their acceptance of the terms laid down.[28]

The situation in the Illinois passed from bad to worse until, in 1787, the records indicate that once again arbitrators functioned in place of judges, and justice was no longer administered by courts or according to law, except at Cahokia. The French law was never to recover from this second disaster. In Kaskaskia, French and American elements in the population opposed each other bitterly. There the final debasement of law and civil authority came in 1782 when Richard Winston, acting county lieutenant, abolished the court for the district. After that, there was no legal authority for any court in the district, at least until 1787.

The five years from 1782 to 1787 are without significance for legal development. However, the period did mark the coming to the Illinois of two men whose names were to be closely connected with the administration of law in future days. John Rice Jones, the lawyer, arrived in Kaskaskia in the fall of 1786. He was the emissary of George Rogers Clark, sent to buy provisions in the Illinois for Kentucky militiamen. There he met and dealt with an American merchant, John Edgar, who had only recently established himself in Kaskaskia.

In 1787, the inhabitants voted to reestablish the old court in the village and elected three Americans and three Frenchmen to the bench. The French judges protested that they could not act with the Americans, and factionalism defeated efforts to establish harmony.[29]

In the whole sorry spectacle of the disintegration of civil authority, the only bright spot was Cahokia. The days of anarchy reduced the population of Kaskaskia materially, but Cahokia showed an increase. There, the court continued to hold regular sessions. Circumstances had isolated Cahokia from the intrigues that so demoralized Kaskaskia. A more cohesive citizenry preserved order without the aid of external authority. The difference was so marked that the people of Cahokia scorned any association with their countrymen to the south.[30] The standing of the Cahokia court was such that it could meet with stern discipline the efforts of citizens of Grand Ruisseau to establish a rival court. The judges at Cahokia ordered the leaders to be put in irons for twenty-four hours, and the *huissier* or French sheriff endorsed the record: "The present sentence has been executed the same day."[31]

These were the conditions in the Illinois when the Congress of the United States passed the Ordinance of 1787. The Ordinance marked the end of the political isolation of the old French villages and the newer settlements that had sprung up to the east and north. The Old Northwest was organized into the Territory of the United States Northwest of the River Ohio. The Ordinance foreshadowed the future. Already the first wagons had crossed the eastern mountains. Time would no longer stand still in the French villages. The westward advance of the land-hungry pioneers had begun, and the streets of Kaskaskia soon would roar with the turbulence of the frontier.

The Ordinance of 1787 provided for a three-judge territorial court to be called the General Court. The judges and the governor exercised the legislative power in the Territory. The direction given them in this regard was conferred in strange terms: "The Governor and judges, or a majority of them, shall adopt and publish in the district such laws of the original States, criminal and civil, as may be necessary, and best suited to the circumstances of the district, and report them to Congress from time to time, which laws shall be in force in the district until the organization of the General Assembly therein, unless disapproved of by Congress; but afterwards the Legislature shall have authority

Cahokia Courthouse. Abraham Lincoln Presidential Library and Museum.

to alter them as they shall think fit."[32] A dispute arose between the governor and judges as to whether the legislative power was confined simply to the adopting of certain of the laws of the original thirteen states or extended to the enactment of new laws.

The Ordinance also contained language relating to the basic law that was to be in force in the Territory. The first provision disclosed that the fundamental requirement of frontier society from law was a set of rules concerning the ownership of property. The first paragraph of the Ordinance (after the enacting clause) contained a statute of descent and dower, a statute of wills and conveyances, provisions for recording such documents, and a provision for the transfer of personal property by delivery. There follows the language: "saving, however, to the French and Canadian inhabitants, and other settlers of the Kaskaskies, Saint Vincents and the neighboring villages, who have heretofore professed themselves citizens of Virginia, their laws and customs now in force among them, relative to the descent and conveyance of property."[33] The General Court had "a common law jurisdiction," and this provision was later thought to exclude it from the exercise of equitable powers.

Congress selected Major General Arthur St. Clair as governor of the Territory and General Samuel Holden Parsons, James Mitchell Varnum, and John Cleves Symmes as judges of the General Court. Winthrop Sargent was appointed secretary.[34]

With the passage of the Ordinance, the way was open for the return of orderly government to the Illinois. Governor St. Clair arrived in the Territory in 1788, but it was not until 1790 that he journeyed to Kaskaskia to establish the civil authority of the United States in the villages along the banks of the Mississippi.

3. *The Coming of the Common Law*

THE ORDINANCE OF 1787 was the first general charter of government created for the mid-continent area named "The Territory Northwest of the River Ohio."[1] The idealism of the Ordinance was beyond the understanding or powers of expression of all but a very few of the inhabitants. Its phrases were written by men to whom the terrors and dangers of the wilderness were distant things. In the passing of time, after the wilderness was gone, the idealism of the Ordinance would shape the thoughts and guide the labors of the lawmakers and the judges.

The second article of the Ordinance used terms that probably were not comprehensible to most of the people in the old river villages in the Illinois. Habeas corpus and trial by jury had no place in the system of law they knew. Nor would they have sensed the high aspiration in the first sentence of the third article: "Religion, morality and knowledge, being necessary to good government and the happiness of mankind, schools and the means of education, shall forever be encouraged." The French way in the Illinois was passing, and it was best for their peace of mind that the inhabitants could not foresee the coming changes.

The Ordinance made provision for two stages of development in the government of the Territory. There would be no representative legislature until there were five thousand free male inhabitants of full age in the Territory. Until that time the general powers of government were vested in a governor and three judges. Following the New England pattern with respect to the division of functions between them, executive power was vested in the governor alone, legislative power was shared by the governor and the judges, and judicial power was granted only to the judges. The convenience and necessity of the people of a new country warranted investing the same officials with the power to make and interpret the laws, but these functions would become separated upon the creation of the territorial legislature. The assent of the governor, however, would always be necessary to the validity of legislation enacted by the territorial assembly.

The Ordinance passed the Continental Congress on July 13, 1787. Nearly a year later to the day, the courtly, unlucky Arthur St. Clair stepped ashore at Marietta, close by the guns of Fort Harmar, where the Muskingum River joins the broad Ohio River. He had come to assume his duties as governor of the Territory.

St. Clair was well qualified by birth and training to be a leader. He had been educated at Edinburgh and had served with distinction under the British general, James Wolfe, in the assault upon Quebec. He had held various offices of public trust in Pennsylvania, including Justice of the Court of Quarter Sessions and Common Pleas for Cumberland County. As a revolutionary officer, St. Clair enjoyed the affection and respect of George Washington. Most recently he had been president of the last Continental Congress.[2] From the record, it is difficult to imagine a more fortunate choice for chief magistrate of the new Territory.

St. Clair was one of the tragic figures of the old Northwest. He was honorable, steadfast, and diligent, but he carried the vices of his virtues to the wilderness he was sent to govern. The graces that had won him social success and a wife in Boston caused him to be misunderstood by the people whose loyalty he needed on the frontier. One reads his correspondence today, letters from the posts that stretched a thin line across the breadth of three future states, and wonders at the lack of humor in the man. His determination was undiscriminating. He could follow a principle with a steadfastness that would overcome all opposition, yet lose an ideal in his inability to yield.

The American frontier dealt unkindly with such men. No demagogue, St. Clair lacked the demagogue's only virtue, the gift of reaching the people's hearts. Throughout his career in the Northwest, luck took sides against him, but he did not merit the humiliation nor the misfortune that marked the end of his service to the Territory. The reestablishment of the administration of justice according to law along the frontier made some gains from his efforts.

We know considerably less of the personalities of the judges who, with St. Clair, framed the first legislation under the Ordinance of 1787. Samuel

Arthur St. Clair was the first governor of the Northwest Territory.
Abraham Lincoln Presidential Library and Museum.

Holden Parsons was a revolutionary soldier and had been a member of the
military tribunal that had tried the gallant Major John André, the British
army major who was hanged as a spy in the American Revolution. He was a
nephew of a governor of Connecticut, had been educated at Harvard, and was
admitted to the New London County bar in 1759.[3] James Mitchell Varnum
came from Rhode Island, where he had practiced law after graduation from
Brown University. His legal career had been interrupted by military service.
John Cleves Symmes had held judicial office in New Jersey, but he was considered the least qualified of the three. His involvement in land speculation
was inconsistent with his judicial duties in the Territory and was a source of
embarrassment to St. Clair.[4]

The governor, Parsons, and Varnum issued a militia law, the first legislative act for the Territory, on July 25, 1788. A few weeks later the same three published an act establishing General Courts of Quarter Sessions of the Peace and County Courts of Common Pleas.[5] Shortly thereafter, they added a Court of Probate for the Territory. Between July 25 and December 28, 1788, the governor and judges passed ten acts. Judge Symmes signed only two of these. No further legislation was announced until July 19, 1790.

The quality of the first legislation in the Territory was poor. The governor and judges were hampered by the Ordinance of 1787 language, which limited their authority to "adopting" such laws of the original states as were best suited to conditions in the Territory.[6]

At the beginning there was a sharp controversy between St. Clair and Judges Parsons and Varnum over the proper interpretation of the words used in the Ordinance. St. Clair was convinced that Congress intended the legislative power to be confined to the verbatim adoption of such of the laws of the original thirteen states as were found most suitable. Judges Parsons and Varnum contended that laws might be created for the Territory as to those subjects for which no laws of the original states were found suitable.

St. Clair was willing to make an exception regarding the militia law, which he thought was required by necessity. He finally acquiesced in the other nine acts that were not true adoptions but reasserted his position in later years with the result that much legislation was created with paste pot and scissors.

The controversy took a curiously academic turn when St. Clair asked the judges what they meant by law. "If your honors will inform me of the precise meaning you affix to the word 'law,' as expressed in the clause of the Ordinance of Congress, referred to in your letter, I shall be better able to explain my sentiments upon the different matters you have opened, which I shall do with the utmost freedom, but not to each other, which is a kind of correspondence that could not be agreeable to either."[7]

The judges dissembled: "The ideas, sir, that we have adopted are that by *law* is meant the legal codes or systems of the original States, in their general nature and spirit, indefinitely as they refer to the vast variety of subjects about which they are conversant."[8] The controversy ended with neither side convinced by the other, and death soon removed two of the participants. Judge Varnum died October 10, 1788, and Judge Parsons met death by drowning in November of the following year.

Major George Turner was appointed in place of Judge Varnum on September 14, 1789. Little is known of his life prior to his appointment beyond the fact that he came from South Carolina and had served in the revolutionary army. Rufus Putnam was appointed April 7, 1790, to the vacancy caused by the death of Judge Parsons. General Putnam, another Revolutionary War soldier, like Judge Symmes, was heavily interested in land speculation in the Territory. Both Turner and Putnam resigned in 1796 and were respectively replaced by Return Jonathan Meigs and Joseph Gilman. Gilman was originally from New Hampshire and little is known of his early life. Meigs had been in the Territory for some time prior to his appointment. He was a graduate of Yale College and probably had legal training. These men actively participated in the drafting of legislation for the government of the Territory and exercised the supreme judicial power. Only one of the judges, George Turner, ever was to have any real connection with the Illinois country.

The Ordinance of 1787 provided that any two of the three Territorial judges might hold a court. A later act of Congress empowered a single judge to exercise this authority. This act caused Governor St. Clair great concern in view of the interest of Judges Symmes and Putnam in the Scioto and Ohio companies, respectively, because they were almost surely to be interested in land litigation that might come before them. Judicial ethics generally in the United States had not then developed to the point at which judges would disqualify themselves because of indirect interest in the causes before them.

There has been little effort to appraise the judicial work of the judges of the General Court of the Northwest Territory. The records of the court have never been published. It sat ordinarily at Marietta and at Cincinnati. A common complaint of the inhabitants and of the governor and secretary was that the judges did not hold court with sufficient frequency and were often absent from the Territory for long periods of time. There was no provision for appeals from the court's decisions or even from decisions rendered by a single judge.[9]

In the Illinois, the courts administering the French law continued to sit after the organization of the Territory. The court at Cahokia unquestionably maintained considerable regularity in its sessions and was respected by the inhabitants.[10] We cannot be entirely sure what was taking place at the time in Kaskaskia, since the record books of the court there appear to have been destroyed. It has been suggested that the destruction of the records was accomplished by certain citizens whose conduct was unfavorably reflected in the proceedings before the court.[11]

Arthur St. Clair arrived in Kaskaskia March 5, 1790. The court at Cahokia was in session two days before he arrived and met again in its accustomed manner on the first day of April. That was to be its last session. Four judges sat to decide the cases heard on that day. Antoine Girardin, who had exacted a good conduct promise from the inhabitants as a condition of his taking office, presided. His associates were Charles Ducharme, Philippe Engel, and Louis Chatel. These men deserve more honor than has been their fate. Through the dark days of anarchy, with no aid from the general government, they kept alive the ideal of justice.

As we examine the decisions they rendered so long ago we can glimpse the French law administered by men who had no technical legal training but who relied upon their general understanding of the traditional rules of the system to guide their decisions. The death of external authority had taken the vigor from the French law. There remained the memory of certain fundamental rules, the intuition of the judges as to the general spirit of the system, and a belief that justice existed when the people were equal before the law.

Thus it happened that justice was still administered according to law when Arthur St. Clair arrived to assert the authority of the United States in the Illinois. But Antoine Girardin did not sense the coming challenge of an alien law when he wrote the last sentence in the record book of the Cahokia Court. *"La Cour est ajournée au 1er may prochain."* (The Court is adjourned to the first of May next.) Never would a French court sit again in the Illinois.

St. Clair might have become a hero to the people of Kaskaskia, Cahokia, and Prairie du Rocher. His courtliness and grace had greater attraction for them than for the backwoodsmen from Virginia and Kentucky with whom he had associated in the settlements to the east, and he spoke fluent French. But his sober Scotch mind could not understand or condone their gaiety. He had no sympathy for their shortcomings, even though they resulted in some part from the breakdown of civil government through no fault of their own.

On April 27, 1790, the governor created St. Clair County by proclamation. It included all of the territory between the Illinois and Ohio Rivers from the Mississippi east to a straight line drawn from the mouth of the Mackinaw River to the mouth of the creek above Fort Massac. The proclamation designated no county seat but divided the county into three judicial districts, one for each of the three principal villages. Courts of general quarter sessions of the peace and common pleas were created, as well as a probate court. These courts were directed to hold sessions in each year at Kaskaskia, Prairie du Rocher, and Cahokia. The governor appointed justices of the peace, a coroner, and designated his cousin, William St. Clair, to be prothonotary and county clerk.[12]

It is important in tracing the development of the law to note the men whom St. Clair designated to act as judges. For the Court of Common Pleas, he appointed Jean Baptiste Barbau, Antoine Girardin, John Edgar, Philippe Engel, and Jean Dumoulin. He named Edgar, Engel, Girardin, and Antoine Louviere as justices of the Court of General Quarter Sessions. The Court of Common Pleas had general civil jurisdiction. The Court of General Quarter Sessions could hear and determine criminal cases in which the punishment did not extend to life, limb, imprisonment for more than one year, or forfeiture of goods or lands.[13]

There was no provision made for appeals from the decisions of these courts until 1795, when a statute allowed writs of error in the General Court. The same statute made provision for the holding of a circuit court in each county during the year by one of the judges of the General Court.[14]

The efforts of Governor St. Clair did not result in the immediate return of orderly civil government to the Illinois. It was too much to expect that the damage of nearly three decades of anarchy could be repaired merely by the enactment of new laws and the appointment of new officials. William St. Clair, the prothonotary, in 1793 reported conditions to the governor at Cincinnati: "There has not been a review these eighteen months past, so that it would appear we have no organized government whatever. Our courts are in a deplorable state; no order is kept in the interior, and many times not held. Prairie du Rocher has had no court this sometime, and Kaskaskia has failed before. The magistrates, however, have taken upon themselves to set it going again. I think they will again fail. The prospect is gloomy."[15]

It is fortunate that enough of the records of this difficult period remain to enable us to discover what was happening to the system of law that was being administered by the courts that came into being with the governor's proclamation. The Ordinance of 1787 provided that the General Court should have "a common law jurisdiction." There are many other passages in the Ordinance that evidence the familiarity of its drafters with the system of the English Common Law. For example, by the terms of Article II, the inhabitants were entitled to the benefits of the writ of habeas corpus, trial by jury, and of judicial proceedings according to the course of the Common Law. And harking back to Magna Charta: "No man shall be deprived of his liberty or property, but by the judgment of his peers, or the law of the land ..."[16]

St. Clair had come to the Territory from Pennsylvania and the first three judges were from Connecticut, Rhode Island, and New Jersey. All four had some considerable contact with courts and all of the judges were trained for the law. In all four of the states just mentioned the English Common Law had been received by the year 1790, but the judges did not think it desirable that the Common Law should be the basic system in the Northwest Territory.

Parsons and Varnum wrote of their misgivings to St. Clair in 1788: "Were we to be confined for any length of time to the principles of common law, we are fearful of very precarious consequences. The common law, as adopted in the States, while colonies, entered essentially into the principles of monar- chial government, and therefore can not, with propriety, be applied here. But upon the present view of the subject, the common law must be applied, or the actions of men be left to the direction of natural licentiousness."[17] Regardless of the feelings of the judges it is clear that the General Court of the Territory Northwest of the River Ohio was required to look to the Com- mon Law of England as administered in the United States for guidance in the decision of cases.

While the General Court was organizing to administer the law under the Ordinance, the judges appointed by St. Clair held the courts established by the Territorial legislation. In the Perrin collection of Cahokia documents there is a fragment of a record that lists the writs returnable to the October term of the Court of Common Pleas in 1790.[18] This record contains the first evidence that attorneys appeared for litigants before the courts in the Illinois. Eighteen cases were recorded, and in at least four of these, counsel represented one or both parties. The names of the frontier lawyers in these cases were Jones, Thruston, and Love.

Although no first names or initials were given, Jones must have been John Rice Jones, traditionally the first lawyer ever to locate in the Illinois. Our first glimpse of this Wales-born American was when he purchased supplies for George Rogers Clark's Kentucky militiamen from John Edgar at Kaskaskia in 1786. Jones was educated at Oxford and received a formal legal training before coming to America. He practiced law for a time in Philadelphia and moved west to become a frontier lawyer. He located in Kaskaskia sometime in 1789 and remained until at least 1800. Thereafter, he returned to Vincennes and later crossed the Mississippi to finish his life in Missouri.

The supplies that Jones purchased for Clark's illegal foray against the Indi- ans in 1786 were detained on the orders of John Dodge, who had instituted a reign of terror in Kaskaskia. Jones returned to the Illinois accompanied by a few Kentuckians with long rifles and defied Dodge in his stronghold, Fort Kas- kaskia on the hill above the village. Jones's courage was effective, for the supplies were released and his conduct was instrumental in breaking Dodge's power.

John Rice Jones was one of the first lawyers to settle in the Illinois country.
Abraham Lincoln Presidential Library and Museum.

The Oxford-trained lawyer must have seemed an extraordinary being to
the simple people in Kaskaskia. Jones, however, had a fine command of the
French language and soon established a considerable following. His career
was not a peaceful one. He served as the first attorney general of the Indiana
Territory and quarreled violently with Indiana Territory governor William
Henry Harrison. He was indicted at least twice for misfeasance in office but
was acquitted. His difficulties with Harrison were based mainly on political
differences. There can be no question that he was an able lawyer and his influence in shaping the course of the law as administered by the courts must have
been considerable. The murder of his son, Rice Jones, in 1808 on the streets
of Kaskaskia, described in chapter 4, provided the most celebrated litigation
tried before the General Court of the Illinois Territory. Another son held office
under the Republic of Texas and a third became a United States Senator.[19]

The Thruston of the Cahokia record was probably Buckner Thruston of Louisville, who became Senator from Kentucky. The identity of the third lawyer, Love, remains a mystery. His name does not appear in the later court records of the period.

What is more extraordinary than the fact that attorneys first appeared for litigants in 1790, is the fact that the Cahokia record listing the writs returnable to the October term gives Common Law names to all the cases. Of the eighteen cases listed, eight were proceedings in debt, five were actions of trespass on the case, four were foreign attachments, and one was an action of ejectment. The records for that year also establish that a grand jury was impaneled and that trial by petit jury was established as a regular institution.

Does it follow from these facts that the French law simply expired upon the establishment of courts with Common Law names? Such a conclusion would be so unusual as to be unsound on its face. In spite of Common Law names, English speaking lawyers and at least one English speaking judge, the old French law was not so easily put out of the way.

It should be noted that all of the judges named by St. Clair in 1790, except one, represented the French element in the population. Men like Antoine Girardin had experience with the French law as it had been administered during the Virginia period. Under these circumstances it was inevitable that the basic French law would continue to be administered in the Illinois courts regardless of what was being done at Marietta and Cincinnati. The extraordinary thing is the manner in which it was administered.

The year 1790 marked the most sudden change ever to take place in the law of Illinois. Beginning with October of that year the records of the courts were written in English instead of French.[20] Almost at once the terminology became that of the Common Law. Terms like debt, trespass on the case, even *scire facias* (a writ to enforce judgments) appeared in the record books. There is very little evidence of the mingling of languages as found in English legal records, although the first time *scire facias* was used, the phrase was *scire facias sur mortgages*, used to describe a writ. There were French terms written by Barrois in the *Registre* that had a certain flavor and descriptive quality that might have led to their appropriation by the invading system, but not a trace of them appears in the records.

This fact is of special significance, for it reveals the weakness of the French law when the Common Law challenged it. The years between 1740 and 1760 marked the period of greatest legal development in Illinois as a French province or district. There apparently existed in the principal villages a considerable number of citizens whose training and education fitted them to understand and to administer a refined and technical legal system. Men like LaLoere, Barrois, and Buchet had a legal competence that deserves respect. It is reasonable to suppose that most of the inhabitants of their generation, since these were immigrants to the Illinois, had some experience with the operation of the Custom of Paris or of Normandy in civilized surroundings. Their children would not have the same opportunity.

There is nothing in the records of Kaskaskia or Cahokia to indicate the establishment of schools or the organization of any kind of training calculated to preserve the refinements of the civilization of Quebec or of New Orleans. Frederic William Maitland's epigram, "Taught law is tough law," suggests its own converse.[21] The generation of Barrois passed. The legal experience of its children was derived from contact with the operation of French law in the wilderness. Even though the system effected a nice adjustment to its new surroundings, it must necessarily have lost coherence and symmetry in the process.

LaLoere, Barrois, and Buchet did not live to see the utter collapse of civil government in the jurisdiction of the Illinois. Others of their generation and tastes moved to New Orleans or across the Mississippi in their discouragement at the downfall of French colonial government. In the thirty years from 1760 to 1790 the French law lost its wise men. There is no evidence that a legal profession had ever existed in the villages along the Mississippi. Responsibility for legal administration rested upon educated men of substance, of whom a last survivor was Jean Gabriel Cerré, and upon professional civil servants like Buchet and Barrois. When death or desertion deprived it of men like these, deterioration was the necessary consequence.

Throughout the thirty years before the coming of the Common Law, the French legal system became more and more primitive. The beginning of the decline is easily discerned in the last poorly made entries of the *Registre des Insinuations*. There were officials who acted as notaries throughout the period, for the familiar means of effecting transfers was always the execution of written instruments before notaries. But they apparently kept no *registres* of these transactions.

It is probable that as men less familiar with the technical terms implemented administrative acts, the terms lost their exact meanings and finally ceased to be used. Their purposes were lost on a social order that no longer required the subtleties of the legal rules they characterized. Thus, terms like *conquet* and *communauté* became unfamiliar, and the distinction between the property that spouses brought to a marriage and acquired after the marriage ceased to be of much significance. Our failure to find the continuation of French legal terms describing important concepts after English became the language of the law in the Illinois country tells us that those concepts had lost their clear contours, and that the French law had ceased to be a systematic and coherent body of rules.

Nonetheless, French law still endured. The Ordinance of 1787 was ungenerous in its treatment of the old law. Virginia had made a gesture toward confirming this law to the inhabitants, first in the act creating the County of Illinois and again in her act of cession. The Continental Congress merely attached a saving clause to the portion of the Ordinance establishing rules of inheritance and for the conveyance of property: "[S]aving, however, to the French and Canadian inhabitants, and other settlers of the Kaskaskies, Saint Vencents and the neighboring villages, who have heretofore professed themselves citizens of Virginia, their laws and customs now in force among them, relative to the descent and conveyance of property." Only in this narrow sphere was the French law to be supported by the sanctions of American authority.

Governor St. Clair first reported to the secretary of state concerning the Illinois country on February 10, 1791. His report indicated the continuance of French customary law as to the matters set forth in the saving clause, noting, "By the Ordinance for the Government of the Territory the Laws and Customs which had prevailed among the ancient settlers are to be continued so far as respects the Descent and Conveyance of real property—the mode of conveyance was an Act before a notary, filed in his office, of which an attested Copy was delivered to the Party—to fulfill that part of the Ordinance it was necessary that Notaries public should be appointed, and one was commissioned at Kaskaskia, one at the Prairie du Rocher, and one at Cahokia."[22]

The Journal of Executive Proceedings shows that Louis Pierre Carbonneaux was appointed notary public at Kaskaskia on June 10, 1790. Carbonneaux had been a notary during the British period and was clerk of the Kaskaskia court under John Todd and Virginia. He was apparently acting as *greffier* when St. Clair arrived in Kaskaskia, for he delivered the archives to the new governor. Joseph Labuxiere Sr. was appointed notary at Cahokia in May of the same year. This and other evidence, such as the continuation of the system of common fields at the villages, establishes the fact that the French system of landholding survived the establishment of federal authority, but it was limited in its application to the French inhabitants. The isolation of the French communities weakened the ability of the French law to obtain a secure hold upon the Illinois country at large.

It is much more difficult to obtain direct evidence about the fate of the rest of French law after the establishment of civil government under the Ordinance of 1787. The adoption of English legal terms was complete and the use of Common Law procedure and forms advanced with extraordinary rapidity. Yet, here and there, the records show that the rules of the older system were still effective. The records from Cahokia afford greater proof of this fact than do the Kaskaskia records, since Cahokia remained more distinctly French for a much longer time.

During the period from 1790 to 1795, the Cahokia court frequently heard proceedings by petition in the old way, instead of by writ. In a petition from this period, parents who had adopted a child sought to be relieved of their responsibility in accordance with the rules of the French law. In other cases, the institution of community property in chattels remained in existence even though in a less developed form than in earlier times. Marriage was still very much a matter of contract and its incidents even as between American inhabitants of Cahokia, at least, were regulated by the French law.[23] Lastly, there were frequent resorts to arbitration in the settlement of disputes. It is clear that the more fundamental rules of the French law that had survived the long years of anarchy were still being administered but through Common Law forms.

However, French law had degenerated to the point where definite rules, outside the law of property, must have been few indeed. The system of law that had served so well the little communities existing like islands in the great wilderness failed completely when the frontier reached them. French law required the submission of every controversy to regularly constituted authority for decision. Except for arbitration, it gave almost no recognition to self-help as a means of settling disputes. Its dependence upon strong central authority was complete. It could not remain the basic system when such authority was lacking and when the more vital element in the population believed that the least law was the best law.

So it was that the French law was overwhelmed and forced to an underground existence. The Common Law moved west with the widening authority of the United States, but the records indicate a greater victory for the Common Law than the fact. The frontier was essentially lawless and although the Common Law was better equipped to cope with its turbulence, it was wholly inadequate to control the licentiousness of the frontiersmen.

In 1790, French criminal justice ceased to be administered in the Illinois country with the establishment of the Court of General Quarter Sessions of the Peace. As has been stated before, the authority of that court was restricted to dealing with crimes, the punishment for which did not involve life, limb, or imprisonment for more than one year, or forfeiture. The justices of the court functioned as committing magistrates when more serious crimes were involved. The grand jury became an established institution after 1790, as did the petit jury for the trial of criminal cases.[24]

But criminal justice, although administered according to law, was not well administered. There were very few instances in which the justices of the peace, in their capacity as committing magistrates, endeavored to curb the violence and brutality of the frontier. The courts did very little to establish order. Even the General Court of the Territory had comparatively little influence in putting down the lawlessness that came with the growing westward movement.

The grand juries, mostly called "grand inquests" in Illinois in the 1790s, occupied themselves principally with matters of morals during the period of the Northwest Territory. Each term, the grand inquest solemnly presented this and that individual (usually a Frenchman) for living in adultery, and many an unfortunate woman was presented for having a "base born" child. Lewdness and nuisance were other offenses frequently mentioned in the records. In the trial of these cases, punishment typically consisted of small fines. There were no jails until 1793, and St. Clair did not believe that military guard houses could legally be used as civil prisons.

Occasionally, however, the judges would try some more unusual form of punishment. Francois Guinett was prosecuted by the United States in the Cahokia court in 1794 for prostituting his wife. "Now come a Jury of good and Lawful men," says the record, giving their names, "Who being duly Called, Tried and Sworn find a Verdict of Guilty—Ordered that tomorrow at ten o-clock in the forenoon Francois Guinett be mounted on horseback with his face to the tail and conducted through the town from the jail to the Church Door and then back to the Jail—then to be liberated."[25]

The justices of the General Court of Quarter Sessions had administrative as well as judicial duties to perform. Grand juries presented roads and bridges for bad conditions as well as inhabitants for immorality. Upon such presentments the justices undertook to order repairs. They also appear to have legislated somewhat after the manner of town councillors. In 1801, when smallpox raged on the Spanish side of the Great River, the justices at Cahokia ordered guards of militiamen set at two ferries and made provision for the punishment of those who attempted to cross to the stricken territory or who sought to return to the Illinois.[26]

While the Court of General Quarter Sessions of the Peace for St. Clair County ineffectively dealt with criminal matters, the Court of Common Pleas administered civil justice according to rules of Common Law and French law. Such rules of French law that survived were rude in form. In 1795, the reorganization of the courts reduced further the chances for survival of the French law. In that year St. Clair, reciting that the division of St. Clair County into districts had not brought expected results, proclaimed the division of the Illinois into two separate counties. The southern county was named Randolph and included Kaskaskia as its seat of government.[27]

The division required the appointment of new judges for the courts of St. Clair County at Cahokia and the organization of the courts of Randolph County. Six judges were appointed to the Court of Common Pleas of St. Clair County. They were Jean Dumoulin, James Piggot, Jean Baptiste Saucier, William St. Clair, Shadrach Bond, and George Atchison. William Arundel was named prothonotary, and William St. Clair judge of probate. These six were also justices of the General Court of Quarter Sessions of the Peace, as were William Biggs and James Lemen. Of this group only Dumoulin had served on the old court. St. Clair had been clerk and prothonotary, and Saucier and Piggot had been justices of the peace.

In Randolph County, the governor appointed John Edgar, Antoine Louviere, Francois Janis, Peter Messerand, William Morrison, Nathaniel Hull, and Jonathan Owsley justices of the peace and commissioned them to hold the Court of General Quarter Sessions of the Peace. The same men, with the exception of Owsley, were appointed judges of the Court of Common Pleas. Lardner Clark was named prothonotary and John Edgar, judge of probate. In all, seventeen men were appointed to offices in the courts of the two counties. Of the seventeen, only four were Frenchmen.[28] It became clear that with the appointment of so many Americans as judges and court officers, the French law—or what remained of it—was presently marked for destruction.

Throughout the life of the Territory Northwest of the River Ohio, there was little connection between the Illinois country and the General Court. Mention has been made of the legislative provisions of 1795 for appeals and for the holding of circuit courts in the counties. So far as the records reveal, the first time a session of the General Court was held west of Vincennes occurred in 1794. In the early spring of that year Judge George Turner, in response to urgings from the governor, arrived in Kaskaskia and proceeded to hold court. He did so despite the fact that the Territorial statute provided that the session of the General Court for St. Clair County should be held in June.

There is a curious obscurity that attaches to all accounts of this session that is difficult to fathom. Judge Turner appears to have become involved in a bitter controversy with William St. Clair concerning the county records that were kept by the latter in Cahokia. Apparently, Judge Turner insisted that they be deposited at Kaskaskia and upon St. Clair's refusal, caused them to be delivered to John Rice Jones. Just what lay behind this dispute is not known.

In his correspondence with the governor, Turner criticized the conduct of the clerk and was sharply rebuked for this and other acts. Most accounts state that Turner aroused the ire of the inhabitants by his refusal to hold court at Cahokia.[29] Again the impression is created that other causes were at the bottom of the trouble. However, a few months earlier Turner had become involved at Vincennes in a dispute with the probate judge, Vander Burgh. It may be that he was lacking in judicial temperament, although he certainly was not lacking in ability. The Journal of Executive Proceedings shows that he made numerous legislative suggestions for desirable reforms that his associates tabled. In 1796, he resigned and left the Territory. He allegedly chose this course rather than face a grand jury indictment resulting from his conduct on the bench.[30]

Whatever may have been the real facts of the Turner affair, it brought Governor St. Clair and Judge Symmes to the Illinois country in September 1795. Judge Symmes, diverted for the moment, at least, from his land interests along the Scioto, appears to have taken up some of the cases that Judge Turner was to have tried and reviewed some of his decisions. St. Clair said that his own efforts and those of Symmes succeeded in restoring some measure of tranquility.

An example that sheds light on the state of the administration of criminal justice on the frontier was a murder case that came before Judge Symmes while he and St. Clair were in the Illinois country. The sheriff arrested two members of the Pottawatomie tribe. Some of the inhabitants killed the Pottowatomies while they were in the sheriff's custody. These events occurred while Judge Turner was in St. Clair County. Upon his report, the governor issued a proclamation reciting that the crime was committed while the Indians were being taken to court under a militia guard, and called for the arrest of the guilty persons.

While Judge Symmes held court in Kaskaskia, St. Clair insisted that the grand jury hear the matter. Witnesses identified two people as the murderers. The grand jury failed to return an indictment. The matter was reopened at Cahokia, and the governor ordered "the persons prosecuting the Public Pleas" to again offer a "Bill for Murder" against the accused, but the grand jury at Cahokia refused to vote a true bill and also refused to indict for manslaughter.

St. Clair despaired of justice being done by white men to Indians. In his report to the secretary of state the next January, he made the suggestion that Congress provide a heavy fine for murder or injury to Indians, to be levied on the county in which the offense occurred. He added from his Scotch thrift, "for it is often seen that the Minds of Men little tinctured with Justice or humanity have a pretty strong sympathy with their Pockets."[31]

The difficulties inherent in the governance of the country composed so largely of wilderness and where the settlements were so widely separated led at last to division. The Territory Northwest of the River Ohio had elected a territorial legislature in 1798. Necessity for travel to the capital at Cincinnati had intensified the problem the wilderness distances created. Congress created the Indiana Territory in 1800.[32] In partial fulfillment of the Ordinance of 1787, Ohio became a state in 1803. Thus the center of federal authority moved west to Vincennes, a settlement with French beginnings just a little younger than Cahokia and Kaskaskia.

The system of government provided by the Ordinance of 1787 continued for the new Territory. William Henry Harrison, who had succeeded Winthrop Sargent as territorial secretary, was appointed governor and John Gibson, another of the veterans of the Revolution, became secretary. The first judges were William Clarke, Henry Vander Burgh, and John Griffin. Clarke's background is unknown. Vander Burgh, a revolutionary soldier, lived in Vincennes for some years and had been judge for probate for Knox County. He originally came from New York. Judge Griffin "was a Virginian, of some elegant accomplishments and fond of social pleasures, a man of no great force, and an intriguer."[33] It seems doubtful whether any of these men had ever studied law.

Clarke died soon after his appointment and was succeeded by Thomas Terry Davis, former Congressman from Kentucky. Judge Griffin was succeeded in 1806 by Waller Taylor from Virginia, who was to become one of the first United States Senators from Indiana. Taylor was a trained lawyer. Judge Vander Burgh resigned in 1807 to accept an appointment to the General Court of Michigan Territory. He was succeeded by Benjamin Parke, territorial attorney-general and representative in Congress. Parke was to have a distinguished career as a state and federal judge. He "was a cultured gentleman, and a lawyer of talent, probity, industry, and conscience."[34] Truly, these qualities were rare on the frontier. The first attorney general, preceding Parke, was John Rice Jones.

The nine years during which the Illinois country was a part of Indiana Territory were years of the development of new problems for law. Most of these problems were unsolved when Illinois Territory began its separate political existence in 1809. The years 1800 to 1809 saw the tide of immigration steadily rising; saw the spread of the sorry, sordid speculation in lands with the attendant degradation of men of decency and ability; and saw the beginnings of the trouble over slavery. These problems were not solved until further legal development occurred after Illinois statehood.

From the standpoint of legal development, the period was one of consolidation of the Common Law as the basic system. By the end of the period, the submergence of the French law was nearly complete. What vestiges remained would continue for a long time. There was an increase in the quantity of litigation and, of course, a closer connection between the Illinois country and the General Court.

It is worthwhile to note that in the middle of the period there came the first formal extension of equity jurisdiction to the territorial courts. In 1805, Congress conferred equitable powers on the General Court. A few months later territorial legislation made provision for a Court of Chancery, but this court did not begin to function until after Illinois Territory had been created.[35] The administration of the Common Law without technical equity in the Northwest modeled the experience of Pennsylvania with some infiltration of equitable principles through Common Law forms. More than likely, the judges who sat in the counties probably had no knowledge of the distinction between equity and law. Much equity in the nontechnical sense was done by them without ever being conscious of the character of their acts.

The Indiana period showed a marked increase in the number of lawyers who practiced in the Illinois. One historian gave a list of seventeen and did not include Thruston or Love, who have been mentioned above.[36] Of the seventeen, a number continued to be prominent after the organization of Illinois Territory, such as William C. Carr, Isaac Darneille, Rufus Easton, and Robert Hamilton.

The period in Illinois legal history that began with the arrival of Arthur St. Clair in Kaskaskia in 1790 and ended with the separation of the Illinois Territory in 1809, was the period of the arrival of the Common Law on the frontier. It was not brought by the frontiersmen in their westerly migration but came with the federal officials and the lawyers. It was not acclaimed, as is sometimes stated, by the American settlers as their birthright. Even the judges of the first territorial court were not convinced that its advent was desirable. It might not have come at all had conditions in the Illinois favored the retention of French law as they did in Louisiana. The parallel legal development of Illinois and Louisiana, to a point, is almost always overlooked.

By 1790, all chance for the Custom of Paris to be retained as the basic law in any part of the midlands was gone. The contributing causes are not hard to find. Anarchy had so enfeebled the French law that in 1790 it scarcely deserved the title of a system. The priests had deserted the temple. Few French remained in the villages along the eastern bank of the Mississippi who knew enough of its essential formulae to be able to expound it, even if the opportunity had presented itself.

However, a much more serious impediment to the retention of French law was the barrier of language. This factor isolated the *habitants* and their ways from the Virginians, Kentuckians, and others who arrived in great numbers. Such a serious barrier to communication between the old settlers and the new was perhaps a sufficient cause in itself, for the French soon became a minority group who did not use the term "Americans" to describe themselves.

There were other causes. The backwoodsmen and pioneers who came into the Illinois in the declining days of French influence were people of a fierce independence. At its best, their independence was the spirit that conquered the wilderness. At its worst, it was a licentiousness that brought unspeakable brutality to every buckskin town on the frontier. The essence of the French law was submission to authority; it gave little place to self-help. Even if they had understood its virtues, the self-reliance of the Americans and their driving energy, which were among the best of their characteristics, would not have allowed them to accept it.[37]

Also we must not overlook the fact that the only law-trained men who entered the wilderness in this period were men trained in the Common Law. It was the trained lawyer who instructed the unlearned judge as to the proper manner of deciding the point at issue, and the French had no professional advocates. The only source materials were the English law books the lawyers brought with them to the wilderness. In the list of books in the library of H. I. Young, who died in Ste. Genevieve in 1810, we find *Barton's Equity, Blackstone's Commentaries, Espinasse's Nisi Prius* and *Comyn's Digest* among the many volumes. There was only one book that could help unravel a problem in French law, the *Laws of Louisiana*, presumably a book of statutes. This volume apparently had no purchaser at the auction sale of his effects.[38]

So ended the influence of French law in Illinois country; not quite ended, for vestiges remained for many years to come. Conditions uncongenial to its survival were most favorable for the development of its rival.

4. A Frontier Court

ON A QUIET STREET in Kaskaskia on the morning of December 7, 1808, a horseman reined his horse close to the picket fence in front of the house of Robert McCall. The horse's hoofs were heavy with the mud that lay deep and black along the center of the street. A hundred yards to the north stood the home of John Edgar with its broad eaves supported by cedar posts sweeping out over a wide gallery, the most imposing house in Kaskaskia. A great elm tree diagonally across the wide roadway from McCall's spread its bare branches black against the gray winter sky.[1]

The rider, a man of slight build, whose face gave evidence of a temper that he could not control, did not dismount but sat chatting idly with McCall. Dr. James Dunlap, physician, was not one of Kaskaskia's most respected citizens. A quarrelsome disposition and an active appetite for strong drink had destroyed whatever influence his medical training might have given him in the frontier community.

The men had talked for a few minutes when the sound of a door being opened across the street caused both to turn in that direction. They watched as the young lawyer, Rice Jones, walked quickly down the path from the house of Robert Morrison and turned up the street toward the Edgar house. As Jones passed, Dunlap's face suddenly contorted. He slipped quickly from the saddle, tossing the bridle reins over a picket in the fence and crossed the street with swift strides. His rapid pace brought him to the other side of the street not more than a half dozen yards behind Jones, who had reached the base of the elm tree. Abruptly, Dunlap called Jones's name and as the young man turned to face him, Dunlap drew a pistol from his belt. There was a brief exchange of words, a cry from Dunlap about revenge, and the sound of a shot. The noise from the hoofs of Dunlap's wildly running horse was in McCall's ears as he lifted the dying Jones from the mud at the edge of the street.[2]

Deeds of violence were not unusual on the streets of Kaskaskia.[3] Even before the coming of the frontiersmen, the ears of Kaskaskia's peace-loving *habitants* had become accustomed to the noise of the roistering *coureurs de bois* and *voyageurs*, and their eyes were accustomed to the flow of blood from the knife fights that so often occurred. But in this instance, the assassination of Rice Jones, son of John Rice Jones, the Territory's first lawyer, had a deeper significance. A struggle between powerful forces had suddenly become overt in the senseless act of a physician without character. The criminal proceeding that followed the murder became the first cause célèbre of the Illinois Territory.

Political events had moved swiftly since the creation of the Indiana Territory. The division of the Old Northwest had increased the agitation for separate government in Illinois. A powerful faction spurred by mostly personal motives, and characterized by an active and outspoken opposition to Governor William Henry Harrison, had made its influence felt in Congress. Two months after James Dunlap's passion overcame the physician in him, the act-making provision for the organization of Illinois Territory became law. The act was approved by President Thomas Jefferson on February 5, 1809, and became effective on March 1, of the same year.[4] The form of government followed the usual pattern. Executive authority was vested in the governor, judicial power in the three judges and a general court, and legislative power in the governor and judges. Old Kaskaskia, which had already seen the authority of two sovereigns, was once again a capital city and the scene of fierce political activity.

For the position of governor, President James Madison chose wisely and well by appointing Ninian Edwards, lawyer and judge from Kentucky, to exercise the executive authority. Madison appointed Nathaniel Pope, also a lawyer and with a faith in the law that led him to compile the first Illinois law book,[5] as territorial secretary. Obadiah Jones, Alexander Stuart, and Jesse B. Thomas were the judges of the General Court.[6]

Edwards had a son to write his biography. Nathaniel Pope left his name on a digest of the laws of Illinois and is remembered for his influence in locating the northern boundary of the future State of Illinois at a point that put Chicago in Illinois instead of in Wisconsin.[7] Of the judges, only Jesse B. Thomas has received just attention from the historians.[8] The men who

Ninian Edwards served as the only governor of the Illinois Territory, from 1809 to 1818. Abraham Lincoln Presidential Library and Museum.

served as members of the General Court, which for a period in its history was also known as the Court of Appeals of Illinois Territory, deserved more recognition of their judicial ability than what was accorded them in the books.

The state and local histories of Illinois contain no information concerning Jones or Stuart.[9] Like so many of the prominent citizens of early Illinois, Obadiah Jones was born in Virginia, probably in 1783. Thus he was only twenty-six years old when he assumed his judicial duties in Illinois. His career indicates he was a man of unusual ability. He was reared in poverty in South

Carolina, near Newberry Court House, and probably had no opportunity for formal schooling.

His ability, however, attracted the attention of a Judge Knight of South Carolina who assisted in his education and obtained a position for him as a school teacher. He studied law with the judge, who took him into partnership. He served less than one year as a member of the General Court in the Illinois Territory. The records do not reveal the identity of his sponsors or the circumstances concerning his appointment. He seems to have preferred the South to the rigors of frontier life in Illinois and was successful in obtaining an appointment as judge of the Mississippi Territory. A few years before his death, he moved to Athens, Georgia, and was appointed receiver of public moneys.[10]

Alexander Stuart was thirty-nine when he assumed his duties as judge in Illinois. Like Jones, he was a Virginian, but unlike him, came from a distinguished family. He was a younger brother of Judge Archibald Stuart from whom was descended the famous Confederate cavalry leader, J. E. B. Stuart. Alexander Stuart studied law in his brother's office and practiced law in Campbell County. He moved to Richmond when he was elected a member of the Executive Council of the Commonwealth. He came to Kaskaskia in May or June 1809 and served as a member of the General Court until 1811, when he established his residence in St. Louis; he died there in 1832. He served with distinction as a circuit judge in the Missouri Territory.

Jones and Stuart were men of more than ordinary ability, but their talents were overshadowed by Jesse B. Thomas, who was one of the most controversial characters of the Illinois frontier. Thomas served as a member of the General Court throughout the entire period of its existence. Future Illinois governor John Reynolds said he was born a politician "and never ceased the avocation until death."[11]

He practiced law in Indiana Territory and became a member of the territorial legislature and was elected speaker in 1805. While a member of the Indiana Legislature, he became a leading advocate of the cause of separation of the Illinois country and, with the help of the Illinois delegation, was elected a member of Congress by the territorial legislature. Governor Thomas Ford said that Thomas's Illinois adherents required him to give bond to further the cause of separation before they would agree to support his candidacy.[12] Whatever may have been his reasons, he proved an able champion of the effort to separate the Illinois country from Indiana Territory, for he was instrumental in obtaining passage of the act of separation. Thomas returned from Congress with a presidential commission as one of the judges of the General Court.

All contemporary accounts concede his ability, mention his capacity for political intrigue, but are silent about his personality. More revealing than anything written about him is the calloused shrewdness of his remark, made when he was serving as one of Illinois' first two senators. "You cannot talk a man down, but you can whisper him to death." Whatever may have been Thomas's capacities as a politician, there was nothing during the long period of his judicial service as a member of the territorial court to reflect upon his integrity. He seems to have been the most conscientious as well as the most influential figure on the court.[13]

There was no courthouse in Kaskaskia when the governor and judges met in the early summer of 1809 to begin their legislative functions. Judges Stuart and Thomas were the first members of the court to arrive in the territorial capital. They met Governor Edwards at the house of Thomas Cox on the morning of June 13. The first legislative act for the Territory continued in force the laws of Indiana Territory until such a time as the governor and judges could prepare legislation better suited to its needs.

Illinois Territory, 13th June, 1809

This day Ninian Edwards, Governor of the Illinois Territory,
Alexander Stuart and Jesse B. Thomas, Judges in and over the
Territory aforesaid, met at the home occupied by Mr. Thomas Cox
in the town of Kaskaskia, and after mature deliberation, they hearby
resolved as their opinion, that the laws of Indiana Territory of a
general nature and not local to that Territory are still in force in this
Territory as they were previous to the first day of March last.

> Ninian Edwards
> Alexr. Stuart
> Jesse B. Thomas

They passed four other acts at this session, three of them concerning the courts to be held in the new Territory. One of these provided that two terms of the General Court should be held each year in Kaskaskia, one to commence on the last Monday in March and the other on the last Monday in August of each year.[14]

Judge Jones put in his appearance at Kaskaskia in July 1809, and the act concerning the General Court, dated July 20, 1809, was signed by the governor and all three judges. This act made provision for two additional terms of the court to be held each year in Cahokia. It also repealed a prior act directing the establishment of courts of common pleas and county courts, and vested their jurisdiction in the General Court.

The governor and judges completed their first legislative efforts on July 22, 1809. The statutes they had drafted and enacted into law were few in number. As might have been expected of lawyers, almost all of these statutes were related in one way or another to the judicial system and to the administration of justice, but the governor and judges were sensible of the growing commercial needs of the Territory over which they had jurisdiction. The first legislative act for Illinois Territory that did not deal with the courts and officers engaged in the administration or enforcement of the law was an act entitled, "A Law to prevent frauds and perjuries. Adopted from the Kentucky Code." This was a version of the familiar Statute of Frauds.[15]

Their legislative duties completed for the time being, the judges waited more than a month before beginning the discharge of their judicial functions. In accordance with the provisions of the act of July 20, 1809, the first term of the General Court began in Kaskaskia on Monday, September 11, 1809. The court convened at the home of Thomas Cox, one of the larger houses in the French style.[16] All three judges—Stuart, Thomas, and Jones—were present at this first term, and all three judges served until the term ended on September 23, 1809.

According to the minute book, William C. Greenup acted as clerk of the court, and B. Stevenson was sheriff. Greenup was the Kaskaskia deputy of William Arundel, who had been appointed by the court as clerk. The very first matter of business before the court was a motion by John Rice Jones, traditionally the first professional lawyer to practice in Illinois, who moved that William O. Allen be admitted to practice as an attorney and counselor-at-law.

The first case to come before the court was that of *United States v. Francis King*. This was a criminal case of assault and battery. A jury found King guilty. On the second day of the term, the court entered an order that "the several attorneys who had practiced heretofore be admitted, etc." The names entered by the clerk in the minute book establish that Illinois, even at that early date, had attracted the talents of able lawyers.

Among the names placed in the court's records were those of Nathaniel Pope, Rufus Easton, John Rice Jones, and William Mears. All of these men were at the beginning of distinguished careers. Nathaniel Pope was territorial secretary. After a long and useful career, he ended life as a federal judge, respected for his ability and integrity. Rufus Easton was probably then living in St. Louis. His name was closely connected with law and politics in the Territory of Missouri. John Rice Jones had been attorney general of Indiana Territory and was to have a distinguished career as a judge in Missouri. He did not remain in Kaskaskia long after the murder of his son, Rice Jones.

There was no contemporary present with the forethought and imagination to describe the appearance of this frontier court as it began its judicial duties in the low-ceilinged principal room of the Cox house in old Kaskaskia. Yet there is evidence from which to reconstruct portions of the picture. The three judges sat at a table near the inside wall of the room that extended across the entire front of the house. The outside sunlight streaming in through the few narrow windows was aided by the yellow light of candles, for there are marks of candle drippings on the record book.

William Greenup, the clerk, wrote with a quill pen. Some of the parings from frequent sharpenings remain between the pages of the book that he or Arundel titled in black letters "Compleat Records of Cases Dicided by the General Court of the Illinois Territory at Kaskaskia." The black broadcloth and white linen of the judges must have contrasted sharply with the garb of the other officials, litigants, and spectators who crowded the room. Buckskin and homespun characterized the frontiersmen of Virginia and Kentucky, while the blue kerchiefs distinguished the French *habitants*.

No picture of Judges Jones or Stuart has been found but a contemporary portrait of Jesse B. Thomas indicates a forceful, dominating personality. He was six feet tall and weighed more than two hundred pounds, of swarthy complexion with dark hair and eyes. He must have occupied the center chair at the table, for any other position would have been inconsistent with his character.[17]

The proceedings of that court, held so long ago in a frontier village, since swept away by the surging Mississippi River, could not have been characterized by the pomp and ceremony associated with court proceedings in the more civilized sections of the country. Nevertheless, the court must have inspired respect, for as the minute book testifies, it disposed of a considerable amount of judicial business in a relatively short time. Interruptions and interferences must have been at a minimum.

The September term lasted twelve days and the court disposed of a total of thirty-seven cases. The records in all of these cases speak of the firm basis on which the Common Law had become established. The court used both grand and petit juries. The names given to the forms of the actions were the old Common Law names that remained in Illinois for more than a century after the General Court ceased to exist.

Nine of the cases disposed of at this term were criminal cases. Of the nine criminal cases, five involved charges of assault and battery, two of murder, one of unlawful assembly, and one of burglary. In the first case, *United States v. Francis King*, in which the prisoner was found guilty, the court sentenced him to be whipped thirty-nine lashes and to be fined $225. Of the twenty-eight civil cases, seventeen were actions of trespass on the case, five were actions of debt, and three were actions of trespass. There was one action in covenant, one domestic attachment, and one action on a recognizance.

On the second day of the term, the clerk called the case of *United States v. James Dunlap*. A grand jury had indicted the intemperate physician for the murder of Rice Jones. Dunlap was never brought to trial because he was never seen in Kaskaskia again after he raced his horse out of town on that early December morning. While Dunlap was never tried, the murder of Rice Jones did give rise to other litigation. On September 15, 1809, the fifth day of the term, the clerk called the case of *United States v. Michael Jones*. The grand jury indicted Jones as an accessory before the fact to James Dunlap's crime. Behind this indictment and the murder of the most promising young lawyer in the Territory was a struggle for power involving greed and dishonesty, graft, and corruption on a scale usually associated with modern-day scandals.

To understand the circumstances that produced the animosities and quarrels culminating in Dunlap's cowardly act of assassination, it is important to remember that on the frontier, the most valuable asset a person could possess was land. The wealth that produced power was in the land that supplied the basic wants of society. While most of the Illinois country was still a wilderness, schemes for control of land had begun. The temptations of those in official positions to use their influence for the recognition of claims to land affected the activities of even so principled a politician as Arthur St. Clair.[18] It has already been noted that he was embarrassed in the performance of his official duties by the financial interest of Judge Symmes in Ohio lands.

The greed and competition for control of land increased as the population grew. The government of the United States, eager to bring about the settlement of the wilderness, had established offices for registering land claims and had made military grants to those who had enrolled in its service.[19] Difficulties inherent in record-keeping on the frontier made possible the forging and duplication of claims and signatures. As fraud piled upon fraud, the realization grew that scarcely one title in the entire Territory could stand unimpeached. St. Clair had attempted to deal with the situation in the days of the old Northwest, and William Henry Harrison, as governor of Indiana Territory, had made some considerable efforts. Neither was successful.

At last in 1804, Michael Jones, newly appointed register of the land office at Kaskaskia, and Elijah Backus, receiver of the same office, were appointed a Board of Land Commissioners to inquire into the claims to lands in the Illinois country. These commissioners worked for six years to unravel and sift the evidence to distinguish valid claims from fraudulent ones. The results of their labors, and that of a second board appointed in 1812, consisting of Michael Jones, John Caldwell, and Thomas Sloo, were extraordinary.

The findings resulted in the disapproving, on the grounds of fraud and perjury, of many claims submitted by some of the most prominent citizens of Illinois Territory. The findings of the boards necessarily had the effect of arousing against the commissioners the unrelenting enmity of such influential men as John Edgar; James Gilbreath; John Rice Jones; William Kelly; Richard Lord; James, Joseph, Robert, and William Morrison; John and Robert Reynolds; and William Whiteside.[20]

In Francis Philbrick's survey of the Laws of Indiana Territory, he concluded that:

> The incredible forgeries, fraud, subordination and perjuries which the commissioners uncovered are explainable only by attributing to the land jobbers an assumption of immunity that led to carelessness or a stupidity of which it is difficult to believe them capable. The discovery of more than seven hundred perjured depositions given before one magistrate in upper Louisiana led to the uncovering of hundreds more. The board, in its own words, struggled "in the very mire and filth of corruption." Almost all of the claims rejected for perjury rested upon the supposed original title or improvements of fifteen persons, attributed to them either by themselves or by others who assumed their names. Some of these fifteen were respectable citizens who disavowed hundreds of their alleged depositions. One tool of the land-jobbers confessed to [was] the wholesale use of another's name. The rest of the fifteen were wholesale perjurers bought and sold by the speculators. Depositions were bought outright, or signatures obtained from drunken men to blank depositions. Among those who gave as many as two hundred depositions each, one was characterized by the commissioners as a "kind of straggling blacksmith,"

another as a "poor wandering wretch, equally destitute of morality or character," several as men "of no education, property or character." Two gave sworn and written confessions. Almost all of the depositions in these fifteen names were given to support claims of John Edgar, Robert and William Morrison, Robert Reynolds, William Kelly—three judges, the clerk, and a former coroner of Randolph—and Richard Lord, a mere (land) privateer. The depositions of one prolific deponent, proved to be false, were signed and sworn to exactly as written in the hand of John Edgar.[21]

The commissioner's report against some of these men was bitter and contemptuous. Robert Reynolds, a justice of the peace with supreme impartiality, forged the names of witnesses, deponents, grantors, and his fellow judges, gave depositions under an assumed name and appeared before a magistrate with deponents who bore false witness. He even allegedly forged a grant to himself from a slave woman.[22]

From the time of the creation of Indiana Territory until Illinois was admitted to the Union as a state, the most influential political faction in the Illinois country was headed by John Edgar and Robert and William Morrison. This group had opposed the Harrison faction in the days of Indiana Territory and had worked continuously for the establishment of a separate government of Illinois.

The dominating personality among its leaders was John Edgar, in 1809 the richest man in Kaskaskia. Born in Ireland about 1733, he arrived in Kaskaskia in 1784 with a considerable stock of money and goods, and immediately went into business as a merchant and miller. His record in support of the American cause in the Revolution in the west is good; and he became a judge in the Illinois country during the governorship of Arthur St. Clair, serving as a member of the Court of Common Pleas and as a justice of Quarter Sessions and as probate judge.

Throughout his life he was prominent in the affairs of the community, but his record as a public citizen is marred "beyond explanation or palliation" by his participation in the land frauds.[23] With William Morrison, he shared the active direction of the most powerful political faction in the Illinois country. Morrison, also a merchant, came to Kaskaskia in 1790 from Pennsylvania and conducted stores in Kaskaskia and Cahokia, engaging on a large scale in the Indian and fur trades. He was in partnership with his uncle, Guy Bryant, of Philadelphia.

Kaskaskia was the social and political capital of the Illinois Territory.
Abraham Lincoln Presidential Library and Museum.

The Edgar-Morrison faction landed on the pro-slavery side of the controversy that was ultimately to light the fire of civil war. This faction—steady
and strong—opposed Governor Harrison. These facts are to be weighed in
considering the course of subsequent events. Not only did the two principal
leaders of the Edgar-Morrison faction become involved in the land frauds,
but also many other prominent members of this group were involved as
well. Their shameful conduct inevitably brought them into collision with the
redoubtable land commissioner, Michael Jones. Little biographical information
concerning Michael Jones is available and there is danger of confusing him
with the lawyer and Shawneetown politician of the same name.

He is said to have come to the Illinois from New Jersey and the evidence
indicates that he was a firm friend and political adherent of Governor Harrison. There is also evidence tending to show that he engaged in considerable
political activity antagonistic to the Edgar-Morrison faction. Nevertheless,
the evidence is overwhelming in favor of his unswerving honesty and steadfast
adherence to duty in office.[24] Failing in every effort to influence him in their
favor, the Edgar-Morrison faction counted it a major purpose to discredit
Michael Jones and to drive him from the Territory.

Rice Jones, the young lawyer whom James Dunlap shot down near the Edgar home in Kaskaskia on December 7, 1808, was the eldest son of John Rice Jones and was born in Wales in 1781. He was educated at Transylvania University and studied law at the Litchfield Law School. Apparently, he began the practice of law in Kaskaskia in 1806. Entering politics in 1808, he represented Randolph County in the lower house of the Indiana Territory General Assembly, being supported by the Edgar-Morrison faction. This faction was then making an issue in the local elections of the division of the Territory. The election produced numerous personal enmities. Rice Jones became involved in a duel with Shadrach Bond, later to be the first governor of the state of Illinois. In this duel, William Morrison appeared as Jones's second and Dr. James Dunlap acted as second for Bond.

The story goes that Jones inadvertently touched the hair-trigger on his pistol before the signal to fire had been given. Dunlap promptly urged his principal to fire at Jones in his turn, but Bond, recognizing that the discharge was accidental, refused to do so. The quarrel was then settled without the duel taking place.

Dr. Dunlap was an adherent of the Harrison faction and a reputed friend of the land commissioner, Michael Jones. The difficulties between Dunlap and Rice Jones may have stemmed from the determination by commissioners Michael Jones and Elijah Backus that the land claims of some of Rice Jones's clients were fraudulent. Rice Jones is reputed to have indulged in numerous attacks upon the character of Dr. Dunlap.

In the proceeding before the General Court of Illinois Territory, it was alleged that Dunlap, smarting under the slurs of Rice Jones, sought the advice of Michael Jones and his fellow land commissioner. The prosecution sought to establish that Jones advised Dunlap to retaliate against his lawyer adversary, but in what way, the evidence did not make clear. It was also alleged that Michael Jones, Backus, and Dunlap made threats against the life of Rice Jones in November 1808. As proof, John Rice Jones offered a letter from himself to Backus, dated November 25, 1808, in which he mentions threats against the life of his son.

The chief defect of Michael Jones's character was his lack of ability to control his temper. It is quite possible that ill-considered words spoken in anger gave the leaders of the Edgar-Morrison faction what they thought was a golden opportunity to discredit the land commissioner and his work. At any rate, they procured his indictment by the grand jury as an accessory before the fact to the murder of Rice Jones, alleging that "he did, on the 6th day of December, 1808, incite, move, aid and abet, feloniously and with malice aforethought, the said James Dunlap, to commit the crime of murder."

The case of *United States v. Michael Jones* was called by the clerk on Friday, September 15, 1809. Judges Jones, Stuart, and Thomas were present. The defendant made a motion for trial, and the attorney general asked for a continuance. The court overruled the motion to continue and fixed "Friday next" for trial. On September 22, the attorney general again moved for a continuance and this time the court granted the motion and set the case over to the April term.

April 9, 1810, the first day of the new term, found only Judges Stuart and Thomas in attendance. Robert Morrison was clerk and B. Stevenson, the sheriff. *United States vs. Michael Jones* was the first case called and in the language of the minute book was "laid over until tomorrow." On the next day the stubborn and uncompromising land commissioner went to trial before a jury, charged with being an accessory to the crime of murder. The verdict, given the same day, was "not guilty."

The records of the General Court of Illinois Territory do not contain a transcript of the evidence. The indications are that there was little to support the charge. Yet on April 11, the court exonerated the attorney general from any obligation to pay costs, a request that could be granted only when the court found probable cause for an indictment. Nevertheless, it is believed that little significance should be attached to this fact, for the records indicate that the court was extremely liberal in relieving prosecutors of the obligation to pay costs.

As soon as Michael Jones was exonerated from the murder charge, he sued William Morrison, Robert Morrison, and John Edgar for libel, the causes of action being alleged to have arisen out of statements made in writing during the course of the criminal proceeding. The case against Robert Morrison was dismissed, but a judgment was rendered against William Morrison for $200 and costs, and John Edgar settled out of court. By the terms of the settlement he was required to make a public declaration "that Michael Jones was entirely innocent of any part in the murder of Rice Jones."[25]

United States v. Michael Jones and the subsequent libel suits involved the most prominent and influential men in the Territory. The judges appear to have acquitted themselves courageously and honorably, without being influenced by the violent contentions of frontier politics.

Throughout the nine years of its existence, no charge of corruption was ever made against the General Court of the Illinois Territory, nor was there any attack upon the integrity of any of its judges. The three places on its bench from 1809 to 1818 were occupied by a total of seven men. Of the three judges originally appointed, Obadiah Jones was the first to leave the court, resigning in 1810. He was succeeded by Stanley Griswold, a Connecticut man who had begun his career as a preacher.

Griswold was a man of considerable experience in frontier politics. He had been commissioned secretary of Michigan Territory by President Thomas Jefferson in March 1805 and served briefly as acting governor of the Territory. In addition to his duties as territorial secretary, he served the United States as collector of revenue. Griswold was a man of substantial talents, but a lack of tact and an inability to express himself candidly without giving offense impaired his effectiveness as a frontier administrator. He became involved in a serious controversy with territorial governor William Hull and was forced to resign as territorial secretary in 1807.

Griswold moved to Ohio after his unhappy experience in the Michigan Territory and served briefly as United States Senator. His appointment as judge in the Illinois Territory came almost immediately after the expiration of his interim term in the Senate. That he was a satisfactory but not a brilliant judge is in the thought behind Governor John Reynolds's quaint language: "Stanley Griswold was a correct, honest man; a good lawyer; paid his debts and sung David's psalms."

Judge Thomas continued as a member of the court until it ended its existence in 1818, thereafter serving as one of Illinois' first two United States Senators. Alexander Stuart, the third member of the original court served until 1813, when he was succeeded by William Sprigg, a Marylander and a brother of a former governor of that state. Sprigg had been a federal district attorney in Chillicothe, Ohio. He declined an appointment to the General Court of Michigan Territory in 1805 but served first as a judge and later as federal land commissioner in Orleans Territory. Governor William C. C. Claiborne, in a letter to President Jefferson, praised Sprigg's ability and integrity, and Reynolds recorded that he was a "fine classic scholar and a well-read and profound lawyer."[26]

Only two other changes in the personnel of the court occurred after 1813. Judge Griswold died at Shawneetown in 1815, and Thomas Towles, who had the backing of Governor Ninian Edwards, succeeded him. Judge Sprigg resigned in 1818, a short time before the court was terminated by the admission of Illinois as a state. He was succeeded by Richard Graham, but the records of the court do not indicate that Graham participated in the remaining sessions of the court, at least at Kaskaskia.

If the decisions rendered by the General Court of the Illinois Territory were in most instances satisfactory to lawyers, litigants, and the public, the diligence of the judges in attending to their duties was not. Travel was difficult and dangerous in the Illinois country, and the judges were not inspired to unusual self-sacrifices by the opportunities for service to the pioneer communities. From the beginning the problem of holding sessions of court with sufficient frequency was a troublesome one.

The governor and judges had endeavored to deal with the problem by legislation enacted in July 1809. Under this enactment the judges were required to hold four terms of court each year, two in Kaskaskia beginning on the second Mondays of April and September, and two in Cahokia on the fourth Mondays of these same months. A further provision stated that the court should have original and final jurisdiction over all cases, both civil and criminal, as was exercised by the General Court, the Circuit Courts, and Courts of Common Pleas of Indiana Territory, except appeals from the judgments of justices of the peace in cases when the sum involved was less than $20.[27]

As the population of the Territory began to increase, the four terms of court provided by this legislation were not adequate to serve the needs of the frontier farmers and merchants, whose aggressive ways offered new problems in the administration of justice through law. As time went on, the judges became less sensible of their duty to provide adequate machinery for the settlement of disputes. Even had the judges been willing to devote themselves more fully to their judicial duties, the rigors of frontier life would have forced frequent postponements and adjournments of court terms.

Once in 1811, Judges Stuart and Thomas postponed the session of the General Court scheduled for September at Cahokia, reciting for the record that there was "great reason to apprehend that the approaching fall will be uncommonly sickly, especially at the town of Cahokia, in the county of St. Clair."[28] As the situation grew worse, the grand juries of St. Clair and Randolph counties presented all of the judges for nonresidence and nonattendance and the matter was brought to the attention of Shadrach Bond, the nonvoting representative of the Territory in Congress, who contemplated laying the presentments before that body.

In 1812, the legislative function passed from the governor and judges to a territorial legislature as Illinois entered the second stage of its territorial development. In 1814, the legislature submitted to the governor a statute entitled, "An act to establish a Supreme Court for Illinois Territory." Prior legislation had attempted to define the jurisdiction of the court. It had stated that such jurisdiction included a general reviewing power over cases determined in any of the inferior courts, original jurisdiction of the more serious criminal offenses, and of all cases in equity where the value of the matter in controversy exceeded the sum of $100. The new act provided that the court should be styled "The Supreme Court of Illinois Territory" and required the judges to hold circuit court in each of the counties. There followed a serious controversy between the judges on one side and the governor and the territorial legislature on the other.[29]

The federal statutes creating the territory and making provision for the legislature did not set forth its powers with respect to the judiciary. Since the General Court had been created pursuant to an act of Congress, serious doubts arose as to the validity of the new legislation, and the General Assembly requested the judges to state their opinion. Judge Griswold remained aloof from the controversy, but Judges Thomas and Sprigg prepared a long opinion in which they emphatically denied the power of the legislature to change the name of the court or to increase or modify the duties of the judges. The legislature then asked Governor Edwards to prepare an answer, which he submitted on December 12, 1814.

Although the arguments presented on both sides were dryly legalistic, it is clear that the opposition of the judges was prompted largely by their desire to avoid the onerous circuit court duties the act imposed upon them. The legal merits of the controversy were never settled. The legislature adopted resolutions transmitting the act, the opinion of the judges, and the answer of Governor Edwards to the Congress, with a memorial requesting "the passage of a law declaring the aforesaid enactment valid, or to pass some law more explanatory of the relative duties and powers of the Judges aforesaid and of this Legislature, in order to remove any future or existing difficulties that may arise between the Judges and the Legislature." The Congress took the matter under consideration and on March 3, 1815, passed a statute titled "An Act regulating and defining the duties of the United States' Judges for the territory of Illinois," which adopted the essential features of the territorial statute.[30]

The new act divided the territory into three circuits, each corresponding to two of the six counties then in existence. The judges were required to allot the three circuits among themselves and to hold two terms of a circuit court annually in each county in their respective circuits. The jurisdiction of the circuit courts was defined to include "all causes, matters or things at common law or in Chancery, arising in each of said Counties" except where the debt or demand was under $20. The circuit courts were also given jurisdiction over all criminal matters. A further provision of the act designated the judges or a majority of them as a court to be styled the "Court of Appeals for Illinois Territory," two sessions of which were to be held annually in March and August at Kaskaskia.

The Court of Appeals was to have appellate jurisdiction only over decisions of all of the inferior courts, including the circuit courts. The act contained no grant of power to the territorial legislature except the authority to change the times of holding any of the courts specified in the act. The last section of the act contained the peculiar provision that "no judge or justice appointed under the authority of the government of the said territory shall be associated with the aforesaid United States judges when sitting as Circuit Court judges as aforesaid." The designation "Court of Appeals for Illinois Territory" was used by the court from the opening of the August 1815 term until the June 1818 term.

The Act of Congress of 1815 did not solve the problem. The controversy between the legislature and the judges continued until the issue of statehood eliminated it. An act of the territorial legislature, approved January 9, 1816, attempted to define the jurisdiction of the circuit courts and to make clear that the United States judges were required to perform the same duties that were vested in and required of the judges of the General Court on December 31, 1814. This act contained a statement that it was the intention of the legislature to confer upon the circuit courts and its judges "such powers and to require of them such duties as the United States Judges for this territory have heretofore from time to time exercised and performed in those cases only in which such powers and duties shall not be repugnant to the before recited Act of Congress."

The legislature also asked the Congress for authority to make such changes in the laws governing the judiciary as might be required in the future. The response of Congress was the act of April 29, 1816, which was obviously intended to grant the request. The wording was such, however, that the judges could claim that the power to make changes would be ineffective at the end of the following session of the legislature. The controversy became one of the most important political issues of the day and the legislature, by an act approved January 6, 1817, attempted to require the judges to perform circuit court duties in three circuits to be allotted between them.

The act organized the counties of Bond, Madison, St. Clair, and Monroe into the first circuit. Randolph, Jackson, Johnson, and Pope Counties comprised the second circuit. The third consisted of Gallatin, White, Edwards, and Crawford Counties. The court entered an order on June 9, 1817, allotting the first circuit to Judge Thomas, the second to Judge Sprigg, and the third to Judge Towles. According to the terms of the order this allotment was to continue until January 10, 1818. The act directed the judges to hold three terms of the circuit court in each county annually, each term to consist of six days. The judges were also required to hold two terms of the Court of Appeals each year at Kaskaskia in June and October.[31]

Judges Thomas and Towles yielded to the legislative will and traveled their circuits, but Judge Sprigg declined to recognize the act and absented himself from the Territory. In 1818, the legislature abandoned the struggle and relieved the judges of their circuit court duties. New legislation divided the Territory into two circuits, for each of which one person "learned in the law" was to be appointed as judge each year at a salary of $1,000. This act, approved January 1, 1818, also provided that the United States judges should again constitute a General Court of Illinois Territory and should hold four terms of this court annually, two at Shawneetown in June and October on the fourth Mondays and two at Kaskaskia on the second Mondays of the same months. The court was to have appellate jurisdiction.

The capitulation of the legislature was not quite complete, however, when it adopted resolutions requesting the territorial delegate in Congress to lay before the House of Representatives charges against Judge Sprigg for his refusal to hold courts as required by law and for absenting himself from the Territory for an unreasonable time.

Perhaps the United States judges should not be criticized too much for their reluctance to undertake the rigors of circuit court duty. Traveling the circuits would have required them to spend the principal part of their time on the road. The dangers to life from Indians and renegade whites were real indeed, and the written statements of travelers in the Illinois country during these years attest the absence of all except the meanest accommodations.

The last term of the General Court of Illinois Territory was held in June 1818 at Kaskaskia, unless possibly a term was held at Shawneetown in that year. The records of sessions held at Kaskaskia are complete from the first term in 1809 until the end of the June term in 1818. Although the court was required by law at various times during the nine years of its life to convene at Cahokia and at Shawneetown, no records of its proceedings at either place have been found and it cannot be stated with certainty that the court ever sat outside the territorial capital.

The earliest of Illinois federal courts was truly a frontier court. The pages of its remaining records provide glimpses of amusing crudities in legal procedure.

The Common Law forms that had come to be adopted in proceedings before the court involved technical refinements that lawyers and judges struggled to adapt to the needs of pioneer communities.

Pleadings were set forth at length in the court's records and one sympathizes with the efforts of the lawyers of the day who endeavored, without the benefit of extensive libraries and precedents, to state their causes of action and defenses in the forms that the Common Law required. In the libel suit that Michael Jones brought against John Edgar, the perspiring efforts of Otho Shrader and Rufus Easton, attorneys for the plaintiff, are almost discernible in the record as they struggled to obey the mandate of the Common Law, as they understood it, regarding the pleading of innuendoes.

There are frequent entries in the records that serve to remind that violence and death in the wilderness imposed a constant strain upon law enforcement and threatened the orderly development of the legal system. Occasionally there is a humorous side to entries in the record. In 1810, Governor Edwards issued a commission to Judge Thomas to hold a special court of oyer and terminer (a court of criminal jurisdiction) to try Moses Cannady and John Gibson on a charge of stealing the sheriff's horse.

The activity in land speculation brought on suits in ejectment to test disputed titles. These cases were often designated "Timothy Peaceable v. Thomas Troublesome" and indicated a developing land law. Arbitration survived from French days as an important means of settling disputes, and the court was frequently asked to enforce the decisions of the arbitrators. There are occasional divorce cases in the records, enough to indicate that judicial divorce was the rule, and legislative divorce, of which there were examples, was the exception.

One such case before the General Court was described as "Libel for Divorce." From the beginning to the end the records indicate completeness of the victory of the Common Law system. No better evidence can be found than the recognition in cases before the court of the distinction between Common Law and equity in the administration of legal remedies.

A case decided at the April 1813 term provides an insight into conditions of life in the wilderness communities. Sarah Curry, an infant, by her next friend, brought an action of trespass *vi et armis* against Jonathan Pettit, for an assault that was alleged to have taken place at the Township of Springfield, in Randolph County, on December 19, 1810. Curry was the indentured servant of the defendant, having been indentured by her mother, a widow, when the plaintiff was four years and ten months of age. The indenture was set forth in the record. In return for obedient services, defendant promised to teach plaintiff to spell and to read in the English language and "shall cause her to be taught how to sew, knit, cook and spin and other farmers housework and at the expiration of said term to provide the said apprentice with two suits of new cloth, one for common were [wear] and one other fit to go abroad in such as is customary in the country by farming people."

The declaration alleged an assault "with fists, clubs, sticks and horse tail" setting forth that defendant tied the plaintiff to a horse's tail, beat her and dragged her over a log. Curry was about twelve years of age when the assault took place. Rufus Easton, attorney for the plaintiff, asked damages in the amount of $1,200. A jury, after hearing the evidence, found the defendant guilty and assessed the plaintiff's damages at $80.

As has been mentioned before, the record of the General Court of Illinois Territory in the impartial administration of justice seems to have been generally satisfactory. The ethics of the day did not require the maintenance of standards that are now regarded as essential to the proper performance of the duties of both judge and advocate. The lawyers of the Illinois country during the territorial period sometimes represented both sides in a controversy, even in litigation, and rarely did a judge of the General Court disqualify himself for cause.

The records provide little information concerning the methods that the court employed in the decision of cases and as to what law books were available for the use of judges or lawyers. They certainly used some collections of the formal precedents, for the language of pleadings in many instances comes too close to what was considered good Common Law practice to be accounted for by reliance on memory.

It is difficult to appraise the contribution of the court to the establishment of the administration of justice according to law. Throughout the first five years of its existence, criminal cases appeared more frequently on its records than during the remaining period of its life. Most guilty offenders during this period were dealt with sternly. It would appear that the court was accomplishing more to control the lawlessness of the frontier than had either of its predecessors, the general courts of Indiana and the Northwest Territories. But the dispute between the legislature and the judges over the performance of circuit court duties impaired judicial ambition, and the zeal that characterized the court during its first years was lacking during the later period. Fewer criminal cases appear in the records and the instances of stern treatment of offenders were rare.

A just appraisal of the work of these frontier judges of a frontier court will take into consideration the fact that the terrors of wilderness life were frequently just outside the doors of the courtroom. On the first day of the September 1812 term, the court caused a letter from Nathaniel Pope, the territorial secretary, to be spread upon the record. The letter, addressed to Judge Thomas, reported a conversation with Governor Edwards in which the governor expressed the opinion that the danger of trouble with the Indians was such that a term of the General Court ought not to be held at Kaskaskia or at Cahokia in that year. The court concluded that conditions were so serious as to require an adjournment until the next term.

As a matter of fact, the court did not sit again until September 1813. The order, written by Judge Thomas, is the nearest thing to a written opinion that the court ever produced. The imagination of the reader can reconstruct from it, some picture of the lives of jurymen and litigants who cleared the land and built their isolated and lonely homes outside of the comparative safety of the frontier towns.

In considering that it is the duty of the court as well as every officer and citizen of the territory to hold in respectful regard any view the executive may entertain, through his superior means of information, respecting the situation of the territory, or any of its inhabitants in point of exterior danger, and also to aid him in repelling or guarding against the same. Considering that the exposure of a single family to be butchered by the savages through the risk of calling the head or a member to attend the Court (as appears to be suggested by the executive) should outweigh in importance the whole mass of civil business which might be transacted in the term. Considering that as one-half of the militia is led out and are ordered to march immediately to the frontier a fair presumption arises that the greater part of the causes docketed for the present term, if now called up must be continued through necessary absence of parties or witnesses, and thus some suitors be put to a useless expense in traveling a great distance to attend such causes: considering finally, that the trials, if proceeded in, could not now be attended to those advantages to the suitors which have been customary and are highly desirable, relating to jurors and bail, inasmuch as the field for the selection of the one and procurement of the other, is materially diminished by the departure of so great a portion of the militia to the frontier as aforesaid: considering these things, the judges now present did, in the vacancy and subsequently to the receipt of the executive information aforesaid, consent to suspend the business of the Court until the next term, and caused information thereof to be extended as much as possible through the territory. It is therefore ordered that all suits, motions recognizances—bills of indictment orders and conditional fines be continued until the next Term. Ordered that court be adjourned until court in course.

5. Lawyers and Law Courts

JAMES MONROE WAS PRESIDENT of the United States when Illinois was admitted to the Union on December 3, 1818. It was a time of impermanence and transition. War with Great Britain had ended on Christmas Eve in 1814, but the Treaty of Ghent left many issues unsettled. Cautiously the government at Washington began to assert itself in the affairs of nations. In another five years the president and his secretary of state would formulate and announce the declaration of policy known as the Monroe Doctrine.[1] In 1819, the first steamship would cross the Atlantic Ocean and the first major business depression would strike the country. It was the beginning of the "era of good feelings," and in politics the two-party system had all but disappeared with the downfall of the Federalists.

Most of these things went unnoticed in the Illinois country. The factional politics of the frontier had little room for political parties or national issues. Not even the passing of one who had been a great leader attracted much attention. George Rogers Clark, old, maimed, and paralyzed, died in poverty on February 13, 1818. The memory of the frontier was short and its impatience too great to keep alive a sense of gratitude or even the vivid memory of one who in a lifetime passed from the heights to obscurity. The devotion of the frontiersman to a man of action needed the constant stimulus of new deeds. When these were lacking, devotion died and the doer was forgotten. There is no question but that Virginia, Illinois, Indiana, and the whole country neglected the talents of one of the most gifted men of the time.[2]

A wave of migration continued to roll westward into Illinois along the principal water highways. The up-country farmers from Virginia and the Carolinas, the backwoodsmen from Kentucky and Tennessee were arriving in large numbers.[3] Cheap land of good quality was largely a thing of the past in southern Ohio and Indiana, and immigrants from the south and east found few bargains to detain them until they reached the prairie country. The children and grandchildren of New England pioneers were coming to the Illinois settlements in increasing numbers and there was the beginning of a small stream of home seekers from England, Germany, and Switzerland that would one day reach very large proportions. As these elements established themselves on the frontier, each contributed something to the development of the legal system under statehood.[4]

There were about 35,000 people within the boundaries of Illinois in 1818. The population was concentrated in the American Bottom because water transportation was easiest and safest and because river bottomlands were fertile and easier to get into cultivation. This land stretched from the point at which the Missouri River empties into the Mississippi southeast to Kaskaskia. Some settlements had sprung up along the Wabash River, others were grouped around the United States salines[5] and on the Ohio River, and some villages were being established along the principal tributaries of the Mississippi.

But the traveler who would go overland from Shawneetown, then the gateway to Illinois, on the way to Kaskaskia must still cross wide tracts of wilderness, broken here and there by trails that would soon become wagon tracks. The old French towns had rivals, some of which, like Belleville, Edwardsville, and Alton, would grow and prosper while others, such as Shawneetown and Brownsville, would decline or disappear.[6]

North of the mouth of the Illinois River was the wilderness—rarely broken by settlements—the prairies, forests, and rivers of the Indian country. East of the Illinois River lived the Kickapoos, who still remembered British influence and the War of 1812. West of the Illinois ranged the Sacs and Fox and hunting bands of other tribes. This latter territory included the Military Grant, where land had been set off to soldiers of the War of 1812. Among the tribes came and went the successors of the *coureurs de bois*, the traders of the American Fur Company, who loaded their mackinack boats with a rich take in pelts.

The once influential position of the French in Illinois had passed when a majority of the important families crossed the Mississippi to the Territory of Louisiana. Many of them were attracted by the high promise of St. Louis, the great trading center and point of embarkation to the West. Only a few of the influential French, like the Menards, saw visions of future greatness in the Illinois and remained to take part in the building of the state. Yet the *habitants* constituted an important element in the population for many years with their descendants remaining in the American Bottom until well into the twentieth century.

Nevertheless, by 1818 French influence had passed and the French way of life was passing too. French speech was to outlast both, but in the years to come the principal influence on government and law would be exerted by Virginians and Kentuckians, New Yorkers, and Yankees from New England.

Before the beginning of statehood, submergence of French law in the growing American Common Law was quite complete. Even in the French villages, French judges no longer sat in the courts nor were proceedings conducted in the language of the people. The Custom of Paris as administered in the Illinois country had degenerated to the point where the only vestiges to be found were primarily in modes of transferring property and in certain rules of family law.[7]

The reasons for the downfall of French law are quite clear. At the most critical period in its development it lost the services of the influential people who might have been able to preserve its spirit and bring about the incorporation of certain of its more important doctrines into the new order. The shock that French law received during the period of anarchy, beginning in 1763, was too severe to permit recovery, especially when it was accompanied by the desertion or death of those whose knowledge of its methods of administration could not be replaced. The temporary resurgence under the rule of Virginia had no secure foundation to support it.

Even if these factors had not been present and even had there been the trained civil servants so necessary to the French system, it is clear that certain characteristics of the French communities would have prevented French law from remaining the basic secondary system. The isolation of the French villages and the inability of their population to absorb the frontier elements appearing on their streets prevented any aspects of French civilization from becoming dominant. So fundamentally opposite were the habits and attitudes of the French *habitants* and those of the frontiersmen from Virginia and Kentucky that no coalescence was possible.

The legislation of the Northwest Territory had imposed courts with Common Law names upon the French population. The terminology of the law became the Common Law terminology. To most outside appearances the legal system appeared to be based upon the Common Law of England. It is easy, however, in appraising these appearances to assume too much. The fact is that in many places in the United States during the last quarter of the eighteenth century, opposition to the Common Law of England had been pronounced and outspoken.[8]

As late as 1807, Kentucky had enacted a statute providing that English authorities since July 4, 1776, should not be read or considered as authority in any of the courts. During the period of the Northwest Territory, Arthur St. Clair had experienced open opposition from the territorial judges to his efforts to bring about a more complete adoption of the Common Law. The frontier elements in the population of Illinois, far from claiming the Common Law as their birthright, were essentially lawless. The frontier period represents the extreme of the philosophy that the last law is the best law.[9]

Nevertheless, the Common Law was ready at hand to be applied when need arose. In the beginning, it provided terminology and machinery for the administration of justice. As long as the needs of the frontier were few, common sense or the social sense of the judges would supply the rules, while the Common Law supplied the forms. It would be a long time after 1787 before English precedents would be cited and relied upon to any considerable extent in the courts of Illinois. In the meantime, interpretation by the judges of the sense of the community began to crystallize into rules. There would emerge in later years an American Common Law in which the law of Coke and Blackstone would be an important ingredient.

The first formal recognition of the Common Law as the basic system of law in the Midwest appeared in legislation for the Northwest Territory. The first reception statute was adopted by Governor St. Clair and Judges Symmes and Turner, July 14, 1795. It was taken from a Virginia Statute of 1776 and provided, "The common law of England, all statutes or acts of the British parliament made in aid of the common law, prior to the fourth year of the reign of King James the first (and which are of a general nature, not local to that kingdom) and also the civil laws in force in this Territory, shall be the rule of decision, and shall be considered, as of full force, until repealed by legislative authority or disapproved of by congress."[10]

In substance this statute has been carried forward into the present law of Ohio, Indiana, Illinois, and Michigan. However, the slow process of adoption and modification of its rules by the judges in the decision of cases, rather than by force of legislative enactments, accomplished actual reception of the Common Law.

In the establishment of any legal system the collective influence of the lawyers practicing in the courts has been at least equal to that of the judges who administer the rules. An examination of the condition of the bar in 1818 is important to an understanding of the state of the law. Considering the times and the pioneer character of its communities, Illinois was served by an able bar when it became a state.

It is probable that there was none among the lawyers practicing in its courts in 1818 who could claim the advantage of cultural and professional training such as had been given to John Rice Jones. That talented leader, whether activated by emotional consequences of the murder of his son or by a belief that larger opportunities were to be found farther west, had left Kaskaskia to establish a place for himself in Missouri Territory. After him came men who made up in ability much of what they may have lacked in educational advantages.

The records that have thus far come to light do not include a roll of attorneys for the Northwest Territory or for Indiana Territory, nor has any such list been discovered among the records of the General Court of Illinois Territory. There is a roll of attorneys at the end of the first order book of the Supreme Court of Illinois, a volume that contains the manuscript records of the last sessions of the territorial court as well.[11]

The roll contains sixty-four signatures and the dates of licenses and entries. The dates of the licenses listed run from 1808 to 1833, while the entries apparently began in 1819. There are names on the list whose bearers rose to fame and fortune. There appear the signatures of William Mears, Samuel D. Lockwood, Sidney Breese, Thomas Ford, Samuel McRoberts, John McLean, Elias Kent Kane, Alfred Cowles, Theophilus W. Smith, George Forquer, Walter B. Scates, and John J. Hardin.

The omission of other distinguished names from the list makes it clear that many of those who had been licensed to practice law in the territorial period did not bother to sign their names to the roll that the first Supreme Court directed to be kept by its clerk. Outstanding among those whose names were omitted was Nathaniel Pope, first territorial secretary, politician, leader of the bar, and federal judge. Missing also is the name of Daniel Pope Cook, for whom Cook County was named and whose efforts were largely responsible for the movement resulting in statehood.

American pioneer communities typically regarded litigation as a game and the courts as arenas where the game was played for the entertainment of the spectators. Victory was something to be achieved by the use of wits and forensic ability and the justness of the result was frequently secondary in the eyes of the community. Amusements were few in the villages of civilization's outposts. Crowds would gather to watch and listen as the lawyers engaged in histrionics and oratory.

Nathaniel Pope was the secretary of the Illinois Territory, the territorial representative to Congress, and a U.S. district judge. Abraham Lincoln Presidential Library and Museum.

Leaders of the Kaskaskia bar when Illinois became a state were John Scott, Rufus Easton, Robert Robinson, and Nathaniel Pope. Scott and Easton were Missourians, and Scott at least was a distinguished and qualified lawyer. The shadow of charges involving unprofessional conduct hangs over Easton's name.

Pope contributed largely to the legal and political life of Illinois during the period when the state was in the making. His forebears had lived in Virginia for three generations and his father had settled in Kentucky at Louisville. Pope had been educated at Transylvania University and in 1803, at nineteen, worked in his brother's law office in Lexington. About 1804, Pope settled in Ste. Genevieve, in upper Louisiana, and directed himself to the practice of law. In 1806, he formed a partnership with John Scott, also a Virginian who had graduated from Princeton University in 1802. He appears to have had an active, if not a lucrative, practice in Ste. Genevieve until just before the organization of Illinois Territory.

It was customary for lawyers of that day to pay little attention to state or territorial lines and Pope appeared regularly in the courts in Kaskaskia. Finally, in December 1808, he took up residence in the oldest of the French settlements in Illinois. That same month he married Lucretia Backus, daughter of the receiver of the land office at Kaskaskia and associate of the redoubtable Michael Jones in the investigation of the land frauds.[12]

Pope's brother had become United States Senator from Kentucky and it was through his influence and that of Henry Clay that the young man gained the appointment as secretary of Illinois Territory on March 7, 1809. John Boyle, who had been appointed governor, resigned without having qualified. As a consequence Pope, as acting governor, undertook the organization of the territory and continued to occupy the chief executive position until June 11, 1809, when Ninian Edwards took the oath of office. Inevitably, Pope became involved in the factional disputes that were characteristic of frontier politics. By marriage and association he was the natural ally of Elijah Backus and Michael Jones, and consequently, the avowed enemy of John Edgar and the Morrisons.

When Edwards left the territory temporarily in 1813, Pope again became acting governor. When the legislature met in November of that year, Pope made the executive recommendations concerning legislation. His compilation and publication of the book familiarly known as *Pope's Digest* was his crowning achievement as territorial secretary. The *Digest* was compiled under legislative direction and was intended to include all of the laws of the Territory then actually in force. It was the first book published in Illinois.

In 1816, Pope was elected to represent the Territory in Congress. A handbill printed by him for use in the campaign and in answer to charges of misconduct is of interest:

> I aspire to the honor of representing the free people of Illinois territory
> in congress, and in that body bear testimony to their patriotism, bravery
> and suffering, and call upon the general government to do justice to those
> who have been so much injured by the unaccountable delay in their pay
> for services.... I should indeed take pride in showing the world what the

sons of Illinois have done to protect an extensive and weak frontier, and then reproach the nation with its conduct towards them. I have other objects; I wish to promote the prosperity and encourage the immigration to this territory; In order to succeed in these objects, I shall endeavor to get the Indian titles extinguished to all the land within the limits that are to be the permanent boundaries of this (will be) state, and especially the lands on this side [of] the Illinois River, including the Sanguemon [*sic*] country, and get it all in the market as soon as possible. Instead of being concerned as has been insinuated with a company to buy the United States' Saline (which I deny) I would oppose such a sale with the most determined zeal. I entertained a hope to be able to prevail on the general government to lay out the money arising from the rents of the U. States' Saline in improvements in the territory such as opening roads, building bridges, &c. in the different parts of the territory. Other things might be done beneficial to the territory, for example, the lands reserved for schools and a seminary, might be placed under some regulations that would make them yield in a short time an income that might be laid out to promote education &c.

Pope was in Washington during the period when Congress decided to give Illinois sovereign existence as a state. While acting as the Territory's representative in Congress, he was able to have the boundary of Illinois moved northward in order to give the new state a harbor on Lake Michigan. Chicago was then unknown; and the northern part of the state was undeveloped. Whatever may have been his dream, Pope has received credit as a man of vision.

He took little part in the affairs that led to the organization of the state government and for a time he made good his stated retirement from politics. He then campaigned unsuccessfully for Congress, and President Monroe appointed him register of the land office at Edwardsville. A short time later, Monroe tendered him a commission as United States judge for the District of Illinois. He held this position until his death on January 23, 1850. Many facts testify that he filled the position with honor and distinction—although not always willingly. He tried once or twice to get back to politics by seeking other offices.

Another leader of the Kaskaskia bar was Elias Kent Kane, who appeared often as counsel before the General Court. Kane was twelve years younger than Pope, having been born in New York in 1794. He practiced law for a short time in Tennessee and came to Kaskaskia about 1814. He served briefly as judge and became the first secretary of state under Governor Shadrach

Bond. In 1824, he campaigned successfully for the United States Senate and was reelected in 1830. He died in Washington near the close of his second term in the Senate, only slightly more than forty years old.[13]

In the southeastern part of the state, Shawneetown was rising to surpass Kaskaskia in commercial importance. The leader of the bar there was John McLean, born in North Carolina in 1791. His oratorical gifts were of a very high order and his services were much in demand in litigation before all of the territorial courts. In 1818, he became the first Illinois Congressman, having defeated Daniel Pope Cook. McLean succeeded Ninian Edwards as United States Senator in 1824 and was reelected in 1828. But like Kane, he died in office.[14]

Although there were able lawyers at the Illinois bar when statehood began, there were rascals and charlatans as well. Traditionally, the second lawyer to establish himself in practice in Illinois was Isaac Darneille, who settled in Cahokia about 1796. For a time Darneille practically monopolized the practice in Cahokia, but in 1797 the Court of Common Pleas of St. Clair County barred him from appearing before it, assigning as reasons "several contempt and disorders in this court and by reason of his horrid moral character." He was the author of the cleverly written Letters of Decius, a series of attacks on Governor William Henry Harrison. His character traits appear to have ruined his practice and caused him to move from Cahokia to Peoria. He later wandered to Kentucky, where he became a school teacher and died in obscurity in 1830.[15]

The typical frontier lawyer had to rely more on oratorical ability and small cleverness than on legal knowledge to win cases and attract clients. Society in Illinois in 1818 had not attained sufficient complexity to render the practice of law burdensome or litigation complicated. Pope, Easton, Scott, and McLean, with Kane and Cook, were the acknowledged leaders of the bar. Yet the volume of practice of none of these was sufficient to occupy his full time or claim his undivided attention.

The profession of the law provided a livelihood, the key to a certain station in society, and a ladder to political preferment. While some of the men who practiced before the Illinois courts may have had the scholar's instinct, few, if any, found in their practice the incentive to excel in legal learning. The development of the law suffered because neither lawyers nor judges were moved to constructive craftsmanship.

Several factors contributed to this absence of demand for legal scholarship. The unrest that followed the American Revolution brought with it public distaste and disrespect for law and animosity toward lawyers. The unpopularity of things English produced outspoken antagonism toward the Common Law.

During the latter part of the eighteenth century and the beginning of the nineteenth, the popular mind regarded lawyers as particularly responsible for most public ills. On the frontier, the fierce independence that characterized the American element in the population considerably heightened the feeling. The very minimum of law was all that could be tolerated.

A writer, who signed himself "Anticipator," expressed the attitude of the country and of the frontier in particular. His long letter was published in the *Illinois Intelligencer* on June 10, 1818. He argued for arbitration as a substitute for litigation in the settlement of disputes:

> Nothing can be more interesting to a community than the simplicity of its code of jurisprudence. That the old ritual of the English common law, handed down with little variation from the barbarous ages of Edward IV, should continue to be the established mode of proceeding in Brittain to this day, is not so strange as might at first be conceived from the rapid stride she has made in other improvements, for there it had not only the prejudices of the people formed, perhaps without examination to support it, but likewise the interest of rulers of the land, who always dread a change in any visual part of their institutions, but it is *strange* that this serpentine and circuitous rotine should be nourished on this side of the Atlantic, after we had thrown off the yoke of political and ecclesiastical operation of the mother country ... but long use has made familiar to our eyes, modes of chicanery and delays of justice in which we are more vitally interested

After making this argument for arbitration he continued:

> It must be an object to all uninterested men to put our legal proceedings on a more simple footing, and in some parts to make it more comfortable to common sense. Lawyers could still live, for men would continue to be vicious, and we must have a criminal court.

The period of time from the organization of Illinois as a state until at least the adoption of the second state constitution in 1848 was characterized by, among other things, a lack of public confidence in judges and courts as guardians of general welfare. There was little prestige attached to judicial office. Reviewing courts were not generally regarded as having any important influence on the development of the law.[16] The state legislatures enjoyed the confidence and faith of those who hoped for improvement in government and law during this period to a greater degree than has ever been accorded them since. Courts and judges still had to earn public confidence and esteem through a series of contests with the legislature.

The general unpopularity of lawyers led to legislative attempts at regulation of the profession beginning under the government of the Northwest Territory as early as 1792. Winthrop Sargent—the strong-willed territorial secretary, acting as governor in the absence of St. Clair—with Judges Symmes and Putnam, passed a statute regulating the admission of attorneys. The statute provided that no person should be admitted or should practice before any of the territorial courts unless he first passed an examination before one of the territorial judges. He also had to obtain a certificate that he possessed "the proper abilities and qualifications to render him useful in the office of an attorney."

The legislation set forth the oath that was required to be taken in addition to the oath of loyalty to the United States. Its language expressed some of the profession's highest ideals:

> I swear that I will do no falsehood nor consent to the doing of any in the courts of justice and if I know of an intention to commit any I will give knowledge thereof to the justices of the said courts or some of them that it may be prevented. I will not wittingly or willingly promote or sue any false groundless or unlawful suit nor give aid or consent to the same and I will conduct myself in the office of an attorney within the said courts according to the best of my knowledge and discretion and with all good fidelity as well to the courts as my clients. So help me God.[17]

The act further provided that the parties to litigation might plead and manage their own causes, personally or with the assistance of counsel, but neither plaintiff nor defendant should employ more than two attorneys in any case. In the modern-day crowded bar, it is amusing to note the provision that where there were only two attorneys attending the courts in any of the counties, neither the plaintiff nor the defendant should be allowed more than one counsel.

Counsel fees seem to have been allowed the successful party to litigation regardless of the subject matter. The statute provided that where there were only two attorneys attending the courts, fees for only one attorney should be taxed. This entire statute, with others, was repealed by the governor and judges by an act passed July 14, 1795.

A more comprehensive statute regarding the admission of attorneys was enacted by the territorial legislature and approved by Governor St. Clair on October 29, 1799. This statute provided for the licensing of attorneys upon an examination conducted by two or more of the judges of the General Court and required the applicant to obtain a rule of that court for the purpose.

In support of the motion for such a rule the applicant was required to produce to the court a certificate from a practicing attorney residing within the Territory. The certificate had to ascertain that the applicant was of good moral character and that "he hath regularly and attentively studied law, under his direction, within the territory for the space of four years, and also, that he believes him to be a person of sufficient abilities and legal knowledge to discharge the duties of an attorney at law."

The clerk of the General Court was required to keep a roll of attorneys, and no person could practice as an attorney unless his name was written on the roll. The legislature was evidently suspicious of the Common Law immunities of lawyers while attending court, for it provided that they should be liable to arrest in the same manner as any other person. The privilege of practicing law was limited to citizens of the Territory. Judges of the General Court, Court of Common Pleas and court officers, sheriffs, and deputies were forbidden to practice.[18]

The statute drew a distinction between attorneys-at-law and counselors-at-law. This distinction apparently corresponded in some degree to the distinction between attorney and barrister and was to be found in Massachusetts, New York, and New Jersey. Subsequent territorial statutes recognized the distinction, but there is no evidence to indicate that it was of any practical significance. Members of the bar appeared in all of the courts in the old Northwest and in Indiana and Illinois territories wherever the business of their clients required their presence.

The fees that attorneys and counselors were entitled to charge were first regulated by an act adopted by the governor and Judges Symmes and Turner from "the New York and Pennsylvania Codes" on June 16, 1795. Some of its provisions are worth noting. The retaining fee for cases in the General Court was limited to $3.50, and 12½ cents was allowed for drawing all processes and returns. The lawyer was entitled to a term fee of 75 cents but no more than three term fees were allowed in a single cause. Clients paid for the drawing of pleadings by the page at the rate of 18 cents for every sheet of seventy-two words. Arguing a special motion was worth $1.50, while the amount of the fee for arguing a demurrer was left to the discretion of the judge. Similar fees were allowed for work in the Court of Common Pleas.

A catch-all provision of the statute took a stand against excessive fees: "For any services actually performed and not enumerated in this law, the judges and justices, respectively, shall certify or tax so much for such services, as the same are really worth, and no more." The act replaced an earlier act of Secretary Sargent and Judges Symmes and Putnam, which had limited pleading fees in cases in the "supreme court" to $2.00 when "council" was employed. The same Act had limited the retaining fee for causes in the Common Pleas and Court of Quarter Sessions to $1.00.[19]

When Indiana Territory was organized, Governor Harrison and Judges Clarke, Vander Burgh, and Griffin repealed the provision of the Northwest Territory statute that required a residence of one year in the Territory for persons desiring to obtain licenses to practice law. They also repealed the provision requiring an applicant to produce a certificate of having studied law for four years.[20]

The removal of these restrictions suggests the fact that the governor and judges, at least, believed that the number of lawyers was too small to serve the needs of the Territory. It is also illustrative of the doubt that existed concerning proper construction of laws of the Northwest Territory with respect to their application in the new territories carved from the old. Did the residence limitation mean residence in Indiana Territory and admitted to practice before the creation of Indiana Territory, eligible to continue to practice before the courts of the new territory?

The new statute was intended to settle the matter. The old statute was further modified in 1804 by eliminating the requirement that the applicant must obtain a rule from the General Court prior to examination. Also eliminated was the section that authorized the governor to grant licenses to attorneys. Thereafter, any judge of the General Court was authorized to examine and license any person "either as counselor or attorney."[21]

Evidently in 1803, the governor and judges had passed legislation regulating the admission and practice of attorneys and counselors. However, this legislation does not appear in the published territorial laws and was repealed by act of the legislature in 1805.[22]

In 1807, the legislature, with the governor's approval, enacted a general statute regulating admission to the bar. In substance, this legislation provided for the obtaining of a license as attorney and counselor-at-law from any two of the judges of the General Court. A prerequisite to such a license was the obtaining of a certificate of good moral character from the "court of some county."

The clerk of the General Court was required to keep a roll of attorneys as part of the records of office. Judges, justices of the peace, coroners, sheriffs, jailers, constables, and clerks of court could not practice, as were persons who were not citizens of the Territory, excepting such as were already licensed as attorneys. The form of oath required, in addition to the oath to support the Constitution of the United States, was taken directly from the short form of oath provided by the legislation of the Northwest Territory.[23]

A statute enacted by Governor Harrison and Judges Davis and Vander Burgh in 1803 regulated fees of lawyers. Counselors and attorneys were entitled to a fee of $7 in cases in the General Court in which the title to lands was not in question. When title to lands was involved, the fee could be $10. For advice when no suit was pending, $3.50 was a permissible fee. In the lower courts in civil actions in which the title to lands was not in question, the fee was limited to $2.50, while $5 was permissible if the title to lands was involved. For advice when a suit was not pending the fee was $1.27.

Legislation of 1807 reduced fees to $2.50 in actions not involving the title to land and $5 in which title was involved, whether the suit was in the General Court or the Court of Common Pleas. For verbal advice in which a suit was not pending the lawyer might receive $1.25. If the advice was written, the fee was double this amount.[24]

Governor Edwards and the judges of Illinois Territory began their legislative duties with a resolution that the laws of Indiana Territory of a general nature were still in force in Illinois Territory. They were apparently satisfied with the Indiana legislation regulating the practice of law. However, they repealed portions of the act of 1807 that prohibited the admission of attorneys and counselors who were not residents of the Territory. This was, of course, a direct recognition of the influence of lawyers such as John Scott, Rufus Easton, and others who lived outside the territory, particularly in Missouri.

Either lawyers were not as troublesome as before or the territorial legislature was too busy with other matters to pass a general statute regulating the practice of law, for the Act of 1807 of Indiana Territory as modified continued to be the law until Illinois became a state. The principle of retaliation motivated the legislature in 1816, when it enacted a statute forbidding persons residing in Indiana from practicing in Illinois Territory. The preamble indicates the basis for the legislation: "Whereas, by a law now in force in the State of Indiana, persons who do not reside therein (although qualified according to the laws of their own state or territory) are not permitted to practice in the courts of the said state, and whereas that restriction is illiberal, unjust and contrary to those principles of liberality and reciprocity by which each and every state or territory should be governed...."[25]

None of the lawyers practicing before Illinois courts in 1818 had enough work to practice full time. The chief reward for members of the bar was enhanced prestige in the community. Practice was a path to political fortune, and most lawyers of that day took advantage of every opportunity to demonstrate whatever forensic ability they possessed. Their homes were their offices or chambers.

Libraries were limited. A few English works such as *Comyn's Digest* had found their way into the hands of the more affluent members of the bar to supply precedents when they were needed. *Blackstone's Commentaries* had been printed in American editions as early as 1780 and was finding its way into use. These and a few other standard works and the statutes were the available books. Law office study was the only means of obtaining a legal education unless a young man could afford the far journey to study at the Litchfield Law School or Harvard University.

The restless energy of a young lawyer, who in 1817 and 1818 had been appearing with increasing frequency before the Kaskaskia courts, supplied the driving force behind the movement that brought Illinois into the Union as a state. Daniel Pope Cook was a son-in-law of Governor Edwards and a nephew of Nathaniel Pope, then the territorial representative in Congress. A Kentuckian by birth, Cook had settled in Ste. Genevieve and engaged actively in the practice of law on both sides of the Mississippi. He moved to Kaskaskia in 1817 when only twenty years old, having purchased from Matthew Duncan the only newspaper in Illinois Territory. He changed its name from the *Illinois Herald* to *The Western Intelligencer*.

Sensing the larger opportunities that would be open when Illinois became a state, Cook vigorously urged the passage of an enabling act through editorials in his newspaper, and induced Nathaniel Pope to introduce such a measure in Congress. In many ways Cook was typical of the young professional men who were beginning to arrive in Illinois in search of wider opportunities for the exercise of their talents.[26]

The enabling act authorized the people of Illinois Territory to form a constitution and made provision for the admission of the Territory as a state. President Monroe approved it on April 18, 1818. Considerable excitement ensued over the election of delegates to the constitutional convention, which was scheduled to meet in Kaskaskia on Monday, August 3, 1818. For many days before the opening of the convention, the roads leading to the old town carried an unusual number of travelers. The members of the convention, thirty-three in number, constituted the largest official body convened in the

Territory during the entire federal period and probably the largest official body ever to assemble in the old French town.

The convention was more than twice as large as the legislative council and territorial house of representatives combined. In addition to the delegates, the convention attracted to the capital a large number of persons who had no official connection with it. For three weeks, beginning August 3, Kaskaskia was the scene of intense political activity. The convention met in the brick building called "the old State House," where the territorial legislature had met and where the General Court and Court of Appeals had been in session.[27]

The convention proceeded immediately to effect its permanent organization. The delegates elected Jesse B. Thomas, shrewd political maneuverer and able territorial judge, as president of the convention, and William C. Greenup, formerly clerk of the General Court, as secretary. A committee was promptly appointed to "frame and report to the convention a constitution for the people of the Territory of Illinois."[28]

For several months prior to the opening of the convention, pages of Cook's newspaper *The Western Intelligencer* (soon to change its name to *Illinois Intelligencer*), had been utilized to argue various questions of importance that would have to be dealt with by the new constitution. More space was devoted to discussion of the slavery question, but a number of writers directed their attention to the system of law and judicial administration that the new constitution would implement.

The administration of justice under territorial officials, at its best, left much to be desired. The enforcement of law and the maintaining of public order had deteriorated in the declining days of the Territory. Pope described the situation in an editorial in the *Intelligencer* of April 15, 1818. He answered the argument of one writer, who wrote under the pseudonym "Caution," advocating the postponement of admission as a state for five years:

> Without courts, and almost without law one-half of our time, Crimes have laughed at the enervated arm of justice—and people have been afraid in many stances to come to the country, lest their property should be taken from them by the swindlers and robbers, who are above the law—our judges pursuing their own private business and neglecting that of the public—everything in a word has been given to ruin, and yet friend Caution would beseech us to wait five years, till his brothers of the north could come with their notions and make a constitution for us. . . .

The Kaskaskia State House is where the 1818 Constitutional Convention met and where the Territory's General Court and Court of Appeals convened. Abraham Lincoln Presidential Library and Museum.

In June, "Anticipator" published arguments for arbitration mentioned elsewhere and "Common Sense" replied with a defense of the law and an attack on the work of legislators in attempting reform. "Old Farmer" said that no reform could be expected from the lawyers, arguing that if you acquire something at great expense and labor, you will not give it up. A writer who signed himself "A Friend to Able Justice" pleaded for careful selection of judges, while "Commentator" wrote criticisms of the Common Law.

The Illinois Constitution of 1818 was produced in this atmosphere of controversy. The delegates shared no unified political philosophy, and the document presents the expected instances of compromise. The provisions relating to courts and the judiciary were modeled somewhat on the provisions of the federal constitution. Article IV vested the judicial power in a supreme court and such inferior courts as the general assembly should ordain and establish.

The Supreme Court should consist of a chief justice and three associate justices, with permission given to the legislature to increase the number of judges after 1824. Jealousy of the power of the territorial governor led to the vesting of the authority to appoint supreme and inferior court judges in the general assembly. The judges were to hold their offices during term of good behavior until 1824. The article also made provision for the removal of judges for "any reasonable cause" by a vote of two-thirds of the legislature.

The Supreme Court was limited to appellate jurisdiction only, except for the provision, now familiar in modified form to every Illinois lawyer, that the Supreme Court should have original jurisdiction in cases relating to the revenue, in cases of mandamus, and in such cases of impeachment as might be required to be tried before it. The chief justice and the associate justices were to have circuit court duties until 1824, with the curious provisions: "but after the aforesaid period . . . the justices . . . shall not hold circuit courts unless required by law."

Article III of the constitution provided that the governor and the judges of the Supreme Court should constitute a council:

> to revise all bills about to be passed into laws by the general assembly; and for that purpose shall assemble themselves from time to time when the general assembly shall be convened, for which nevertheless they shall not receive any salary or consideration under any pretense whatever; and all bills which have passed the senate and house of representatives shall, before they become laws, be presented to the said council for their revisal and consideration; and if, upon such revisal and consideration, it should appear improper to the said council or a majority of them, that the bill should become a law of this State, they shall return the same, together with their objections thereto, in writing, to the senate or house of representatives (in whichsoever the same shall have originated), who shall enter the objection set down by the council at large in their minutes and proceed to reconsider the said bill. But if, after such reconsider-ation, the said senate or house of representatives shall, notwithstanding the said objections, agree to pass the same by a majority of the whole number of members elected, it shall, together with said objections, be sent to the other branch of the general assembly, where it shall also be reconsidered, and if approved by a majority of all the members elected, it shall become a law.[29]

The framers had high hopes for this provision, that it would eliminate con-fusion and ambiguity in the law and make of the body of statutes a coherent code of laws.

"A Friend to Able Justice" published a letter in the *Intelligencer* on October 7, 1818, writing: "The strong reason for uniting the judges with the governor, for the purpose of revising the acts of the two houses, was, that if legal experience and political information, should at any future day be found wanting in the legislature, salutary assistance might be found in a standing body of officers, which it was expected would always contain the first talents of the state. The perfection of our code of laws, is expected to result for this salutary union. Encroachments on the constitution will be stopped in their incipience—and that unfortunate practice of passing laws on the same subject so frequently it is expected will be corrected."

Illinois became one of the United States, admitted on an equal footing with the original states, by a resolution of Congress approved December 3, 1818. Organization of the government began immediately. Shadrach Bond became the first governor, and Pierre Menard, almost the last representative of French influence, became the first lieutenant governor. Elias Kent Kane became the first secretary of state, and Jesse B. Thomas and Ninian Edwards were the first U.S. Senators. The assembly convening for its first session in December proceeded to accept statehood and adjourned until February 1819, after having chosen the first Illinois Supreme Court.

Small praise is due that pioneer legislature for the wisdom of its selections. The names of Philips, Browne, Foster, and Reynolds cause no stir in lawyers' imaginations with thoughts of great causes and influential decisions. Of the four, Reynolds and Browne were accounted successful at the bar. Philips might have become a legal scholar had legal scholarship counted for much on the frontier. Foster was not even a lawyer. In future years Reynolds would become governor of the state, Philips would leave the state with the taste of election defeat for the same office bitter in his mouth. Foster would become a pleasant thief in a career of crime. Only Browne, inarticulate about legal principles, would make a career of his judgeship.

Joseph Philips, the first chief justice, had been secretary of Illinois Territory. He was born in Kentucky but his family moved to Tennessee where he received a substantial, and Reynolds says "classical," education. Philips was licensed to practice law in Rutherford County, Tennessee, in 1809. In 1812, he led a regiment to Fort Massac in Illinois in the War of 1812. After the war he moved to Kaskaskia. He was a man of ability with instincts for scholarship whose talents might have brought him distinction on the Supreme Court. However, he resigned in 1822 to become a candidate for governor, and left the state to return to Tennessee after his defeat by Edward Coles.[30]

Thomas C. Browne was to be a member of the Supreme Court for many years. He was born in Kentucky and came to Illinois Territory in 1812. Settling in Shawneetown in 1814, he became a member of the territorial legislature and a member of the legislative council in 1816. He had fair ability as a judge and possessed high personal integrity. Although he served on the court until 1848, he did not exercise his talents beyond the observance of the requirement that a judge act impartially in the trial of cases. He delivered few opinions during his tenure. Like all lawyers of his time he engaged actively in politics, and the judicial ethics of the period was such that it was not expected that he refrain from political activity even when he became a member of the court.[31]

Of the four appointments made by the legislature, the most extraordinary was that of William P. Foster. A Virginian by birth, he came to Illinois a few months before its admission as a state. The record seems to bear out Governor Ford's statement that he was "a man of winning, polished manners," for without legal training or judicial experience he was able to induce the legislature to elect him associate justice of the Supreme Court. The record indicates that he never participated in any of the deliberations of the Supreme Court and he resigned in July 1819, after having drawn his salary.

It has been said that although a circuit was assigned to him, he never fulfilled any of his judicial duties. However, county records indicate that he did carry out some acts as a circuit judge. He left the state shortly after his resignation. Ford is the authority for the statement that he thereafter became "a noted swindler, moving from city to city and living by swindling strangers and prostituting his daughters, who were very beautiful." Unfortunately, Governor Ford gave no indication of the source of his information and subsequent inquiries have failed to prove or disprove his statement.[32]

The fourth member of the court was John Reynolds, about whom considerable biographical data exists. He was to serve his state as jurist, governor, and author, and will be remembered as "The Old Ranger" as long as any interest in Illinois history exists. He was born on February 26, 1788, in Montgomery County, Pennsylvania, the son of Irish Protestant immigrants. Soon after his birth his family removed to Tennessee where he lived until 1800. In that year his father, Robert Reynolds, with his family of six children, set out for Spanish Territory across the Mississippi River from Kaskaskia. Partly from desire to avoid Catholicism and partly due to the urging of Kaskaskia citizens, including John Edgar, the Reynolds family settled in Illinois a few miles east of Kaskaskia.

John Reynolds was educated in Knoxville, Tennessee, and read law with a lawyer of that city. He served under Captain William Whiteside in the War of 1812, whose company ranged the Illinois border to intimidate the Indians. From this experience came the sobriquet "Old Ranger." In 1814, he entered the practice of law at Cahokia. He served on the Supreme Court of Illinois from 1818 to 1825 and was a member of the Illinois General Assembly of 1826 and 1828. He was elected governor in 1830. In 1817, he had married a daughter of Julien Dubuque. With this connection and his fluent knowledge of the French language, he soon acquired a substantial and successful law practice.[33]

Reynolds had considerable legal ability, but his talents as a politician frequently obscured his soberer qualities. He was an experienced campaigner. In dealing with the backwoodsmen of the Illinois forests and the pioneer families of the prairies, he successfully disguised his education and cultural attributes. He served briefly in Congress from 1834 to 1837 and again from 1839 to 1843, but will be better remembered for his two books on Illinois history: *The Pioneer History of Illinois* and the autobiographical *My Own Times*. After his term as governor of Illinois, he prospered financially and died at Belleville on May 8, 1865.

His father, Robert Reynolds, was associated with the Edgar-Morrison faction in Illinois politics and was seriously involved in the land frauds. In his declining years the father's taste for strong drink further impaired his record. The son's historical works contain few references to his father. It is entirely probable that John Reynolds's rigid honesty in public affairs, his withdrawal from land speculation when he assumed judicial office, and his abstinence from the use of liquor were due in considerable part to the object lesson of his father's career.

Of the four members of the original court, Reynolds was unquestionably the most colorful. His skill as a political campaigner and his interest, in common with all lawyers and judges of his time, in political preferment led him to adapt the rude speech and crude manners of the backwoodsmen upon whom he relied for support. In the light of his record, the bad taste of some of his acts and words may be forgiven and forgotten. Stories about him will persist as long as there are traditions among Illinois lawyers. He himself supplied some of the more vivid pictures of the pioneer courts in operation.

Too honest to assume a pose of judicial decorum foreign to his nature, Reynolds frequently marred his effectiveness as a circuit judge by his lack of dignity. On one occasion when holding court in Washington County, both the clerk and the sheriff had served in the same company with him in the War of 1812. When court convened, the sheriff, without moving from his position astride a bench in the courtroom, announced, "The court is now opened,

John is on the bench." One glimpses backwoods efforts to attain dignity in Reynolds's own anecdote of the deputy sheriff in Union County who opened court by saying "Oh, yes!" three times, then, solemnly, "The Honorable Judge is now opened."

Law, legal matters, and duties of the judiciary occupied a share of the attention of the first General Assembly of Illinois, which convened for its second session at Kaskaskia in 1819. One of its earliest legislative acts was the passage of a statute declaring the Common Law of England to be the rule of decision in Illinois.

At the same session the legislature enacted a general statute regulating the admission and practice of lawyers. The statute provided that a license must be obtained from two of the justices of the Supreme Court and required the applicant to obtain a certificate of good moral character from one of the county courts. Justices of the Supreme Court, coroners, sheriffs, county commissioners, deputy sheriffs, and jailers and constables were all declared ineligible to practice before the courts. The statute further provided the form of oath that should be taken and in this respect, followed to the letter the Act of Indiana Territory in force when Illinois was admitted as a state.

The law directed that the clerk of the Supreme Court keep a roll of attorneys, but many well-known names were missing from the list. In fact, not one of the four members of the Supreme Court signed his name to the roll. This fact is probably attributable to the clause in the statute that exempted from the duty of renewing their licenses persons who had been admitted as attorney or counselor in Illinois Territory.

In March 1819, the legislature, exercising the power conferred upon it by Article IV of the Constitution, proceeded by statute to define the duties of the justices of the Supreme Court. The form of oath directed to be taken by the members of the court was prescribed: "I, A. B., Chief Justice (or associate justice as the case may be) of the Supreme Court, do solemnly swear (or affirm) that I will administer justice without respect to persons, and do equal right to the poor and to the rich, without sale or denial, promptly and without favor, affection, or partiality to the best of my judgment and ability."

The statute made provision for two terms of the Supreme Court to be held each year at the seat of government in July and December. Review of lower court decisions was to be had by writ of error or appeal and there was a specific grant of power to the court to issue writs of mandamus.

It was further provided that there should be two terms of the circuit court held in each county during the year to be conducted by a justice of the Supreme

Court. The state was divided into four circuits. St. Clair, Madison, Bond, and Washington Counties comprised the first circuit; Crawford, Edwards, and White Counties the second circuit; Monroe, Randolph, Jackson, and Union Counties the third circuit; and Gallatin, Franklin, Pope, and Johnson the fourth circuit. Each justice had responsibility for a circuit. The General Assembly assigned the justices to the various circuits but made provision for Reynolds and the other judges to exchange when there were cases presented in which they had been counsel.

Looking forward to the time when the court would shape the law, the legislature also made provision for a reporter to the Supreme Court and for written opinions in all cases of appeals and writs of error. The quaintly worded legislative description of the reporter is worth repeating: "And the said court shall, when they deem it expedient, appoint some fit person learned in the law, to minute down and make a report of all the principal matter drawn out at length with the opinion of the court in all such cases that may be tried before the said court, where a question of law not before decided by the said court, shall be settled. And the said reporter shall have a right to use the original opinion after it shall have been recorded by the clerk." There was a further provision authorizing the justices of the Supreme Court to publish their reports.

The duties placed upon the judges by this legislation were a considerable burden. While the volume of appellate work was small, the amount of litigation in the circuit courts alone was sufficient to occupy substantially all of their time. Travel being what it was, the circuit court duties must have been no more pleasant to perform than those that had led the judges of the General Court of the Territory to refuse to undertake them.

Before the court convened to decide its first appellate cases, William P. Foster resigned to seek doubtful distinction elsewhere, and the legislature appointed William Wilson in his place. Wilson was also a Virginian, having been born in Loudoun County, April 27, 1794. After serving a while as apprentice in law to John Cook, who had been minister to France, he came to Illinois by way of Kentucky, locating near Carmi in White County. He served on the court as associate justice until 1825, when he became chief justice. He continued in this capacity until 1848, when he retired after twenty-nine years of service on the bench.

The first attorney general of the state was Daniel Pope Cook, who held office only for a short time, resigning on October 19, 1819, after being elected to Congress. William Mears, the former attorney general of Illinois Territory, succeeded Cook. His was a recess appointment by the governor.

It has been frequently said that the Supreme Court did not convene until December 1819. However, the order book shows that the first term began on Monday, July 12, 1819, and that Chief Justice Philips and Associate Justice John Reynolds were the only members of the court present. At this term the court ordered the appointment of James M. Duncan as clerk pro tempore.

The first case to appear on the court's docket was that of *Michael Sprinkle v. Jonathan Taylor,* which came before it on appeal from the judgment of the circuit court of Gallatin County. The honor of being the first lawyer to appear before the court belonged to Elias Kent Kane, who was given leave by the court to file the transcript of the record in *Sprinkle v. Taylor.* After the entry of this order, and a similar order in four other cases, the court adjourned until Monday, December 13, 1819.

The first session of the Supreme Court of Illinois was not an event of sufficient importance to justify a description of the proceedings in the local newspaper. There is merely the formal and colorless entry in the record book that Chief Justice Philips and Associate Justice Reynolds appeared and entered several routine orders. Inferentially, the court must have met in the old state house at Kaskaskia. It is probable that the formal *oyez* of orthodox English and American procedure announced the opening of the court. A description of the proceedings, if available, would be interesting to place alongside the description of the opening of the first term of the Supreme Court of the United States.

The first Supreme Court of Illinois, excepting Foster, was composed of men of fair ability as lawyers. Not one of the four could be called a scholar, but all possessed considerable native common sense that assisted them in the performance of their judicial duties. They made no important contribution to the law, but the service they rendered in the performance of their ordinary judicial duties was, in the main, satisfactory.

Apparently not one of the five who had been appointed prior to the opening of the December 1819 term looked upon judicial service as a career. Philips left the court to become a candidate for governor. Foster, possibly finding the legal pace too swift and a judge's duties not very exciting, may have preferred the more uncertain existence of a confidence man. Even William Wilson, of the five probably the most appreciative of the duties and opportunities of his position, aspired to leave it for the more active sphere of national politics, trying for the United States Senate in 1830. Reynolds attained the governorship and lived to write history and autobiography, both volumes full of pungent expression and opinions strong in their likes and dislikes.

Monday July 12th 1819

At a Supreme Court began and held on the Second monday of July in the year of our Lord One thousand Eight hundred and nineteen, And of the Independence of the United States Forty fourth, at Kashaskia the seat of Government for the state of Illinois in Conformity with the Constitution of of said state and the act of assembly entitled and act regulating and defineing the duties of the Justices of the Supreme approved 31st of March 1819

Present the Honble Joseph Phillips Chief Justice and John Reynolds one of the Justices of said County

It is Ordered that James M Duncan be appointed Clerk of this court protempore

Mikeal Sprinkle } On an appeal from the the Judgment
vs } of the Circuit Court of Gatalin County
Jonathon Taylor

On motion of Elias K Kain Leave is given to file the transcript of the record in the above Suit And the Cause is directed to be put upon the Docket

Monday July the 12th 1819

Daniel Figgins } upon an appeal from the Judgment of the Circuit
vs } Court of Madison County.
Fanny Colean

On motion of Elias K Kain leave is given to file transcript of the record in the above Suit, And the Cause is directed to be to be put upon the Docket.

Francis Scott Admr of the Estate of Rebeca McCann
vs } Upon an appeal to reverse a Judgment of
William Beggs } the County Court of St Clair

William Mears attorny for the plaintiff Suggested the death of Franc Scott the plaintiff and moved the Court to admit Levi Scott administrator of Rebeca McCann to prosecute the Suit — which motion was continued until the next term of this Court

George Leach Francis Cain & Marshall
Executors of Isaac White Dec'd } In Chancery
vs
Jonathon Taylor Charly Welkins and James Morrison

It is Ordered that this Cause be continued until the next term & that the order of the June term 1818 be revived

The first orders from the first term of the Illinois Supreme Court, July 1819. Illinois State Archives.

Browne was probably most content with his position than any of the others, but whether he was an asset or liability during his long stay on the court is a disputed point. Reynolds, years later, praised Browne's honor, integrity, and fidelity. Others have seriously questioned his abilities as a judge. It has been said that in the conference room he never attempted to argue any question, possibly for lack of ability to express his views in a sustained or logical form and he contributed no opinion in any important case that came before the court. Caton, who served with him on the bench, praised his ability to reach a sound decision in a controversial case and mentions his lack of ability clearly to express his views.

Allegedly, as Judge Browne was sitting as circuit judge at Dixon, in Lee County, a prominent lawyer, Burton C. Cook, tried a case before him and obtained a verdict to which he thought he was fairly entitled. When his adversary made the customary motion for a new trial, Cook, thinking the motion clearly without merit, declined to argue it. His consternation was considerable when Judge Browne, assuming a look of judicial seriousness, said, "Well, Mr. Cook, let us give him a new trial. Maybe he will be better satisfied next time."

Caton said that Browne's relationship with the bar was pleasant and that he administered justice as satisfactorily as any of the other judges holding circuit courts, adding, "He evidently appreciated that while he could plainly see how a question should be decided he might not readily be able to assign the best reason for that decision, and so he prudently declined to assign any reasons. Probably all of us would have got along better at times had we adopted the same wise course."[34]

Whatever may have been Browne's values and defects as a judge, he maintained, as did all the other judges, a close association with state and local politics. He was a member of the faction that actively supported Ninian Edwards. The bitter factional disputes, which were characteristic of the politics of the day, led to an unsuccessful attempt to impeach him.[35] In 1822, he was an unsuccessful candidate for governor, as was Chief Justice Philips. Both were defeated by Edward Coles, with Philips running second and Browne third.

There was no important legislation affecting the Supreme Court between 1819 and 1824. There was a new division of counties into the third and fourth circuits in 1821 to take care of additional counties that had been created. Difficulties had been caused from the beginning by the fact that certain of the judges, particularly Reynolds and Browne, had been of counsel in numerous cases that would normally come before them as circuit judges.

The legislature in 1821 by statutory provision required Reynolds to make out a complete list of all suits that remained undetermined in the circuit courts of St. Clair and Madison Counties in which he had been engaged as counsel or attorney so that such suits might be transferred to another court. In 1823, because of the press of the circuit court duties of the justices of the Supreme Court, it was provided that thereafter there should be but one term of the Supreme Court, to be held on the fourth Monday in November. The judges were also given the privilege of interchanging circuits with each other.

The work of this first Supreme Court from 1819 to 1824 is not difficult to appraise. The printed opinions in the cases before it occupy sixty-five pages of Breese's Reports. At first, all of the opinions were per curiam.

At the December 1819 term, Browne, Reynolds, and Wilson held the court. They disposed of five cases, and Justice Wilson allegedly wrote all of the opinions. None of the points involved in these cases had any special significance in the development of the law. In only one case does the report show the names of counsel who were engaged by the parties.

At the July 1820 term, Chief Justice Philips and Justices Reynolds and Browne were present. Again they disposed of five cases, and none of the points involved were of any real importance to the law. Technical questions of pleading and procedure were the issues most frequently raised in the Supreme Court.

Kaskaskia hosted both of these terms, but when the court convened for the December 1820 term, the capital had been moved to Vandalia, and the court occupied temporary quarters in a log building in that place. Removal of the capital from the old French town on the Mississippi was the end of strife for Kaskaskia, and it was not even a county seat when the river finally overcame it. Interest in land speculation was probably the basic reason for the move, but Vandalia itself did not long enjoy whatever benefits are attached to being a capital city.

The court disposed of six cases at this term, and the only really significant point about any of them was that in one, *Cornelius v. Boucher*,[36] the court for the first time cited and relied on authorities. The action was covenant. A New York case from Johnston's Reports was cited along with an English case as authority for deciding a rather technical question of procedure.

Judge Sidney Breese, whose volume of Reports was published in 1831, stated that the records of cases decided at the December 1821 term were consumed when the bank house in Vandalia burned and it is not known how much work was before the court at that term. At the December 1822 term, the court had gotten down to business and disposed of a total of sixteen cases.

At this term the record indicates that Thomas Reynolds had succeeded Chief Justice Philips. Reynolds became associate justice on August 31, 1822, and Governor Bond appointed him chief justice on January 14, 1823. He was born in Kentucky on March 12, 1796, and came to Illinois about 1817. He was a district attorney in Randolph and Union Counties and became chief clerk of the Illinois House of Representatives. He was a man of some considerable ability. His opinions are in substantially better literary form than most of those written by other members of the court.

There are indications that he acquired a reputation for rowdyism and bad personal conduct. He was dropped from the court when it was reconstituted by the legislature in 1824 and shortly thereafter went to Missouri, where he had considerable political success. He became a member of the legislature, then a judge and finally rose to be governor of the state. While holding this latter office and a candidate for the United States Senate, he committed suicide on February 9, 1844. It was said that political involvement drove him to end his life.[37]

Most of the cases decided at the December 1822 term were cases involving technical questions of pleading and practice. But others indicate that the court was beginning to develop a sense of the importance of its function in determining the rules of the Common Law. Also from the cases decided at this term, commercial interests began to find expression in law. There were two cases decided at the term that involved promissory notes and one of these was a case in which the court determined the applicability of New York law.[38]

For the most part the court continued to dispose of the cases before it without reference to specific authorities to support its decisions. The court cited no authorities in any of the cases decided except for reference to Illinois statutes. At the November 1823 term, the eleven cases decided were also for the most part unimportant. The court passed upon the usual technical procedural questions, decided what constituted due diligence by the holder of a promissory note in making demand for payment, and passed upon the sufficiency of a will to create an executory devise. In the latter case, the court cited and relied upon authorities from New York and English reports.[39]

The court passed the first four years of its existence without the determination of a single constitutional issue nor to exercise the functions as arbiter between the various organs of the state government. In summing up the work of the first Supreme Court there remains only the need for inquiry into the activities of the judges as members of the Council of Revision to the Constitution of 1818. The legislature in 1819, probably due in part to the urging of Justice John Reynolds, undertook a revision of the statute book. The result was the Laws of 1819, which was intended to be a restatement of the territorial laws with the inconsistencies and contradictions removed and certain necessary additions made.

The work was the product of a committee, none of whom appear to have been trained lawyers. Reynolds said that the judges of the Supreme Court in their capacity as members of the Council of Revision participated in the preparation of the so-called code. The committee also appears to have called to its aid the able lawyer, Elias Kent Kane. The result was far from satisfactory and it is doubtful whether the judges of the Supreme Court, in view of their individual tastes and abilities, contributed very much of value to its preparation.

6. Law and Politics

THE POLITICAL SITUATION in Illinois in 1824 was still characterized by division in terms of local issues and factions. Separation into national political parties was of little consequence in local elections. As in territorial days there were still two major factions, but most of the old leaders were missing. The aging John Edgar still lived in his wide-galleried house in Kaskaskia, but his political power was gone and his voice no longer heard in the councils of the alliance he once led.

Edgar passed from the political scene when the removal of the capital left Kaskaskia to drowse in the sun beside the river that had given it life and was to be the instrument of its death. With him into obscurity went the Morrisons, Robert and William, and others who had fought the battles of politics against the Harrison men in the years before statehood. Some, like John Rice Jones, had taken their political ambitions west of the Mississippi, others discovered that frontier politics was a young man's game.

There remained to rally the divergent elements of the old Edgar-Morrison faction the shrewd and capable Jesse B. Thomas, seasoned now by his service in the United States Senate. Surpassing him in intellectual powers if not in political acumen was the lawyer Elias Kent Kane. Kane had vision and a capacity for work that made him the leading lawyer in the state. If his political leadership was sporadic, it was also brilliant. Of all the men of law and politics of this period, the character and personality of Kane are the most elusive. Contemporary accounts invariability praise his ability but say nothing to make him live and breathe. As a lawyer his practice was large and his accomplishments impressive.[1] His record in the Illinois Supreme Court was not long but was creditable, for he won four of the six cases he argued there. Changes had also occurred in the leadership of the other important faction in Illinois politics. Governor William Henry Harrison of Indiana Territory was gone and the years had carried away Michael Jones and Elijah Backus, his lieutenants, whose work in exposing the land frauds had so embarrassed the Edgar-Morrison men. In place of these came to power the handsome and unstable Ninian Edwards, judge in Kentucky, governor of Illinois Territory, and now junior Senator from Illinois. Edwards's personal charm and family ties attracted to him two of the state's ablest lawyer-politicians: Nathaniel Pope, a federal judge, and his nephew, Daniel Pope Cook. Had the qualities of their leader been more solid and less susceptible to the misleading effect of self-flattery, this faction might have maintained the dominant position in Illinois politics for many years.

Most of the issues dividing the two factions were local in character and many of them can be described principally as excuses for tests of strength. Lines of cleavage over questions of national importance usually did not exactly coincide with the alignment of the two factions. More than a few people in Illinois during the period from 1821 to 1824 had experienced financial distress. Many of these began to believe that the removal of legal restrictions against slavery afforded the solution to their economic problems.

A considerable portion of the population of Illinois in 1824 lived in the southern section of the state. Most of them had the Southerner's attitude of the day toward blacks. Slaves of the French still lived in the villages along the Mississippi and the indentured servant, slave for a term of years, was to be found in towns and on farms throughout the state. The Illinois country was aroused over the question of the introduction of slavery into Missouri, and Jesse B. Thomas, who had drawn the long term in the Senate, helped draft the Missouri Compromise.[2] Under these circumstances it was inevitable that there would occur in Illinois a battle for the reestablishment of slavery.

When drawn, the battle lines would not coincide exactly with the lines between the Edwards and anti-Edwards factions. Edwards himself would not take sides, although he voted with Thomas for the Compromise, and others of his faction, such as John Reynolds, were with the pro-slavery group. The struggle that was coming would provide tense and exciting moments but would die down in the lull that preceded the great conflagration.

Meanwhile across the whole country, the great, popular "Jacksonian" movement gathered forces. The movement spread over Illinois like the wind across the prairies. Out of this and the slavery question eventually came a consciousness on the part of Illinois people of their position as part of the nation. With that realization finally came a recognition of the significance of party lines.

Storm signs on the national horizon were not generally perceived when the Fourth General Assembly convened for its first session at Vandalia late in 1824. Local matters left unsettled at the formation of state government required immediate action. The Constitution of 1818, in making provision for the first Supreme Court, had set forth that the judges should hold office upon good behavior until 1824 when the legislature had the authority to select new judges.

In December of that year the General Assembly reorganized the judiciary. The new statute provided that the number of judges on the Supreme Court should remain at four, one of whom should be chief justice. With some sense of the function of the court in formulating a system of law for the state, it was provided that the jurisdiction of the court, except in cases involving the collection of state money from public officials, was limited to reviewing the decisions of lower courts. Five circuit court judges assumed the circuit court duties that had been performed by the Supreme Court judges. The five circuit court judges were directed to hold two terms of a circuit court in each county of the state during each year.[3]

Pursuant to the authority conferred by the Constitution of 1818, the legislature named the new judges. Of the old court, only Wilson and Browne, both Edwards men, remained. The legislature elected Wilson as chief justice. The picturesque John Reynolds of the same faction was dropped from the court, though for what reason is not clear. Reynolds wrote afterward that he and Thomas Reynolds had been conspicuous in advocating the calling of a constitutional convention to settle the slavery question and that this cost his return.[4] The two new judges were Samuel D. Lockwood and Theophilus W. Smith. Of these, Lockwood was an anti-slavery leader of the Edwards party, and Smith, of the opposition, had supported the pro-slavery men. Both had come to Illinois from New York.

Samuel Drake Lockwood was born in 1789. He studied law in a lawyer's office in New York and was admitted to the bar in that state in 1811. He came to Illinois by way of Shawneetown in 1818 and moved on to Kaskaskia, later changing his residence to Carmi. Beginning in 1821, he served for a short time as attorney general of Illinois. While in this position he became connected with one of the celebrated criminal cases of the day.

Two Belleville men, Alphonso Stewart and William Bennett, had arranged to fight a duel. The seconds had arranged it to be a sham duel in order to ridicule Bennett, the challenger, and the rifles were loaded with blank cartridges. Stewart was in on the secret, but Bennett apparently was not. The latter, suspecting a trick, put a ball into his gun without the knowledge of his adversary or the seconds. When the word was given to fire, Stewart was killed. Bennett escaped to Arkansas but was later brought back to Illinois and tried for murder. He was convicted through the efforts of Judge Lockwood, who prosecuted the case in his capacity as attorney general. Governor Ford says that the hanging of Bennett made dueling discreditable and unpopular.[5]

In December 1822, Lockwood resigned as attorney general to become commissioned as secretary of state. He also resigned this office a short time later when President James Monroe appointed him receiver of the Edwardsville land office. He was an unsuccessful candidate for United States Senator in 1823, and became active in the faction opposing the calling of a constitutional convention to determine the question of slavery in 1823 and 1824. He was again a candidate for United States Senator in November 1824, but Elias Kent Kane defeated him. The legislature elected him as associate justice of the Supreme Court on December 30, 1824, on the sixth ballot after the election of Browne and Smith. He served until 1848.[6]

All contemporary authorities agree in placing a high value on Lockwood's ability and integrity. Gustave Koerner, who saw him first in 1835, described his appearance: "Judge Lockwood, from the State of New York, was very tall and very thin, held himself very erect, and, though at the time hardly more than forty-five years of age, had thick, stiff snow-white hair. His complexion was dark, his eyes black and of brilliant lustre. He made the impression of an intellectual, benignant person. An excellent lawyer, he was clear-headed, conscientious and eminently just."[7]

Theophilus W. Smith, the other newcomer to the bench, was born in 1784. He came to Illinois in 1816 and was admitted to the bar in the following year, though there is no reference to him in the legal records of any county preceding his election to the Supreme Court. However, he appeared before the Supreme Court in five cases during 1823 and was successful in two. Prior to his election to the Supreme Court, he served as cashier of the Edwardsville Bank. Smith was an active pro-slavery leader along with Judge Philips and Judge Thomas Reynolds. Governor Ford said of him: "Judge Smith (I regret to say it of a man who is no more) was an active, bustling, ambitious and turbulent member of the democratic party."[8]

Ninian Edwards singled out Smith with characteristic lack of tact for attacks and charges of corruption in connection with the mismanagement of the affairs of the Edwardsville Bank. In his position as cashier he was reputed to have filled kegs with old iron covered with coin in order to deceive the bank examiners. These charges were probably the cause of Smith's having drawn a pistol on Edwards, who snatched it and struck Smith in the face, breaking his jaw. Throughout his public career, Smith was a partisan political maneuverer with a positive talent for intrigue. The legislature impeached him in 1832, but conviction failed by the narrowest of margins.

Thus reconstituted, the Supreme Court of Illinois took up the work of declaring the law of the state. There would be no new judges until 1841. Cases of importance, some involving constitutional issues, came before Wilson, Browne, Smith, and Lockwood for decision. The real work of the court was done by Smith and Lockwood, whose physical strength exceeded that of Wilson, and whose capacity for work certainly exceeded that of Browne.

Browne may be pictured sitting at the conference table, his quick eyes searching the faces of his more articulate colleagues as they argued their views. Then, exercising his peculiar quality, whatever it was, of interpreting and applying the common sense of his time and place, he would state his vote but not his reasons.

It is of Browne that Linder tells the tale that wishing a not-too-well-qualified candidate admitted to the bar, he arranged for an examination by Browne in his hotel room. The most important question asked by the jurist of the candidate was "Are you a judge of good brandy?" The hint being taken, the candidate received his certificate.[9] Gustave Koerner, whose discernment was generally good, said of Browne: "He was a large, portly man of great levity of character, and in his widower-days a great ladies' man, fond of gossip, an epicure, and never refusing to drink with anyone. He was a plausible man, with engaging Southern manners, and popular with the crowd."[10]

The picture just given, of a bar examination in the court's first years could not have been typical. John Dean Caton, who was to be a member of the court through many years, described far differently his own examination by Justice Lockwood:

After supper he invited me to take a walk. It was a beautiful moonlit night; we strolled down to the back of the river, he leading the conversation on various subjects, and when we arrived at a large oak stump, on either side of which we stood, he rather abruptly commenced the examination by inquiring with whom I had read law and how long, what books I had read, and then inquired of the different forms of action, and the objects of each, some questions about criminal law, and the law of the administration of estates, and especially of the provision of our statutes on these subjects. . . .

I do not think that the examination occupied more than thirty minutes, but it had the effect of starting a pretty free perspiration. I think I would have got along much better had it commenced in a more formal way. However, at the close he said he would give me a license, although I had much to learn to make me a good lawyer, and said I had better adopt some other pursuit, unless I was determined to work hard, to read much and to think strongly of what I did read, that good strong thinking was as indispensable to success in the profession as industrious reading; but that both were absolutely important to enable a man to attain eminence as a lawyer, or even respectability.[11]

Koerner, who also was to become an associate justice, was examined by Chief Justice Wilson and Justice Smith. To him we are indebted for almost the only contemporary description of the chief justice:

Wilson, complaining of being sick, was stretched on one of the beds, held a phial of medicine in his hand and swallowed once or twice in the course of the conversation a few drops. It was opium, which he was in the habit of taking for a chronic disease of the stomach. Judge Smith was sitting near the bed. It was a warm day and both were in their shirt-sleeves.

Wilson was from Virginia. He must have been a very noble-looking person when young, but his health was evidently much broken. His voice had an unnatural, cracked sound. He was a man of fine education and a good lawyer, and, as his opinions will show, a fine writer. It was said, however, that he merely jotted his ideas down on small slips of paper and then handed them to an amanuensis who put them in shape, Wilson revising the composition.[12]

The court over which Wilson presided was not a distinguished court. Its judges had too many ties to factional politics, but it was a court that in dealing with people and their affairs brought to its decisions the hard judgment of the frontier. To most people at the outreaches of civilization, the least law was the best, and where law was necessary, law should be certain. Extraordinary respect for the written law is characteristic of the pioneer community. Codification of law was under serious consideration in New York and Louisiana. The Illinois legislature was sensible of the chaotic condition of Illinois statute law. By an act approved January 10, 1825, the judges of the Supreme Court were required to digest "in one or more volumes, all the statutes of this state of a general nature which shall be in force after the close of the present session of the general assembly and to arrange all the statutes on the same subject under one head in appropriate order, condensing the matter as much as practicable, but preserving the sense."

A second section of the same statute required the judges to suggest alterations and amendments "to enable the next general assembly to adopt a permanent statutory code for this state." The legislators also wanted to know what English statutes were in force in Illinois and whether it would be advisable to have the English statutes published along with the Code. For their labors in carrying out the legislative intent the judges were to receive a reasonable compensation. This was the substance of the statute pursuant to which the Revised Code of Laws of 1827 was prepared.

The judges probably began the work of revision promptly after the passage of the statute. Certainly Wilson and Lockwood would have realized the magnitude of the task that was set before them. It was not until December 1826 that the judges reported to the legislature. The report stated that it was not deemed desirable to digest all of the laws of the state and that they had therefore endeavored to prepare a code of laws "to embrace such parts of all our present statutes, and to incorporate therewith, the substance of such British statutes, as were conformable to the genius and spirit of our institutions." The report advised the General Assembly that it was not practicable to carry out the suggestion to digest and print the English statutes in the statute book, since there was no set of such statutes then available in Illinois.

It was partly because the judges were sensible of a task unfinished, and partly because after two years they recognized the dangers of haste in drafting statutes that led them to include in the report an appeal to the legislators to delay enactments of any code until an examination could be made of the Livingston Code of Louisiana and the statutory revision nearing completion in New York. Later events showed their fears to have been well-founded.

The judges submitted drafts of laws for inclusion in the new code, which accompanied the report. Unfortunately the report did not list them, and it is now impossible to determine just how many drafts covering what subjects they had prepared. It is probable that more than thirty of the some sixty titles in the published code were covered by drafts submitted by the judges. The evidence indicates that the bulk of the work was done by Judges Lockwood and Smith, and that Lockwood unquestionably contributed the greater portion, for Smith was ill for an extended period during 1826. Judge Browne certainly could not have been expected to be any more articulate in the preparation of statutes than in the writing of opinions, and there is no evidence that Chief Justice Wilson assumed any large share of the work.

Lockwood must be credited with having the instincts, if not the techniques, of a scholar, and he deserved the recognition of having prepared the sections of the code dealing with criminal law. Many of the ideas expressed, particularly regarding definitions of various crimes, remained a part of the written law of Illinois for decades.

The General Assembly did not heed the judges' plea for delay. There was at the time throughout the country a movement toward codification of law expressing the popular desire that law be certain even before it is just. The causes underlying this movement intensified in the pioneer communities, where the people, most of whom were themselves semiliterate, had a disproportionate respect for the written word.

The General Assembly of 1827 was unable to withstand the pressure and rushed into preparation, through committees, the titles of the code the judges had not yet had time to draft. With equal haste the legislators rushed consideration of the drafts that the judges had submitted. The result was an attempt at a complete revision of the statutory law of Illinois in a single legislative session. The finished product was ample proof that this haste was mistaken.

Moreover, the most serious faults of the Revised Code of Laws of 1827 were first, that it did not include all of the statutory law of Illinois, and second, that it did not supersede in authority all prior enactments.[13] Indeed the legislators of 1829 felt it necessary to issue an additional, although smaller, volume, which unfortunately was also called the Revised Code of Laws of Illinois. The 1829 volume was merely a supplement to that of 1827, and the two together constituted a single code.[14]

No copies of the drafts of statutes that the judges prepared can now be found, but it is probable that these were enacted without very many changes by the General Assembly. It must be kept in mind that the judges of the Supreme Court were members of the Council of Revision who could and did exercise veto powers over legislation. It is not unreasonable to expect that the judges protected their own work.

In spite of its faults, the code of 1827–29 was a considerable accomplishment. By comparison with previous statutory enactments the draftsmanship was good. There was considerable condensing and simplifying of the language of older statutes, and there were many new provisions that served to adjust the rules of law to conditions as they then existed in Illinois. The arrangement was logical and useful and, considering the haste with which the materials were put together, those who participated could take much credit for their work.

Thus Lockwood and Smith produced the first important contribution of the Supreme Court to the law of Illinois. One of these judges was modest, sincere, and competent with a capacity for learning beyond the opportunities afforded for its exercise; the other was a politician whose acute mind concerned itself most actively with the machinations of factional politics and whose shrewdness never turned toward the furtherance of great causes. Yet the combined efforts of these men resulted in an important contribution to the law of Illinois.

The same legislature whose zeal for statutory reform produced the Revision of 1827–29 rewarded the Supreme Court judges for their work on the code by sending them back to duty on the circuits from which they had been freed by the legislation of 1824. Conditions of travel and of accommodations for the wayfarer had improved little since territorial days when the federal judges had refused their risks and discomforts. Their successors must have had doubts whether salaries and whatever prestige their positions gave them were worth the cost. Possibly the legislature of 1824 had expected much more from the Supreme Court in the declaring of the rules of law than the court had been able to contribute.

Even had the selection of judges been of the best, youth and lack of judicial experience required more than three years for the Supreme Court to come to a full exercise of its powers. Unfortunately, the representatives of the people in 1827 were impatient of delay and hasty in action. They convened at Vandalia in December 1826, and in January 1827 they turned the circuit judges out of office and directed the chief justice and associate justices of the Supreme Court to take over their duties. The legislature paid no attention whatever to the complaint of the unfrocked circuit judges that this was the path to destruction of an independent judiciary. The new law stipulated that terms of the circuit courts begin in the early spring, with a second term beginning in the fall, and one term of the Supreme Court held annually on the first Monday of December.

Ex-justice John Reynolds, who later wrote that the duties of the Supreme Court judge when he was on the bench were laborious because of circuit court duties, related serenely how, when he was no longer a member of the court, he worked assiduously to put his former colleagues back on the circuit. He offered economy as his reason. The four judges, he said, referring to the period after the legislature of 1824 had dropped him from the court, "had not much services to perform."[15] The legislature intended to compensate the judges for their additional duties by increasing their salaries from $800 to $1,000 per year.

The Revised Code of Laws of 1829 contained a comprehensive statute relating to the Supreme Court. It was, in effect, a reenactment of the prior statutes in force as modified by the legislature in 1827. The statute prescribed the form of oath to be taken by the judges in the following language: "I. A. B., chief justice (or associate justice as the case may be) of the Supreme Court (or judge of the Circuit Court as the case may be) do solemnly swear (or affirm) that I will administer justice without respect to persons, and do equal right to the poor and to the rich without sale or denial, promptly without delay, conformably to the laws, without favor, affection or partiality to the best of my judgment and abilities." The statute further provided that the Supreme Court might institute such rules of practice and prescribe such forms of process as should be deemed most conducive to the due administration of justice.

Another statute enacted at the same session provided for a circuit court to be held north of the Illinois River. It made provision for the circuit judge to be elected by a joint ballot of both houses of the General Assembly. Apparently at this time the Supreme Court was meeting in the log building in Vandalia known as the banking house because another statute set aside the southeast room on the lower floor for the exclusive purpose of holding the Supreme Court. It directed that the state treasurer keep his office in the front room on the same floor.

Whatever may have been the opinion of the members of the General Assembly of 1827 of the ability and accomplishments of the Supreme Court, the court began to make decisions important to the legal development of the state shortly after it was reconstituted in 1824. Chief Justice Wilson and Justices Browne, Lockwood, and Smith first held the Supreme Court at Vandalia at the June 1825 term. Beginning with the opinions written in cases decided at that term, there was a noticeable improvement in the quality of the work done. This was due in large part to the fact that at least three of the four judges possessed sufficient ability and awareness to qualify them as judges of a reviewing court. It is noticeable too, that from this point forward, the issues involved in the cases before the court became increasingly important and required, if not more careful consideration, at least greater attention to the formulating of opinions.

They disposed of only five cases at the June 1825 term. Of these, three opinions were written by Justice Smith, and the other two by Justice Lockwood. The first case, *Chandler v. Gay*,[16] involved the interpretation of the statute relating to arbitration and indicated that the proper method of enforcing arbitration awards was by contempt process. The other cases involved no issues of any great legal importance.

These four judges who began the real work of the Supreme Court in shaping the law of Illinois remained exclusively responsible for its work until 1841, when the court became the center of a political storm that led to its reorganization.

From the June 1825 term until the December 1840 term, the court handed down written opinions in nearly 500 cases. During this period, Smith submitted a total of 194 opinions; Lockwood, 157; Wilson, 81; Browne, 45; and 22 were per curiam. No statement has been found concerning the method of work of the judges but it is clear that the court had not yet adopted the system of assigning cases in rotation.

It is easy enough to account for the fact that Browne wrote so few opinions, but it is a little more difficult to discover why Wilson, who held the position of chief justice throughout the entire period, should have given opinions in little more than 15 percent of the cases. By training and education, he was at least as well qualified to speak for the court as either Smith or Lockwood. There are frequent references in contemporary accounts to the poor state of his health and this may account for his failure to carry his full load. It is significant that no contemporary reported hearing either Smith or Lockwood complain of the fact that they did much more of the court's work than the other two members. Apparently, experience had shown them that they could expect nothing better from Browne. They must have counted it their good fortune in the rare instances when he was induced to prepare the court's opinion.

The very absence of complaints lends some support to the view that the state of his health prevented Wilson from taking a more active part, although he seems to have discharged his circuit court duties regularly throughout the period. Another contrast between Wilson and Browne should be noticed. Wilson wrote opinions in some cases that presented complicated issues and in others where political considerations made the case difficult to decide. On the other hand, Browne wrote forty-five opinions in cases involving pedestrian matters that required very little research.

William Wilson served as chief justice from 1825 to 1848, the longest tenured chief justice in the state's history. Illinois Supreme Court Historic Preservation Commission.

None of these four judges wrote with any special distinction. The opinions of Wilson are for the most part clear and without pretension. Lockwood's style was more fluent but there are no passages that capture the imagination or stir the emotions. Yet, occasionally there is evidence of a scholar's mind at work, and he may have done more for the development of the law had public confidence in courts made a judicial career attractive and had the judges been less occupied with strenuous circuit duties.

There are 326 of the 414 pages of Breese's Reports (1 Illinois) taken up with the opinions of these four judges. From the December 1825 term onward, the number of cases involving important questions of substantive law, as distinguished from procedural matters, steadily increased. When the opinions cited authorities, most of the citations were to English and New York cases. For the English cases, the court may have relied on some of the various digests; it is possible that the reports were not available.

Important cases began to appear on the docket in 1825, and in 1826 the court decided that the rule of the civil law as to the ascertainment of the next of kin of a deceased person should be adopted in construing the Illinois statute of descent. This rule followed consistently after that.

Some of the cases, such as *The People ex rel. William D. Ewing v. George Forquer*,[17] involved issues of a political nature. Edward Coles had become governor of Illinois in 1822. The lieutenant governor was Adolphus F. Hubbard, a political buffoon and the not-unwilling tool of the opposition faction. Governor Coles's three-month absence from the state beginning in July 1825 afforded Hubbard an opportunity to assert a comic opera claim that he was entitled to be considered the acting governor for the entire balance of the term. The Constitution of 1818 provided that, "In case of an impeachment of the governor, his removal from office, death, refusal to qualify, resignation or absence from the state, the lieutenant governor shall exercise all the power and authority appertaining to the office of governor, until the time pointed out by this constitution for the election of governor shall arise, unless the general assembly shall provide by law for the election of governor to fill such vacancy."

Hubbard, anxious to please his friends and to exercise the power he thought he possessed, appointed William L. D. Ewing to the position of paymaster-general of the state on November 2, 1825. On the same day he executed and delivered Ewing's signed commission to George Forquer, secretary of state, requesting Forquer to countersign and seal the commission. Since Governor Coles had returned to Illinois two days before, Forquer refused Hubbard's request. Thus began the Illinois caricature of the great case of *Marbury v. Madison*.[18] Ewing obtained in the Supreme Court a rule on the secretary of state to show cause why a mandamus ought not to be issued requiring him to sign and seal the commission.

The case presented the issue of whether Coles or Hubbard was the lawful governor. Although the issue was presented, it was not decided, for, like the Supreme Court of the United States in *Marbury v. Madison*, the court avoided a direct interference with the executive department. Justice Lockwood wrote the opinion of the court in which the principal reason given for refusing the mandamus was that the office of paymaster-general had never been filled and the power given to the governor to make vacation appointments was limited to filling offices in which a vacancy had occurred.

The opinion followed the outline of *Marbury v. Madison*, which was cited with approval. Justice Lockwood took great pains to show that the court was not given sufficient opportunity to consider the questions involved, saying:

> The questions supposed to grow out of this application have been elaborately argued, and the discussion has occupied several days, yet it is expected that this court will, in less time than was employed in the argument of the case, make up and deliver an opinion, which in its consequences may determine the question whether Edward Coles or A. F. Hubbard is, according to the constitution, the governor of this state. A question of such immense importance, whether we regard the interest and dignity of the persons interested in the result, or the right of the people to have the government administered by the person to whom they have delegated so important a trust would seem to require that the court ought to have more time for deliberation and examination, than the remainder of the present term. As, however, decision has been anxiously pressed upon the court, they have determined to give the subject on the investigation which the shortness of time, and the almost total absence of law books and other sources of information will permit. If the court, laboring under such great disadvantage, together with the unprecedented nature and novelty of the case, should err in the conclusions to which they shall arrive, they have no doubt that the error will meet, in the bosoms of the intelligent and honest, with a ready and satisfactory apology. In the great case of Marbury and Madison, secretary of state for the United States, in the supreme court of the United States (a tribunal filled with an enlightened and as able jurists, as ever graced the judgment seat in this or any other nation, the questions which, in some respects are similar to those in this case, were pending before that court for two years. Yet the opinion delivered in that case, although conspicuous for its luminous displays of deep research and constitutional learning, has not given universal satisfaction. Can it then be reasonably expected, that this court, without any pretension to the great and distinguished talents of the judges of that court, and destitute of even the ordinary means of forming an opinion will be able to arrive at a determination that will be universally satisfactory?

Justice Smith filed a separate opinion in which he pointed out that Ewing had not shown a clear legal right to the mandamus.[19]

Ewing was represented by four counsel, among whom were Thomas Reynolds and Robert Blackwell, while Forquer appeared on his own behalf. Forquer was an Edwards man politically. He had come from Pennsylvania and was a half-brother of Thomas Ford, who was to become associate justice of the Supreme Court and later governor of the state. He was a politician by profession and served previously as attorney general and in the state senate. Forquer was a reasonably competent lawyer but was a man of violent temper and suspicious nature.

Coles v. County of Madison[20] was decided at the June 1826 term. In this case the court for the first time considered an important constitutional issue. The case arose out of the strenuous efforts of the political enemies of Governor Coles to discredit him. A provision of the black code required a bond of a person bringing slaves into the state and setting them free. Governor Coles had liberated his ten slaves but through oversight had omitted to give the required bond. The action was brought by the county commissioners of Madison County to recover a statutory penalty of $2,000.

While the case was pending, the legislature aided Coles by passing an act releasing all penalties incurred under the provision mentioned, including the ones in suit. Chief Justice Wilson wrote the opinion of the court. He pointed out that the act of the legislature was not an ex post facto law and did not impair the obligation of any contract. Judge Smith was said to have first suggested the claim against Coles. Lockwood had been counsel for Coles in the lower court and recused himself.

There were no cases before 1831 in which the court declared any act of the legislature to be in contravention of the provisions of the Constitution of 1818. The court successfully avoided passing upon the constitutionality of the act creating the state bank.[21]

As term followed term, the issue of the continuance of slavery, already of first importance in national politics, began to appear in cases in the Supreme Court. Not counting the case involving Governor Coles, Breese's Reports contain four cases involving the status of blacks in Illinois. Judge Lockwood was an avowed enemy of slavery, and Wilson held similar views. In three of the four cases the court appeared to make every effort to limit the institution, which in Illinois remained legal through indentured servitude.

In one of these three cases, *Phoebe, a woman of color v. Jay,*[22] the court held an act of the Territorial Legislature of Indiana invalid as conflicting with

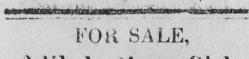

FOR SALE,
A likely Negro Girl,
16 years of age.
For further particulars, enquire at this Office.
Kaskaskia, Dec 12, 1826.   21-8t

PUBLIC NOTICE.

THIS day was committed to the custody of the Sheriff of Randolph county, State of Illinois, as Runaway, a Negro Man who calls himself

Martin Barker,

about forty-three years of age, about five feet nine inches high, a scar over his right eye, and also one on his right leg above his ancle, his make and his appearance active ; he states that he once belonged to Lewis Barker, of Pope county near the Rock-in-Cave but that he is now free. If any person has any legal claim to him, they are requested to exhibit the same and pay all charges, according to law.
        ANT. DUFOUR, *D. Sheriff*
        For THOS. J. V. OWEN, S R C.
Kaskaskia, Dec. 11, 1896   21-6t

Advertisement in a Kaskaskia newspaper demonstrates that slavery and indentured servitude were synonymous in Illinois. Abraham Lincoln Presidential Library and Museum.

provisions of the Ordinance of 1787. By a somewhat devious course of reasoning, the court upheld the validity of the provisions in the Illinois Constitution authorizing the indenturing of servants. It was said that the Act of Congress admitting Illinois into the Union was the consent of Congress to the abrogation of that portion of the Ordinance with which the constitution was in conflict.

In another case, *Fanny, a woman of color v. Montgomery,*[23] the court had occasion to consider the application of the fugitive slave law. On technical grounds the court reversed and remanded a lower court judgment refusing damages for assault and battery on an indentured servant. With respect to a technical question concerning a certificate under the fugitive slave law, Justice Lockwood concluded the opinion, "We are not required, from the state of the pleadings, to go into any such inquiry; on this point, therefore, I forebear; for 'sufficient unto the day is the evil thereof.'"

Whatever may have been the views of Justice Lockwood and his associates on the moral and social aspects of the institution of slavery, their decision in the case of *Nance, a girl of color v. Howard*,[24] left no doubt that the status of the indentured servant and that of the slave were substantially identical, except for the duration of the servitude. The court held that an indentured servant might be sold upon execution like any other piece of personal property.

This court, or at least three of its judges, were definitely opposed to the continuance of slavery as an institution whether it appeared disguised as indentured servitude or not. A review of its decisions establishes that the court neglected no opportunity to interpret the constitutional provision in such a way as to require strict compliance if an indenture was to be upheld.

In a case decided at the December 1836 term, the court held that the minor children of blacks registered under Indiana and Illinois territorial law were free, notwithstanding the language of the sixth article of the constitution to the effect that such children should become free, "the males at the age of twenty-one years, and the females at the age of eighteen years."[25] The territorial laws subsequent to the Act of 1807 of the Indiana Territory imposed no restrictions upon the freedom of registered servants. Therefore, the language of the constitution was intended merely to impose a restriction on the rights of the master to the services of such children, and these rights did not legally exist.

In another case decided at the same term, the court repeated its prior declaration that the Act of 1807 of the Indiana Territory was void because it violated the Ordinance of 1787.[26] It was pointed out that the Constitution of 1818 confirmed only those indentures that were made in strict ordinance with the Act of 1807. One of its requirements was that the indenture be made and entered into within thirty days from the time the black person was brought into the Territory.

The greater number of the opinions of Chief Justice Wilson and his three associates are to be found in the first and second volumes of Scammon's Reports (2 and 3 Illinois). Lawyers who scan these volumes, even if they look only to the headnotes of the cases, are rewarded by a view of the rapid expansion and development of the legal system of a state. From the narrow questions of pleading and procedure that characterize so many of the cases in

Breese's Reports, the issues before the court after 1831 broadened. They now presented problems that made the court conscious that it was laying down principles to guide business people and ordinary citizens as well as lawyers and judges in the future.

There were cases that prescribed the rules for dealing with commercial paper and cases determining the validity of titles to land. Now and then one of these would recall dramatic events in the history of the state, such as in *McConnell v. Wilcox*,[27] in which the court passed upon the title to the site of Fort Dearborn in Chicago. This case was decided at the June 1837 term, and Justice Smith wrote the longest opinion, thirty-three pages, produced by any of the judges up to that time. Names that capture the imagination appear on these pages: George Rogers Clark, Mark Beaubien, and Robert A. Kinzie.

A disbarment case at the December 1834 term allowed the court to require strict proof if it was to mete out severe justice to an erring member of the bar.[28] There were criminal cases, including one case of murder in which the court held that the inclusion of an alien as a juror would have rendered the verdict void had not the trial court ordered the juror withdrawn.[29] This signified its approval of the Common Law viewpoint that it is better that a guilty person go free than that the innocent one be convicted.

This court also was required to pass squarely upon the question of whether or not it had power to declare an act of the legislature invalid. The decision was given in a case involving the ill-omened State Bank of Illinois. The court held that the bills issued by the bank were "bills of credit" within the meaning of the prohibition in the federal Constitution.[30] The court followed the decision of the Supreme Court of the United States in *Craig, et al. v. The State of Missouri*[31] and in so doing overruled its own prior decision in *Snyder v. The State Bank of Illinois*.[32]

By the end of 1834, all of the judges had served at least ten years on the court. An interested person, whether lawyer or not, reading the court's opinions after ten years of experience in putting down the foundations of the judicial system is impressed with the thought that the court had come of age. Even the scattered opinions of Justice Browne proceeded with assurance. Those of the other judges indicated a full realization of the court's responsibility in the development of the law.

In the disbarment case, just referred to, the language of Chief Justice Wilson's opinion is the language of mature judicial experience: "It is not upon every idle rumor put forth with the garb and semblance of truth, aided by feeling of hostility, that a member of the profession should be arraigned for supposed misconduct. It is the duty of the court to guard with vigilance every member of the bar from such assaults, while at the same time it should not shrink from inflicting exemplary punishment upon those who are guilty of acts of delinquency."[33]

The judges must have felt some encouragement in their efforts when in 1835 the General Assembly once again relieved them of their circuit court duties. Yet subsequent events were to prove that the court was approaching a crisis in its history. There was no tradition of a career judiciary in Illinois. Not one of the four judges had been able to withstand the attractions afforded by other political offices. Not one seems to have thought that the prestige of the Supreme Court was sufficient for his ambitions. Participation in the bawdy game of pioneer politics was to mar the court's influence, and the political activity of certain judges would stand between them and the attainment of judicial greatness.

In 1826, the great figure on the national political horizon was Andrew Jackson. All along the frontier his name and military exploits were on the peoples' tongues. His qualities attracted the frontiersmen, farmers, and "butcher knife boys" who made up the bulk of the population in Illinois. Not surprisingly, Daniel Pope Cook's action was unpopular when he cast the Illinois vote for John Quincy Adams when the House of Representatives decided the presidential election of 1824. There can be no doubt that this contributed to the downfall of the Edwards-Cook faction in state politics. Cook was defeated for reelection to Congress in 1826 and Ninian Edwards narrowly escaped defeat in his campaign for the governorship.

With the rise of Jacksonianism came a consciousness of party politics. It is true that in the campaign of 1828 the people were mostly pro-Jackson or anti-Jackson on a personal basis, but after that the growth of alignment as Democrats or Whigs was noticeable. Three of the judges of the Supreme Court became Whigs; Smith became the lone Democrat. Smith's political activities more than equaled, at least in energy, the combined activities of all the other judges.

Smith had been an aggressive leader of the pro-slavery convention group before he became a judge. As a judge he became the acknowledged leader of the remnants of the Edgar-Morrison group, in time dividing the leadership of the Illinois Democrats with Elias Kent Kane. The events of 1832 and 1833 nearly brought his career to an end and severely damaged the prestige of the Supreme Court. The General Assembly received numerous petitions recommending Smith's impeachment, and the House of Representatives finally

Theophilus W. Smith, Illinois Supreme Court justice from 1825 to 1842, was impeached by the Illinois House of Representatives but acquitted in the Senate. Illinois Supreme Court Historic Preservation Commission.

undertook the investigation. The result was formal articles of impeachment that charged him with selling a circuit clerk's office; swearing out vexatious writs returnable before himself for the purpose of oppressing innocent men by holding them to bail, and then continuing the suits for several terms in a court of which he was a judge; imprisoning a Quaker for not taking off his hat in court; and suspending a lawyer for advising his client to take a change of venue from his court.[34]

The trial before the Senate lasted for many days. The court was shaken by the attacks on Justice Smith. The story, true or not, was told that while the impeachment trial was in progress, he procured someone to collect the scraps of paper from the desks of the Senators after each adjournment in order to see what they had scribbled during the proceedings. When the vote was taken it was found that while two-thirds of the Senators voting had believed him guilty of some of the charges against him, there had been no concurrence of the requisite two-thirds in any particular charge or charges. The greatest number to agree that he was guilty of particular charges was twelve, while fifteen was required for a conviction. The House of Representatives, after the failure of the impeachment proceedings, sought to remove him by address but the Senate did not agree.[35]

There can be no doubt that public confidence in the court was shaken by the attacks on Justice Smith. Even though his party became dominant in state politics, the Supreme Court remained unpopular with the people for some time to come. The unpopularity increased when cases appeared in the court that involved issues upon which the two parties divided.

The court rendered an unpopular decision at the December 1835 term in the case of *The People v. Mobley*.[36] The question arose when Stephen T. Logan, newly elected judge of the Circuit Court of Sangamon County, appointed Mobley clerk of that court in place of Matheny, the incumbent. The court held that the tenure of the circuit clerks was not limited by law and that they could not be removed except for misbehavior. The doctrine of free tenure approved by the court was a forecast of its decision in a case that was destined to make it even more unpopular.

Illinois voted for Martin Van Buren, the Democrat, in the presidential election of 1840. Governor Edwards had been succeeded by John Reynolds, a member of his own party, who in turn had been succeeded in 1834 by Joseph Duncan, a Democrat. When Thomas Carlin was elected governor in 1838, he found the office of secretary of state occupied by Alexander P. Field, a Whig who had been appointed by Edwards. Claiming the right to name a secretary from his own party, Governor Carlin appointed John A. McClernand to succeed Field. Field refused to surrender the office, and McClernand filed an information in the nature of a quo warranto in the Circuit Court of Fayette County where Judge Sidney Breese presided.

The circuit court decided in favor of McClernand, and Field appealed the judgment to the Supreme Court. The best legal talent of the state argued the case. Cyrus Walker, Justin Butterfield, and Levi Davis appeared for Field, while Jesse B. Thomas Jr., Stephen A. Douglas, James Shields, and the attorney general, Wickliffe Kitchell, argued on behalf of McClernand.

Chief Justice Wilson and Justice Lockwood, at the December 1839 term, held that the governor possessed no constitutional power to remove the secretary of state and appoint a successor at will.[37] Justice Smith dissented, relying principally upon the doctrine of federal constitutional law that the power to appoint includes the power to remove. The report of the case occupies over one hundred pages in the second volume of Scammon's Reports (3 Illinois).

In addition to the unpopular doctrine of *The People v. Mobley*, here reaffirmed, the division of the court along party lines inflamed popular feeling against the Whig judges. It is doubtful that Wilson and Lockwood were influenced by the considerations that were imputed to them, but there was no way of refuting the charges.

At the same term another case was argued that heightened the popular excitement and feeling against the court. The population of Illinois in 1839 included possibly 10,000 aliens, and Governor Ford said that nine-tenths of the alien vote was Democratic.[38] An agreed case from Jo Daviess County presented to the Supreme Court the issue of whether aliens could vote in the state elections. The Democrats regarded it as a foregone conclusion that the Whig majority on the court would render a decision adverse to their wishes, and they began plans to "reform" the judiciary. So positive were the Democrats that the Whig judges would adhere to the party line, that the Democratic lawyers, among them Stephen A. Douglas, obtained a continuance on the ground of a defect in the record.

The court announced its decision at the December 1840 term. The Whig judges decided that election judges under the law had no power to pass on the citizenship of prospective voters.[39] However, instead of turning popular opinion in their favor, the Whig judges then found that most people believed they had discovered an excuse to avoid the real issue in order to stave off the reform measures that threatened the court.

There is, of course, no direct evidence for or against such a view. It can only be considered whether the characters of Wilson, Lockwood, and Browne were consistent with such conduct. It is true, however, that further discredit came to Justice Smith from this case. Stephen A. Douglas disclosed that he had been in constant touch with Smith during the time the case was pending before the Supreme Court and that Smith had pointed out the defect in the record on the basis of which a continuance was obtained. It seems likely that Smith was giving information about the probable outcome of the case.[40]

The proposed judiciary reform bill provided for an increase in the number of judges of the Supreme Court from four to nine, which would give the Democrats a majority of six. The measure also provided once more for sending the judges back to duty on the circuits. After much opposition, the legislature finally passed the bill. Before the end of the December 1840 term, Sidney Breese, Thomas Ford, Walter B. Scates, Samuel H. Treat, and Stephen A. Douglas took their places with Wilson, Browne, Lockwood, and Smith.

7. Giants in the Prairie

"PRAIRIE LAND REQUIRES a strong team, and a large plow kept very sharp, to break it up thoroughly. This must be done well, and every particle of sward turned over; or it had better be let alone." By 1839 Illinois had become the Prairie State. The frontier was west of the Mississippi and civilization had begun in the midlands. A last, small Indian war had been fought, and Blackhawk had made his sad speech and was dead in Iowa of humiliation and despair.

There was a ludicrous side to the Black Hawk War. There had been marching up and down, and politicians who never fought a battle had gained reputations as warriors. Some had even perpetuated their reputations by nicknames earned in the supposed defense of the border. Only one, Abraham Lincoln, whose tall shadow was beginning to be cast across the Illinois prairies, saw no dignity in playing at soldiering. He would make capital, with a master storyteller's art, of the ludicrous aspect of this most unwarlike war.[1]

The legislature moved the capital of Illinois from Vandalia to Springfield in 1839. Such was the restlessness of the people that neither the provision in the schedule of the Constitution of 1818 guaranteeing Vandalia a full twenty years as a capital city, nor the attractions of a new brick capitol building were sufficient to overcome the determined horse-trading of the "Long Nine."[2]

The National Road pushing westward from Cumberland across Ohio and Indiana had reached Vandalia, but public interest flagged before it could stretch to St. Louis. Indifference to its condition and the high cost of maintenance prevented it from bringing the expected advantages to Illinois' second capital city.[3]

Kaskaskia was already falling into obscurity. Vandalia would become another pleasant town in the Illinois countryside with a "Madonna of the Trail" to remind the visitor that here passed the wagons of the pioneers pushing the frontier west. Only a brick courthouse, with a tale of a tall man who dropped from a second story window to break a legislative quorum, would remain to remind generations of citizens and tourists that from this place a state was once governed.[4]

The capital moved from a village in the wooded wilderness to another village on the prairie, a move that symbolized the importance of the prairies in the development of the state. Woodsmen and hunters from Kentucky and Tennessee had been afraid of the Illinois prairies. Even the experiences of the French with the rich lands of the American Bottom had failed to convince them that land that did not grow trees could be expected to grow anything worthwhile. They were afraid of the lonesomeness of the prairies at night, of the winds that seldom stopped blowing except in the heat of summer, of the lack of wood for houses and fuel, and of the prairie grasses that in places in the low lands grew taller than a person on horseback. More than anything else, they were afraid of the terrible prairie fires that roared through the tall grass fanned by the wind.

But farming stump patches was hard work, and the rewards were small. The Germans, Italians, Irish, and Norwegians who came to settle in Illinois in the 1830s did not have the woodsman's instinctive mistrust of the prairies. Besides, Johnny Appleseed made trees grow as well on prairies as anywhere. Gradually it was understood that prairie lands could produce in abundance if properly farmed.

Like the woods, streams, and knolls, the prairies came in time to have names, the characteristic names that pioneers gave to features of the country just behind the frontier. The most widely known prairie in Illinois was Looking Glass Prairie in St. Clair County on the way to St. Louis. There was Long Prairie, Flat Prairie, and Strong Prairie, and prairies such as Twelve-Mile Prairie and Four-Mile Prairie, whose names described their size. Some of the names carried the particular flavor of the American frontier: Squaw Prairie, Horse Prairie, Gun Prairie, Lost Prairie, and Elk Prairie. Some like Goose-Nest Prairie became part of the tradition surrounding the name of men who lived and struggled there, the giants of their time.

With the breaking of the prairies came the establishment of towns and villages on their edges. Trails were becoming roads and transportation over land became as important as transportation by water. The town would be counted fortunate that had prairie at its door to furnish food to eat and grain and meat to trade with the outside world. Even Chicago, which in seven years was to spring from obscurity to the largest city in the state, had its Burnt Prairie, memories of which were still alive in the minds of elder citizens in the twentieth century.[5]

Springfield became the prairie capital of the Prairie State, and there were other towns for which the prairies were the source of strong life. Woodland towns like Shawneetown, Carmi, Palestine, Brownsville, and Equality became eclipsed by Jacksonville, Danville, Belleville, Carthage, Mt. Vernon, Springfield, Decatur, and Bloomington. And there were fast-rising towns whose locations afforded advantages of water transportation and prairie land support, such as Alton, Chicago, Beardstown, Quincy, Peoria, Ottawa, and Joliet.[6]

The law growing up in Illinois as the "Long Nine" allegedly log rolled the capital away from Vandalia, was a prairie law that laid emphasis upon such problems as drainage of surface waters, destruction of crops by grazing cattle and foraging hogs, and the form and validity of deeds to prairie land. Moreover, it was a law troubled by knotty questions inherited from the misdeeds of the days of John Edgar and the Morrisons. Cases confronted the courts involving the title to lands in which the evidence went back to the charges of fraud and worse, which were embodied in the reports of the uncompromising land commissioners, Michael Jones and Elijah Backus.

It was a prairie law that still could not cope with the essential lawlessness of a considerable element in the pioneer population. The days of Kaskaskia as a capital city had been marked by the violence that was the worst side of frontier character. The days of Vandalia as the seat of government had seen that violence curbed only slightly. The men with ox teams, bull whips, and prairie breaker plows who had replaced "the tall lank visitors, brown as snuff" were only slightly less turbulent. The basic idea still prevailed that the least law was the best, and personal arguments were better settled with fists or knives, or sometimes even with guns, than in the courts.

Courts were places where land titles were settled, notes and debts collected, estates administered, and sometimes horse thieves, sneak thieves, and murders by stealth were dealt with. Juries did not convict a man who killed his adversary in a fair fight or who proved himself handier with knife or pistol than a slower-witted opponent with an equal chance.[7] The important work for judges was to determine fairly the questions of law presented in such cases, maintain a reasonable degree of order in proceedings before them, and use common sense in adapting legal rules to the conditions of pioneer life—a not inconsiderable assignment. People on the prairies had little money and much land, and judges were expected to be understanding with respect to delays in the payments of debts.

As important as anything else, legal contests were entertainment, courts were shows, and lawyers were actors. Litigation was a game as well as a show. The rewards frequently went to the skillful player who might or might not represent the person whose claim was just. The idea of justice according to law in a pioneer community insisted that every person be equal before the law in all except ability to prevail in a contest in which the terms were fair. In court as elsewhere, victory might properly go to the most skillful at the game of litigation. The injustice of the result was frequently forgotten when a lawyer with a bad case was able to win it by cleverly disguising subordinate issues as important ones. Courts and judges were not expected to be reformers. The hope of the underprivileged was the legislator, not the jurist. Few made careers of being judges, for the honor of the bench was still in the future.

The restraints the courts provided against violence and lawlessness were only somewhat more effective than such restraints had been in territorial days. The grosser forms of brutality were no longer condoned by juries, and judges had better means of enforcing their orders, but this is merely to say that communities were in general more law-abiding.

Three years before the capital went to Springfield, a spectacled man with the air of a minister of the gospel and a Puritan conscience came to Alton from St. Louis. Alton had seemed a good place for a man whose conscience was troubled by slavery—especially if that conscience made him speak his mind in print instead of holding to his views and being quiet about it. St. Louis had been unfriendly to Elijah Lovejoy.[8] Too many people in St. Louis had plantation connections and were willing to justify them forcibly. There were no slaves in Alton. There were immigrants from Germany with positive convictions that appealed to a man who was troubled that other men and women were bought and sold as property.

Elijah Lovejoy became a newspaper editor in Alton and began the publication of the *Alton Observer*. The reaction of lawless elements, presumably from St. Louis, was swift. His press was destroyed before it was set up. Not daunted by this vandalism, Lovejoy promptly ordered another and began the expression of his views. At a public meeting in Alton he denied that he was an abolitionist but insisted upon his right to express his views without restraint, even if the subject was slavery.[9]

The *Alton Observer* was out of place in that Illinois community. It is doubtful that Lovejoy's denunciation of slavery alone brought upon him the disaster that was to occur, but in any case, Illinois had no New England conscience to be appealed to. The prairie lands were then the West, with the characteristic easy-going attitude that, when aroused, could take the form of extreme intolerance toward all reformers. So Lovejoy, whose conscience could accept no middle ground, was destined for martyrdom. His third press was destroyed on September 21, 1837, and he ordered a fourth. Threats were made against his life, and the shadow of mob violence hung over him continually.

There were those in Alton who sincerely tried to avoid the inevitable catastrophe. In November, citizens held a public meeting, which gave Lovejoy an opportunity to speak in his own defense. His was no friendly voice. He was as uncompromising as his Puritan forebears. Even so, there was something in Lovejoy's strict insistence on his right to speak as he pleased that appealed to the spirit of independence of the community. His fearlessness and obvious honesty might possibly have saved him had not the attorney general of Illinois taken the platform in what today seems a needless display of oratory.[10]

There had been no warmth in Lovejoy's speech and the Puritan conscience makes no emotional appeal. Whatever good Lovejoy's words might have done for the cause of law and order, Usher F. Linder dispelled that good with inflammatory courtroom oratory. When Lovejoy's new press arrived at an Alton warehouse, a mob organized for its destruction. Lovejoy and a small group of associates armed themselves for its defense. The mob attempted to rush the warehouse, but the little group of defenders repelled it. In that first attack defenders mortally wounded one of the mob. The mob then attempted to fire the roof of the warehouse. They backed the attempt with bullets, and Lovejoy received wounds from which he died.

There was an immediate and unfavorable reaction against mob rule and against the city of Alton throughout much of the United States, but public response in Alton was otherwise. Lovejoy was hurried to an obscure grave without ceremony the day after his death. The defenders of the warehouse who had stood with him were indicted for unlawfully "resisting an attack made by certain persons unknown to destroy a printing press," and for "unlawfully defending a certain warehouse." Usher Linder, whose speech had inflamed the public meeting that Lovejoy had addressed, prosecuted as attorney general. The defendants were acquitted.[11]

Thus Lovejoy became not only the first martyr in Illinois since statehood, but a martyr to the whole cause of abolition. His case is a plain example of the weakness of law enforcement that could protect neither his property nor his life. One of the most pathetic incidents in Illinois history is the story of how his wife defended him from the mob when his third press was destroyed. To Mrs. Lovejoy also belonged the "red badge of courage."[12]

Some years later a stone was placed over the obscure grave in the cemetery on one of Alton's seven hills. The inscription was like a cry of anguish: "Hic Jacet Lovejoy Jam Parce Sepulto" ("Here lies Lovejoy. Now that he is buried, let him be"). His may have been a restless ghost. Long after bullets settled the question of abolition, litigation arose in Alton, bitter and protracted, involving the right of blacks to attend public schools.[13] Alton sought to rival St. Louis in commercial importance. How much of the failure of justice according to prairie law set back its ambitions is a matter of conjecture.

These were some of the characteristics of the prairie law when Springfield became the seat of government, and the Supreme Court of Illinois took up its duties there in 1840. The weaknesses of that law were chiefly weaknesses in administration. The rules of law as they had evolved were pretty well adapted to community needs.[14] With the hard common sense that took the place of much of legal learning, the Supreme Court judges had refused to apply rules of Common Law that seemed poorly adapted to the needs of a pioneer community. There was little effort at conscious judicial statesmanship. When the law needed changing, the biennial sessions of the legislature were provided by the constitution for that purpose. The year 1839 began the period of the decline of the influence of legislatures and the beginning of the influence of courts.

The four-judge Supreme Court, which in 1840 decided the alien case, was composed of three Whigs and one Democrat. When the Democratic legislature passed the bill to reorganize the judiciary in 1840, it increased the membership of the court from four to nine, proceeded to elect five Democrats to the bench, and returned the judges to circuit court duties.

In the matter of assignments of circuits, the legislature dealt kindly with Chief Justice Wilson and Justice Lockwood, as if in recognition of their years of satisfactory service. Justice Lockwood, who lived in Jacksonville, received the first circuit, which included his home county of Morgan among eight counties.[15] The chief justice likewise received his home county with the assignment of the fourth circuit, which included White County, of which Carmi, his place of residence, was the county seat.[16]

But it appeared that the legislature reserved its vindictiveness for inoffensive and inarticulate but courageous and honest Justice Browne. Like a conscientious policeman disciplined for offending politicians, Judge Browne, who resided in Shawneetown, Gallatin County, in the extreme southeastern part of Illinois, was assigned to the sixth circuit, which included Jo Daviess County

Jo Daviess County

Gallatin County

In an effort to get Illinois Supreme Court justice Thomas C. Browne
to resign, the legislature assigned him to the Sixth Judicial Circuit in
Jo Daviess County, four hundred miles from his home in Gallatin County.
Map prepared by Matt Burns.

in the extreme northwesterly corner of the state.[17] He took up residence in
the picturesque lead mining town of Galena. The important seventh circuit,
which included the fast-growing city of Chicago, went to Justice Smith, the
only Democrat already on the bench.

The reorganized court met for its first session in Springfield on February
15, 1841. All of the new judges were present except Douglas, who did not
join the court until the end of the term.[18] This nine-judge court of 1841 was
worthy of careful notice even though its membership would change rapidly
in the months immediately ahead.

There were men on the court for whom the future held positions of high importance. Two would satisfy in part their desires for political preferment by attaining to the United States Senate, and one of these, whose misfortune it was not to be a man of destiny, would be a candidate for president. Another would leave the Supreme Court to become a federal judge and would serve with distinction for many years. A fourth would resign after a few months to become governor of the state and would also have the misfortune not to be a man of destiny. Of the new judges, only one would consider his judicial position a career in itself.

One day in 1833, in the little river town of Meredosia, a farmer from the Illinois prairies took notice of a small man with a big head and a big voice. The man was young, and since he weighed scarcely more than a boy, the farmer helped him up behind him on his horse, and they headed southeastward from Meredosia to the village of Exeter. Here, the young man hoped to put his big voice and his eastern accent to work teaching school.

Stephen Arnold Douglas had journeyed far in search of fame and fortune. He was born at Brandon, Vermont, on April 23, 1813, the son of a physician. His opportunities for formal education were limited by his father's death when he was a young boy, and he learned the cabinetmaker's trade. A step-father brought better times to the family, and Douglas moved to New York, where he acquired some formal education. With characteristic positiveness of purpose, he soon decided upon a career at the bar. Lacking the means of obtaining a formal education, he began a journey westward that took him to Cleveland and Cincinnati, to Louisville and St. Louis, and into Illinois.[19]

Douglas came to Illinois in 1833 with no funds and no prospects, but soon he was befriended by Murray McConnel, then one of the most active lawyers in practice in the state. Young Douglas studied the law books that McConnel lent him and sought a job teaching as a means of supporting himself. Despite the efforts of the friendly farmer who took him to Exeter, no school was available for him to teach, and he made his way to Winchester, county seat of Scott County. There the story is told that he went into a tavern and announced in his big voice that he had no money but intended to have a bed. Throughout his life his characteristic aggressiveness, his small stature, impressive head, and penetrating eyes attracted men and women too. It is related that the landlord not only gave him the bed but found him forty pupils and a school to teach.[20] During his Winchester days, he studied Murray McConnel's books at night and "pettifogged" before a justice of the peace on Saturdays and eventually gained admission to the bar.

Douglas moved to Jacksonville, in Morgan County, where he attracted the notice and interest of Captain John Wyatt, a local Democratic leader. Wyatt was a bitter political enemy of John J. Hardin, the state's attorney. Wyatt conceived the audacious idea of humiliating Hardin by legislating him out of office. Accordingly, Douglas drafted a bill that provided that the legislature—instead of the governor—should fill the office of state's attorney. Wyatt maneuvered the bill through the General Assembly and likewise maneuvered the appointment of Douglas as state's attorney for Morgan County.[21]

Douglas's ambition was bigger than his voice. He remained as prosecutor for only a few short months when he resigned to become a member of the lower house of the General Assembly. Thereafter, he was successively a candidate for Congress and secretary of state. During this period of life he was not only a successful politician, but also a successful lawyer. He was of counsel in the case of *People ex rel. McClernand v. Field*,[22] involving the right of the governor to appoint his secretary of state and was also of counsel in the alien case that did so much to make the Supreme Court unpopular.

Stephen A. Douglas was only twenty-eight years old when, in 1840, he was selected as an associate justice of the Supreme Court of Illinois, one of the youngest judges in the history of the court. He remained on the bench only long enough to earn the title, for he resigned July 28, 1843. It was characteristic not only of Douglas, but of his times that his success in becoming a member of the Supreme Court should merely make him aspire to further political preferment. The immediate purpose of his resignation was to enable him to go Washington as Congressman, his eyes already focused on the United States Senate.

Douglas's circuit as a member of the Supreme Court was the fifth, which included the counties of Schuyler, Brown, Adams, Hancock, McDonough, Warren, Henderson, Knox, and Fulton. He held court in the brick courthouse at Quincy where there appeared before him such able lawyers from the fifth circuit as Cyrus Walker, Orville H. Browning, and Lewis Ross, and Stephen T. Logan, Lyman Trumbull, and Edward D. Baker from other circuits.[23] In a majority of the cases decided by Douglas on the circuit and that were taken to the Supreme Court for review, his rulings were upheld. Now and then a case appeared in which the Supreme Court found it necessary to reverse him. In some of these, Douglas himself wrote the opinion of the court.[24]

Douglas was as restless as the pioneer communities that took him to their hearts and made him the "Little Giant" when he moved into the wider sphere of national politics. There was in him a turbulence that the career of a successful lawyer and competent judge could not quell. His ability was tremendous and his energy without limit. He was personally ambitious but not more so than the other "giant in the prairie" who in a few years would contend with him for the highest of national honors. But his ambition craved satisfaction through the acclaim of the crowds who would gather to hear him speak wherever he appeared. The audiences of a trial lawyer were too small to satisfy his need, and the judge of an appellate court had no audience at all.

Thus Stephen A. Douglas appeared a short while to preside competently on the circuit and to write opinions that were clear and direct in his full share of the cases before the Supreme Court. Then he left the scene of legal history to appear in the larger theater of national politics at a time when great issues attracted the attention of prairie giants.

At Peoria, Thomas Ford became circuit judge in 1835. A governor of Illinois from 1842 to 1846, he became one of the state's more tragic figures. Ford was born near Uniontown, Pennsylvania, on December 5, 1800. His father, Robert Ford, was killed by highwaymen and his mother's first husband, named Forquer, had been killed in a coal mine accident. In 1804, his mother, with her large family of children, set out for St. Louis and after a short stay, moved to the village of New Design in what is now Monroe County, Illinois.

The most abject poverty was characteristic of Ford's early life. His schooling was extremely meager. His guiding spirit was his elder half-brother, George Forquer, who made enough money in St. Louis as a carpenter to go into business. When financial failure attended Forquer's efforts as a merchant, he established himself as a lawyer, entered Illinois politics, and became secretary of state by Governor Edward Coles. Forquer sent young Ford to Transylvania University in 1818. He attended there for almost a year before the financial reverses of his benefactor made it necessary for him to give up his education. He started the return journey home to New Design on foot when only eighteen years of age. While passing through Indiana he persuaded people in one of the pioneer settlements to erect a schoolhouse and engage him as school master.

He returned to Illinois a short time later, did farm work, taught school, and studied law until 1824, when he obtained a position on a newspaper in St. Louis. After six months of this, he entered the practice of law at Edwardsville in partnership with George Forquer. In 1828, he married Frances Hambaugh, daughter of a German farmer living near Edwardsville. In 1829, Ford terminated his partnership with Forquer and, attracted by the hope of a new career in the undeveloped northern section of the state, set out for Galena, where the lead mines brought a new prosperity. Things went badly for him, and he was again rescued from financial distress by Forquer, who procured his appointment as state's attorney of the fifth judicial district, which then embraced the entire territory between the Illinois and Mississippi Rivers.

Meanwhile, his wife's parents had moved to Versailles Township in Brown County, and Ford returned to establish himself in Peoria. In 1835, he was elected judge of the circuit court, assigned to the ninth judicial circuit in the northern part of the state. Upon assumption of his new judicial duties, he located in the town of Oregon in Ogle County because of its central location in his circuit.[25]

Ford was a scholar by nature and considerate and kindly in disposition. He was conscientious in the discharge of his duties. He possessed perhaps to a greater degree than any of his colleagues that elusive quality called judicial temperament. He was too diffident and too sensitive to be a successful politician. Yet only two years after he took office as a Supreme Court justice, he found himself selected as the Democratic candidate for governor following the death of the regular candidate. Reluctantly he allowed himself to be persuaded to join the campaign and resigned his position on the Supreme Court.

The rest of his life is tragedy. Too conscientious and forthright to become the Reynolds type of backwoods politician, he was too diffident and retiring to become a real leader of his party. He assumed the governor's position at a time when the state was practically bankrupt, and many people seriously urged the repudiation of public debt. In order to defeat repudiation he called upon his friend, Stephen A. Douglas, for aid. Douglas left a sickbed and with a characteristic gesture, taunted the members of the legislature assembled in joint session. He told them that their children and their children's children would curse their names if they should dare to blacken the reputation of the state by repudiation.[26] Ford's efforts at economy were successful and under his leadership the state began gradually to return to sound financial condition.

When his term as governor ended in 1846, he returned to the Hambaugh farm in Brown County to write the history of Illinois for which he is best remembered. Ford completed the history in 1847 but was unable to make arrangements for its publication.[27] He had planned to resume the practice of law at Peoria, but whatever personal fortune he had dissipated during his term as governor. He remained on the Hambaugh farm in poverty until 1850. On October 12 of that year, his wife died of cancer at the age of 38, and three weeks later, November 3, Ford himself was dead. Misfortune continued to follow his children who were left to depend upon homes provided by friends of their father. One daughter died a public charge at Lincoln, and his two sons were put to death by "regulators" in Kansas.[28]

Breese, Scates, and Treat, the other three judges whom the Democrats added to the court in 1841, had less controversial careers than either Ford or Douglas and with results far happier than in the case of Governor Ford.

Sidney Breese came to Illinois from New York in 1818. He was a graduate of Union College and was admitted to the bar in 1820. He established himself at Kaskaskia and studied law with Elias Kent Kane. He became assistant secretary of state, and in December 1820 was employed to remove the archives from Kaskaskia to Vandalia. He made the trip in a wagon for which he received the sum of $25. Like Ford, he became a circuit judge in 1835, holding this position at the time of his election to the Supreme Court. Breese presided over the second circuit, which included the old French settlements in St. Clair and Randolph Counties. He served until 1843, when he resigned to become United States Senator, but returned to the Supreme Court again in 1857.[29]

The third judicial circuit was assigned to Walter Bennett Scates. Scates had been attorney general of the state and later a circuit judge. Of all the judges on the court at that time, Scates was least attracted by political advancement. He regarded the bench as a worthy career and the position of associate justice of the Supreme Court as sufficient honor to satisfy a lawyer's ambition.[30] His circuit took him to the valleys and hills of the extreme southeastern section of the state.

The fifth Democrat selected in the reformation of the court was Samuel Hubbel Treat, a New Yorker by birth. Treat spent his early years in the state of his birth and came to Illinois in 1834, taking up his residence in Springfield, where he became one of the able group of lawyers on the first judicial circuit. He became a circuit judge in 1839 for the newly created eighth judicial circuit and served continuously on the Supreme Court from 1841 until 1855, when he resigned to become judge of the United States District Court for the newly created Southern District of Illinois. Although his judicial career was not distinguished by any of the incidents that perpetrate lasting fame for judges, he was sincere and capable in his work. Like Scates, being judge was to him a career. It is not surprising that he preferred the certainty of life tenure on the federal bench to the uncertainty of an elective position on the highest court of the state.[31]

The nine-judge court that the Democrats created by the legislation of 1840 continued until the adoption of the Constitution of 1848. The court was composed of men of considerable legal and some judicial experience. Wilson, Browne, Lockwood, and Smith contributed a combined judicial experience of great value. Of the new judges, Treat and Scates were good lawyers with

Two politically charged Illinois
Supreme Court cases caused
the Democratic-controlled
legislature to expand the court
from four to nine members,
with all five new justices being
Democrats. The new members
were (*from top, left to right*)
Sidney Breese, Thomas Ford,
Samuel H. Treat, Walter B.
Scates, and Stephen A. Douglas.
Illinois Supreme Court Historic
Preservation Commission.

experience as trial court judges. Thomas Ford was sincere and intelligent with a scholar's instincts. Sidney Breese had the makings of a great judge, but his career was dominated by excessive zeal for participation in local politics. Stephen A. Douglas may have had mental powers unequaled by any of his colleagues, but the field was too narrow for his soaring ambitions and judicial duties too restricting for the restless energy of his mind and temperament. Had the court remained thus constituted for a longer time, it might have made an impressive contribution to the growth and development of the administration of prairie justice according to prairie law. This nine-judge court combined the talents of men of ability. Had a judicial career offered prestige, security, and some substantial financial advantages, most, if not all, would have been content to remain on the bench. Events brought rapid changes, and judicial workmanship suffered in consequence.

First to leave the court was Thomas Ford. Illinois Democrats met in convention in Springfield on December 5, 1841, to select candidates for the offices of governor and lieutenant governor for the 1842 elections. The choice of the convention for governor was Adam W. Snyder, who lived at Belleville, in St. Clair County. Snyder was one of the ablest men of his time and an excellent lawyer. His running mate was John Moore of McLean County. However wise may have been the choice of Snyder from the standpoint of ability and probability of future success, the choice was unwise in the light of subsequent events.

Snyder, long threatened by tuberculosis, succumbed to the disease on May 14, 1842, leaving the Democrats without a candidate for governor and the crucial election but a short time away. The party had been able to unite behind the candidacy of Snyder, but its divergent factions were at odds over the choice of a successor. In June, leading Democrats of the state met in Springfield, and after considerable argument and discussion selected Judge Ford as the successor candidate. Ford did not seek the office, but he was finally persuaded to accept the nomination. The election was scheduled for August 2, and Judge Ford accordingly resigned from the Supreme Court as of August 1. The demoralized state of the Whig party in Illinois assured his election and although he did not campaign very strenuously, he received a plurality of more than 8,000 votes.[32]

It was then true of the office of governor, as has since been said of the office of United States Senator, that a poor man has no business being elected to it. Governor Ford was without means other than his earnings, and was in no position to carry the large financial burden of the office for which the salary was grossly inadequate. Moreover, he had the misfortune to become governor at one of the most difficult times in the history of the state. Illinois had been bankrupted by the fantastic program of internal improvements inaugurated during the 1830s. It was Ford's unpopular task to place the government on a sound financial basis. He had the ability but not the temperament for his job. He was too conscientious to be a successful demagogue and too sensitive to be a successful politician. The opinions of others worried him quite as much as events, and criticism impeded his sincerest efforts. Controversy was distasteful to him, and had he resisted the party draft and remained on the bench he might have avoided being drawn into controversies that troubled his sensitive nature so deeply.

At Nauvoo, in Hancock County, a drama began that, like the Lovejoy affair, would point out the inadequacies of law and law enforcement. To this place on the bluffs above the Mississippi, about ten miles north of the point where the great Keokuk dam now widens the river into a lake, in 1839 came Joseph Smith, the prophet, and his followers who called themselves the Latter Day Saints. Trouble had followed their efforts to establish a community first in Ohio and then in Missouri,[33] and the peaceful wood and prairie land around Nauvoo offered the haven from suspicion and misunderstanding that they were seeking. Nauvoo grew rapidly as news of the establishment of the community reached Ohio and the east. By 1844, there were probably 17,000 people living there, the largest city in the state.

Increase in size brought political importance to Nauvoo and political influence to its leaders. Joseph Smith used his influence to obtain privileges for his followers and "home-rule" for Nauvoo.[34] In 1840, the General Assembly granted a charter to the inhabitants, who "constituted a body corporate and politic," with powers through their mayor and council to do almost anything they chose, consistent with state and federal constitutions.[35]

The mayor and aldermen possessed the same jurisdiction as justices of the peace and appeals from their decisions went to the municipal court, which consisted of the mayor and the four aldermen. The city council was also given the power to organize the inhabitants into an independent military body to be called the "Nauvoo Legion." The Legion performed the same amount of military duty as was required of the regular state militia, and its members were exempt from all other military duty. It served at the disposal of the mayor in executing the city ordinances.

The causes of the misunderstanding and antagonism between the Mormons and non-Mormons that led to the "Mormon War" were many. Differences in religious faith alone would never have brought on the conflict. It is true that certain of the Saints' beliefs were regarded as outlandish by the rest of the population, but there was nothing of a religious crusade in the movement to drive the Mormons out of Illinois.[36]

In the beginning both Whigs and Democrats sought to capture the vote of Nauvoo. When one party was temporarily successful in securing it, the press of the other party became vituperative. Joseph Smith and his elders used their unique position to obtain special privileges and immunities for their community. This was bound to stir resentment in the other pioneer settlements in the surrounding country. Also, dissident groups developed within the church, some of which had few scruples as to the means used to defeat the group in power.

Thus the Saints developed enemies within and without their organization. These found weapons within easy reach. There were ugly stories that had followed the Mormons from their difficulties in Ohio and Missouri and there were more sinister stories of debauchery and crime in Nauvoo.[37] Whether any of these were true remains a matter of conjecture. But whether they were true or not, the conduct of the leaders was not such as was calculated to win over their enemies or disarm them. They took a course of action that to the rest of the state seemed to spring only from arrogance. By force, the Mormons suppressed an opposition newspaper in Nauvoo, destroying its press; they passed a series of ordinances to establish the church as a super government; and Joseph Smith in 1844 announced that he was a candidate for the presidency of the United States.[38]

Popular resentment against the prophet had arisen in the state when in 1843 Missouri sought to extradite him and Orrin Porter Rockwell to answer a charge of having attempted to murder Missouri governor Lilburn Boggs. Governor Ford issued a warrant, which was placed in the hands of a constable and Missouri's agent for service. The constable arrested Smith and delivered his prisoner to the Missouri agent. The prophet was rescued by the faithful and returned to Nauvoo where he appeared before the municipal court, represented by Cyrus Walker, the Whig candidate for Congress. He was discharged on a writ of habeas corpus, although the court was clearly without jurisdiction.[39] The representative from Missouri immediately appealed to Governor Ford to call out the militia to take Smith into custody again. Ford declined, adding to his growing unpopularity.

In 1844, a rebellious faction in the church removed from Nauvoo to Carthage and a delegation from that place again asked Ford to call out the militia in order to restore regular government at Nauvoo. Ford, with characteristic conscientiousness determined to go to the scene of the trouble to investigate conditions first hand. Finding a considerable part of the militia assembled there, he placed them under command of their proper officers. He requested the Mormon leaders to appear before him to present their side of the situation. Ford addressed the men under arms at Carthage on behalf of law and order and apparently secured their acclamation for his course. Word was sent to the Mormon leaders that they would receive protection of the law if they surrendered and that the militia would be called out if they would not.

Meanwhile, Joseph Smith had declared martial law in Nauvoo and had summoned the Nauvoo Legion to arms. Upon the arrival of the governor's message and a constable and ten men, martial law was abolished and the mayor and the council of Nauvoo agreed to present themselves at Carthage the next morning. On June 24, Joseph Smith and his brother Hyrum, and other Nauvoo officials came into Carthage and surrendered themselves to the constable who had a warrant charging them with riot. They were next charged with treason on account of the declaration of martial law.[40]

The prisoners were confined in the stone jail building in Carthage. Ford, unaware of impending tragedy, ordered the troops dispersed except for two companies retained to guard the jail. With a third company he departed for Nauvoo. While the governor spoke to the assembled Mormons at Nauvoo on June 27, a mob attacked the jail at Carthage and Joseph and Hyrum Smith were shot to death.[41]

Ford acted throughout with a sincere desire to avoid bloodshed and to maintain orderly justice. Characteristically, he was almost naive in his trust of those around him. From his own account it appears that the misfortune and ill chance that followed him most of his days were present on this occasion also. There followed the disgraceful events of the so-called Mormon War and the expulsion of the Mormons from the state.[42]

Governor Ford's words at the end of the description of these sorry events in his written history are those of a bitter man: "But it is a fundamental law of man's nature from which he cannot escape that despotism is obliged to grow out of general anarchy, as surely as a stone is obliged to fall to the earth when left unsupported in the air. Without any revealed special providence, but in accordance with this great law of Man's nature, Cromwell rose out of the disorders of the English revolution; Charles the Second was restored to despotism by the anarchy which succeeded Cromwell; and Bonaparte came forth from the misrule of republican France. The people in all these cases attempted to govern; but in fact did not. They were incapable of self-government; and by returning to despotism admitted that they needed a master. Where the people are unfit for liberty; where they will not be free without violence, license, and injustice to others; where they do not deserve to be free, nature itself will give them a master. No form of constitution can make them free and keep so. On the contrary, a people who are fit for and deserve liberty cannot be enslaved."[43]

The administration of justice according to law failed under the stresses of conflict between Mormons and non-Mormons. Many questions that bear upon the causes of the failure remain unanswered. Was the community established at Nauvoo successful from an economic point of view? The records of the finances of church and city are unavailable or nonexistent.[44] Was the apparent prosperity of the Mormons real or feigned, the result of intelligent direction of sober industry, or the consequence of spending by the church government of money collected through the efforts of elders of the church in many parts of the country? Was there truth in the ugly stories of graft and debauchery circulated among those only too ready to believe? Or were these tales merely canard formulated by the malcontents within and the envious outside the church? These and other questions seem to defy positive answer.

However, certain conclusions seem fully supported by the evidence. Joseph and Hyrum Smith and the other leaders were overzealous in securing special privileges for themselves and their followers. Resentment flared as incidents accumulated. Nauvoo all but achieved complete autonomy in the management of its governmental and financial affairs. What Carthage and the rest of Hancock County took for arrogance seemed to be the basis of many official and private actions of the church leaders. Suspicion, mistrust, and jealousy usually follow the determination of a minority group to maintain social and religious barriers against intercourse with the rest of society.[45]

These and other forces produced the stresses that the faults in the structure of law enforcement were unable to withstand. A long process is required to insure complete acceptance of the belief that violence is the peculiar monopoly of organized government and that democratic action is its only legal and moral substitute. Illinois was made up of pioneer communities and this process had proceeded only a small way. It is not necessary to conclude that mob violence at Carthage and Nauvoo was the only means by which difficulties could be resolved, but it is certainly true that what occurred revealed how short a way the legal system had progressed toward the goal of peaceful settlement of controversies according to the rules of law.[46]

Following the resignation of Ford on August 1, 1842, vacancies on the nine-judge Supreme Court occurred rather rapidly. In December of the same year, turbulent Judge Smith resigned. On January 1, 1843, Sidney Breese resigned to become a candidate for United States Senator. John Dean Caton of Ottawa replaced Ford and took office on August 9, 1842, but left on March 6, 1843, when the legislature elected John M. Robinson of Carmi. Richard M. Young of Jonesboro replaced Smith January 14, 1843, and James Semple of Edwardsville replaced Breese on January 16 of the same year. Semple remained on the court only until August 16, 1843, when he resigned and James Shields of Randolph County replaced him. John M. Robinson died in office on April 27, 1843, and Caton returned to the bench after only a two-month absence on May 2, 1843.

Next to leave the court was Douglas, watching national politics with a shrewd eye from Springfield and the circuit bench in Quincy. He resigned on June 26, 1843, to go to Washington as a Congressman, and Jesse B. Thomas Jr. of Springfield, a nephew of the territorial judge and pioneer Senator, succeeded him.

Four other vacancies occurred before the Constitution of 1848 reorganized the court. Shields resigned in 1845, at the beginning of his extraordinary career, to become commissioner of the General Land Office at Washington. Gustave P. Koerner, the German-born future lieutenant governor from Belleville, succeeded him. In the same year, Judge Thomas left the court, and Norman H. Purple of Peoria, whose name is most frequently associated with statutory compilation, succeeded him. Richard M. Young resigned in 1847 to succeed Shields as commissioner of the General Land Office in Washington, and Judge Thomas returned to the court. In that year also, Judge Scates resigned, and William Denning took his place.[47]

The events just related clearly indicate an important obstacle in the way of legal development in Illinois before 1850. The position of a judge of the Supreme Court was not sufficiently eminent to satisfy the ambitions of most of the men of ability who attained the office. Of the five judges whom the Democrats added to the court in 1841, only Samuel H. Treat served until the drastic revision of the judiciary under the Constitution of 1848. The three Whig judges of the old court, Wilson, Browne, and Lockwood, likewise remained on the court; it is probable that advancing age and declining health were the factors inducing Wilson and Lockwood to remain. Certainly if the prestige of the position was not a considerable inducement, neither was the meager salary that went with it.[48]

Participation in the work of the court could not have been a particularly stimulating intellectual experience in the period that came to a close with the adoption of a new constitution in 1848. Great causes were few and the issues in cases before the court were mostly pedestrian. But there was legal development. The rules of law multiplied in number, and the diversifying interests of the people of the state brought new situations to the court's attention. Moreover, the court itself was increasing in influence. As cases increased in number the judges became increasingly conscious that their opinions stated the law as it would be applied in subsequent cases.

The nine-judge court was much more particular to cite authorities to support the principles it propounded than was its predecessor. A comparison of opinions announced in 1843 with those handed down in 1823 shows that the intervening years furnished the court with more and better tools with which to work. Texts and reports cited by the judges established that law libraries had assumed respectable size. Still, in 1845 Judge Scates said regretfully in an opinion that he could not procure certain volumes of English reports.[49]

During the whole existence of the Supreme Court of Illinois from 1818 to 1848, the most celebrated case to come before it was probably *Wilcox v. Jackson*.[50] This case involved the validity of the Beaubien claim to the tract of land in Chicago extending from the Chicago River south to Madison Street and from a line just east of State Street east to Lake Michigan. The tract included the site of Fort Dearborn and a portion of the military reservation surrounding it.

Jean Baptiste Beaubien, a French-Canadian from Detroit, established himself on the military reservation near the fort in 1817. He filed his application for a patent to the tract in 1831 at the land office at Palestine in Crawford County, tendering the sum of $94.61 in payment. His first and second applications were rejected as invalid. But his third, filed in Chicago in 1835, was accepted and sent to Washington. After waiting a year without action, Beaubien and others with whom he was associated began an ejectment suit against Wilcox, Commandant of Fort Dearborn. Thomas Ford, sitting in the circuit court in Chicago at the October 1836 term, ruled against Beaubien, who took the case on a writ of error to the Supreme Court of Illinois.

In an opinion by Judge Smith, the court reversed the circuit court decision, upholding Beaubien's claim. The Supreme Court of the United States reversed the judgment, however, on the ground that the tract was a military reservation and had been withdrawn from entry.[51] In the Supreme Court of the United States, Felix Grundy, then Attorney General, represented the government, and Daniel Webster and a Mr. Key, most likely Francis Scott

Key, represented Beaubien and his associates.[52] Beaubien was defeated by the absence of a preemption law at the time he endeavored to establish his claim.

From the time of the decision of the Beaubien case until the nine-judge court ceased to exist in 1848, only four other Illinois Supreme Court cases went to the United States Supreme Court. In two of these cases, the Court affirmed the rulings of the Illinois court and in the other two held that it was without jurisdiction.[53]

The opinions of the nine-judge court are contained in volumes 2, 3, and 4 of Scammon's Reports and in volumes 1 through 4 of Gilman's Reports (3–9 Illinois Reports). During the period covered by these reports the judges produced about 600 opinions dealing with a wide variety of subjects. Of course, cases dealing with titles to land predominated, but there were enough other cases to establish a considerable body of law. Many of the opinions show the prairie influences at work in the development of the law. For example, one opinion stated that the Common Law rule requiring the owner to retain his domestic animals on his own property was inapplicable.[54]

The court heard and decided on several cases involving slavery and indentured servants. The most celebrated of these was the case of *Jarrot v. Jarrot*.[55] The court held that the descendants of slaves held by the French of the old river towns were no longer slaves, but free. In its dealings with the slavery issue the court acted with judicial decorum that was above reproach. It upheld existing statutes such as the state fugitive slave law, but adhered to a strict construction of the laws regarding indentured servants. It remarked in one case that it must not be forgotten that Illinois was admitted as a free state.[56]

Almost no information is available on the methods employed by the court to decide cases. It is clear that the system of assigning cases in rotation for the writing of opinions did not then prevail. In the case of the nine-judge court, a few judges carried the burden of producing opinions. Most extraordinary is the record of Judge Treat, perhaps the first judge on the court to regard his position as a career in itself. Of the 601 "opinions of the Court," he wrote 181. Judges Scates and Caton also carried more than their share of the load, the former producing 72 majority opinions and the latter 70. Scates was also the principal dissenter, writing eight dissenting opinions and noting his disagreement in two other cases. With characteristic energy Stephen A. Douglas contributed majority opinions in 22 cases during his short term on the court. Chief Justice Wilson and his contemporary, Judge Lockwood, were content to leave the bulk of the work to the younger men, producing 29 and 27 majority opinions, respectively.

Least active of all the judges in the production of written opinions was Judge Browne. During the six years from the reorganization of the court in 1842 to the effective date of the Constitution of 1848, he produced only three opinions and these in cases of minor importance. Yet he was the central figure in one last dramatic episode. Sent to the outlands by the Democratic legislature of 1841 in what was probably an attempt to make him resign, he bore the calumny with a self-restraint that merits respect. He took up residence in Galena and continued to be diligent in the discharge of his circuit duties. His enemies in the Democratic party continued their determined efforts to eliminate him from the court. It is difficult to ascertain the real reason for his persecution.[57]

In 1842, four Galena lawyers introduced a petition into the lower house of the General Assembly praying for his removal "for want of capacity to discharge the duties of his office."[58] After some maneuvering, Orville Browning of Quincy introduced resolutions requiring the petitioners to set forth a bill of particulars concerning their charges. At this point the proceeding took on a special significance, for the author of the resolutions and counsel for the defense was Abraham Lincoln, the prairie giant whose lengthening shadow would someday spread across the nation.[59]

The petitioners replied to Lincoln's demand for specific charges with a document in which they insisted that they charged "nothing derogatory to his character as a man of integrity," but based their charges "on the natural infirmity and feebleness of his intellect, over which he has no control." They charged that he lacked legal and literary learning, that opinions purporting to be written by him were in fact written or revised by others, that on the circuit his decisions were "the mere echo of some favorite attorney," and that he was "by nature, education and habit" wholly unfit for his position.[60]

Meanwhile the senate refused to sit with the house and to hear the charges, and the house resolved itself into a committee of the whole and voted to allow counsel for the parties to participate in the examination of witnesses. Josiah Lamborn and Giles Spring represented the petitioners. Sidney Breese, who had resigned from the court three days before, was the only witness called.

Breese was asked his opinion of Browne's general competency and the question plunged the house into an argument over the admission of opinion evidence. The argument continued into the second day. Breese was finally allowed to testify but could recall no facts showing Browne's incompetency. The whole matter ended when the committee of the whole was discharged

The Illinois legislature attempted to remove Illinois Supreme Court justice Thomas C. Browne in 1842. Illinois Supreme Court Historic Preservation Commission.

from further consideration with only three dissenting votes, party lines being overlooked entirely.

The evidence as to Judge Browne's value to the court is inconclusive. His inability to express himself in writing contributed most to the charges of incompetency. His contemporaries generally agreed that he was a man of honor and a judge of integrity. The significance of the entire episode is the failure of attempted legislative control of judicial officers even though the Supreme Court of Illinois had not yet established its independent position as an organ of government. The Constitution of 1818 made possible legislative removal of judges without impeachment proceedings. Yet in an attempted exercise of the power, public opinion was on the side of the judge and against accusers who could charge only "general incompetency." The result contributed largely to the growing popular respect for the court.

A new constitution ended the life of the nine-judge court and ended in Illinois the choice of judges by the legislature. The Constitution of 1848 established popular election of members of the Supreme Court and subjected the judicial system to drastic reorganization.

8. *Trails of the Circuit Riders*

A QUARTER CENTURY lies between the effective date of the Constitution of 1848 and the decision of the Supreme Court in the case of *Munn v. People.*[1] The powerful and conflicting forces that affected the law of Illinois during this twenty-five-year period brought about greater changes than in any other similar period from the beginning of statehood to the economic depression of the 1930s. The changes in economic and social life brought about by new methods of transportation and communication and by the rise of mining and manufacturing challenged the supremacy of the prairie law. Over the whole country spread the movement for expansion brought about by the end of the war with Mexico. It expressed itself in talk of "the halls of Montezuma" and in the slogan "Fifty-four forty or fight."

Much that was simple and picturesque in the lives of the people was passing. The steadily accelerating pace of living moved with an exhilaration that was untempered by any spirit of nostalgia. Common men with light of empire in their eyes had no time or inclination for the contemplative process that weighs present values while planning for the future. The emphasis was on the here and now in the material aspect of life.

The frontier had rolled west of the Mississippi and the pioneer state was changing. The struggle for bare existence shifted to a striving for the acquisition of wealth. Great obstacles were to be overcome as they were met—by great effort. Allan Nevins suggested that the spirit of Illinois at the beginning of this period in its legal, political, social, and economic history was exemplified in the career and character of Stephen A. Douglas. "Hurry, hurry!—Improvise,

148

improvise!" These were the words the Little Giant lived by during much of his lifetime and these were the words that characterized so much of the life and activity around him. His prodigious concentration of headlong vigor and swift improvisation that met each problem in its time and not one second before, expressed the ideal of the midlands to the inarticulate thousands who cheered his every public appearance.[2]

In the second half of the period of 1848 to 1873, the great catastrophe of civil conflict occurred, scoring deep grooves in American political thought and changing the course of American constitutional law. The shock of civil war and the confusion of its aftermath strengthened the forces that changed the law and intensified the challenge to prairie domination.

The prairie element in law was at the height of its influence when the new constitution became effective on April 1, 1848. A great westward movement of migration had swept over the state, and settlers from the northeastern United States and from Europe had proved the wonderful fertility of the prairie lands lying north of the Shelbyville Moraine. Fear of the flat country was gone. The great prairie-breaker plows improvised by the people who settled the grasslands were turning the heavy prairie sod. Prairie farms were larger than woodland farms. Compelled self-reliance continued the spirit of independence that had been a principal contribution of the frontier to the development of law.

Government under the new constitution was barely under way when the reorganized Supreme Court gave positive expression to prairie influences. In May 1847, John Dean Caton, justice of the nine-judge Supreme Court then in its last days, held the circuit court in Peoria. There appeared on his docket the case of *Seeley v. Peters*, which was an appeal from a judgment of a justice of the peace in an action of trespass.[3] The facts as presented to Judge Caton and a jury indicated that Seeley's hogs had damaged Peters' wheat shocked in a field enclosed by a fence. Seeley proved in defense that the field was poorly fenced and that the hogs "could go in and out at pleasure," and that the side of the field where the fence was defective was bounded by "unoccupied and unenclosed prairie."

Judge Caton instructed the jury: "That if they believe from the evidence, that the defendant's hogs went into the plaintiff's enclosure and did damage to his crops, they will find a verdict for the plaintiff, and assess his damages to amount of the injury actually done, and it matters not what was the condition of the plaintiff's fence, so far as his right to recover some damages is concerned, inasmuch as the owner of a field is not obliged to keep up a fence around his inclosure to keep out his neighbor's cattle or hogs, but the owners of cattle permit them to run at large at their peril." The jury brought in a verdict for Peters and awarded damages in the amount of $4.10. Seeley promptly sued out a writ of error to reverse the judgment in the Supreme Court.

Meanwhile, the Supreme Court was reorganized with three judges pursuant to the provisions of the new constitution, and Treat and Caton, veterans of the old courts, and the newcomer, Lyman Trumbull, held its first term in December 1848.

Seeley employed the frail and ailing ex-justice and ex-governor Thomas Ford to represent him before the Supreme Court. The redoubtable William H. Herndon was counsel for Peters. In his brief, Herndon cited eleven cases and Kent's Commentaries as authority for the rule that "by the Common Law all persons were bound to keep up their own cattle, and if they went upon the grounds of others the owners were liable in damages, unless the owners of the cattle could show that the lands trespassed upon should have been fenced either by prescription, agreement or assignment." His co-counsel, Onslow Peters, cited eighteen cases, Blackstone, Chitty, Lord Hale, Kent, and Dane's Abridgment in support of the doctrine that "by the Common Law, one need not inclose his fields, but they were 'bounded by law'; the law was his fence."

The published report of the case does not contain Ford's brief or argument but he must have been persuasive, for Judges Treat and Trumbull concurred in reversing the judgment, while Judge Caton supported his own decision in the circuit court.[4] Judge Trumbull wrote the opinion of the court and found the Common Law rule inapplicable to the "condition of our country and people." He said:

> However well adapted the rule of the Common Law may be to a densely populated country like England, it is surely but ill adapted to a new country like ours. If this Common Law rule prevails now, it must have prevailed from the time of the earliest settlements in the State, and can it be supposed that when the early settlers of this country located upon the borders of our extensive prairies, that they brought with them and adopted as applicable to their condition a rule of law, requiring each one to fence up his cattle; that they designed the millions of fertile acres stretched out before them to go ungrazed, except as each purchaser from Government was able to inclose his part with a fence? This State is unlike any of the Eastern States in their early settlement, because, from the scarcity of timber, it must be many years yet before our extensive prairies can be fenced, and their luxuriate growth sufficient for thousands of cattle

must be sufferd to rot and decay where it grows unless the settlers upon their borders are permitted to turn their cattle upon them.

Caton, too, saw the broad prairies of Illinois as he wrote his long dissent and thought the majority might be mistaken on the issue of whether the Common Law rule was inapplicable to conditions in a prairie state.[5] In any event, the reception statute did not authorize the judges to decide the question.

Whether it would be better for each one to take care of his own stock, and allow these "extended prairies" capable of producing grain, sufficient to feed a nation, to be reduced to a state of cultivation, without the onerous expense and great delay of fencing them, where timber is scarce, would be but matter of opinion, which the people's representatives are much more capable of forming than we are. I think it quite as probable that the settlers located on the borders of the prairies, that they might cultivate farms, without the expense and delay of clearing off a heavy growth of timber, as that their moving object was to obtain a range for their cattle. Notwithstanding the privilege which it is said they have always enjoyed, not one part in a thousand of this luxuriant growth of grass, but was rotted and decayed where it grew, or more generally been consumed by fire. So it will ever be, for the want of thousands of cattle to crop it, until brought into cultivation by the husbandman's plow. One acre in tillage is of more value than many acres of wild grass, which would seem to show, that as a question of political economy, it were better to allow the land to be cultivated without the expense of inclosing it, to keep off strangers' animals, than to impose so onerous a tax upon the tillage of the soil, for the sake of the small value of grass consumed by the cattle.

Caton was troubled by the ease with which the majority eliminated the Common Law by holding its rules inapplicable to the conditions of men in Illinois and was fearful of the precedent that the decision would establish. Out of his training had come a true reverence for the Common Law and its tradition. "This principle of the Common Law is most unquestionably the law of natural justice, whence it originated, for it secures to each one the quiet enjoyment of his own, without intrusion or molestation from another."

He was deeply distrustful of the accuracy of the judicial instinct for interpreting the understanding of the community. He voiced the feelings of generations of judges in the Common Law tradition against decisions predicated upon public policy. To him the word "applicable" in the reception statute referred to the relation of the rules of the Common Law to the political institutions, form of government and Constitution of Illinois, not to the domestic habits, wants, and necessities of its people.

Despite his fears, the rule that permitted the owner of cattle to run them at large upon the unfenced prairies became the established law of Illinois. Nearly three years later in the case of *Misner v. Lighthall*,[6] the court reaffirmed its conclusion that the owner of land damaged by cattle running at large must prove that his property was protected by a good and sufficient fence in order to entitle him to damages from his neighbor. In this case, Caton concurred in the opinion of the court written by Chief Justice Treat, probably regarding further dissent as useless.

The Constitution of 1848 accomplished a sweeping reorganization of the judicial system. Economy in public spending was the popular demand of the day. Illinois farmers remembered the financial collapse that followed the fantastic program of internal improvement initiated by the legislation of 1837. A flood of public spending had precipitated frantic efforts at financing that had broken the state banks and ruined the credit of the state. A quotation from Article X dealing with corporations is sufficient to show the temper of the people with respect to public financing: "Sec. 3. No state bank shall hereafter be created nor shall the State own or be liable for any stock in any corporation or joint stock association for banking purposes, to be hereafter created."

With economy as the watchword, the nine-judge Supreme Court had to go. As if to directly rebuke the legislature that had increased the number of judges for political reasons, the new constitution fixed the number of judges at three.[7] The Supreme Court had not yet risen to a position of prestige to rank it with the legislative and executive branches of the state government in the popular mind. While this was still true in 1848, nevertheless there was evidence that there was popular response to the ideal of an independent judiciary.

The legislature had come off second best after the Browne affair. Moreover, it had on occasion used its power to require circuit duties of the Supreme Court judges for reasons other than those connected with improvement of the administration of justice according to law. There was a feeling, too, that the legislature had not always done too well in the matter of selection of judges. As if in reaction against these failures, the Constitution of 1848 provided for the popular election of judges of the supreme and circuit courts; it made no provision for the performance of circuit duties by the Supreme Court judges; and it took from the legislature control of the number of judges on the Supreme Court.

The reasons assigned above were not necessarily the only ones for the action just outlined. The public sense of propriety was outraged by the spectacle in 1840 of the legislature increasing the number of judges from four to nine for political reasons, and that this contributed directly to the changes in the organic law. Even with these changes, the judicial victory was not quite complete, for the convention retained the provision of the Constitution of 1818 that made it possible for the legislature to remove judges of the supreme and circuit courts for "reasonable cause, . . . which shall not be sufficient ground for impeachment," by a two-thirds vote of each house.[8]

But even in this instance the removal power was restricted in three ways. First, the "reasonable cause" had to be entered upon the journals of each house. Second, a two-thirds vote of the members elected to each branch was required, instead of merely a two-thirds vote of the members present, the latter being a plausible interpretation of the language of the Constitution of 1818. Third, the requirement of notice and hearing, now essential to due process of law, was made explicit by the language that required that the judge complained of be served with a copy of the complaint and be given an opportunity to be heard in his own defense.

Of special interest are the provisions of the Constitution of 1848 that provided for election of Supreme Court judges, who were designated as "judges" not "justices" as in the Constitution of 1818. The state was divided into three grand divisions. One judge was to be elected from each division and must have resided in the division for at least two years preceding his election. No youthful "Little Giant" could again use the Supreme Court as an advance post in the beginning of a political career with the minimum age for election fixed at thirty-five years.[9]

The new constitution provided no change in the original jurisdiction of the Supreme Court in cases relating to revenue and in cases of mandamus but added original jurisdiction in habeas corpus cases.[10] It also omitted the provision that required the judges of the Supreme Court to act with the governor as a legislative council of revision.

Thus, the Constitution of 1848 helped to establish for the Supreme Court a position of independence that it had not enjoyed under the Constitution of 1818. There could be no doubt that the judicial sense, hard work, and instinct for justice of such men as Philips, Wilson, Lockwood, Ford, Breese, Treat, and Caton had done much to increase popular confidence in the court as an effective organ of free government.

Not all of the provisions of the judiciary article of the new constitution were as helpful to the court as those just mentioned. As noted, the state was divided into three grand divisions. The southern tier of counties was designated as the first division, the counties of the central part of the state were designated as the second division, and the northern tier of counties was grouped as the third division. Three terms of the Supreme Court were to be held each year, one in each of the grand divisions.

The result of these provisions was that for the next twenty-two years the court became, as one judge expressed it, "a court on wheels," moving during each year from Mt. Vernon in the first division to Springfield in the second division and from there to Ottawa in the third division. The drafters of the constitution revealed a striking lack of understanding of the nature of judicial work and a failure to appreciate the real importance of the contribution of government that can be made by a state court of last resort. Illinois was a Common Law state, yet the lawyers of the constitutional convention were insensitive to the traditional methods and techniques of a matured Common Law.

The role of the Supreme Court as lawmaker and the possibilities in the development of an enriched case law were not discerned. There had been no John Marshall on the court to assert its independence, no dramatic settlement of controversies with the executive department by judicial decision, and no formulation of great constitutional principles in its written opinions. Then as now, the fact is mostly unrealized that decisions of state courts of last resort touch more closely the small affairs and personal concerns of the people who lived in those states, than most of the great constitutional decisions of the Supreme Court of the United States. The application of ordinary legal principles to the facts of legal controversies is not a process that fires the popular imagination, however profoundly important it may be.

The provisions in the Constitution of 1848 for the popular election of judges and for the establishment of the grand divisions proved two things. First, the Supreme Court was considered primarily as a court for the correction of the mistakes of the trial courts, not as the architect of a legal system. Second, its function in the decision of cases was to follow intelligently the will of the legislature and to interpret accurately the popular sense of justice.

Credit is due then, to the judges through whose efforts the court rose above the position assigned to it and established its position of independence. In this accomplishment and in the work of building a system of law for the state, the work of the three-judge court created by the Constitution of 1848 is of greatest importance.

The constitution also provided for the division of the state into nine judicial circuits with one circuit judge to be popularly elected in each circuit.

The three grand divisions: the 1848 constitution provided that the Supreme Court meet in three geographic regions of the state. Map prepared by Matt Burns.

The legislature could increase the number of circuits to meet future needs.[11] Under these provisions the circuit system expanded, and the judicial machinery of the state became better adjusted to the requirements of the increasing volume of litigation following a rapidly increasing population.

The year 1848 belongs to the era of the circuit lawyer, a figure as colorful in his way as the wigged and robed barrister of the English courts. From 1842 to 1848, the Supreme Court judges held the terms of the circuit courts and laid the foundations of the system that sent the leading lawyers of the state traveling in groups from county town to county town, eating, drinking, and sleeping together at night and fighting each other with all their energies at the bar by day. The years that followed the adoption of the Constitution of

1848 saw the circuit system most completely developed. When the nine-judge Supreme Court passed into history, its judges were replaced on the circuit by judges elected from the communities that they served. Thereafter, the social side of life on the circuit gained a greater development.

The period beginning in 1848 was the era of greatest prominence of the fabled eighth judicial circuit and the period when the shadow of a prairie giant grew longer and longer across the plains. Practice on the eighth circuit provided the training and the knowledge of people and their ways that sent Lincoln along the path to the presidency.[12] He traveled the circuit differently than most attorneys, and he met and made friends of all conditions across the breadth of the state. In addition to the law, life on the circuit taught Lincoln the lessons of politics. It was while traveling the eighth circuit that he became closely associated with such personalities as Ward Hill Lamon, Judge David Davis, and others whose lives became linked with his all the way from Springfield to Ford's Theatre in Washington.

During all but the last three years of the period under examination, the growth and development of the law was the special charge of a Supreme Court composed of three judges. In twenty-two years a total of nine men filled these positions. The nine-judge court that went out of existence with the Constitution of 1848 was composed of Wilson and Browne, the two old Whigs of the four-judge court; David Woodson, who only served for one month after Lockwood, another old Whig who resigned a month before the new Court convened; Treat, last remaining of the five judges added by the Democrats in the 1841 reorganization; and Caton, Koerner, Purple, and Denning.

The economy-minded framers of the Constitution of 1848 fixed the salaries of the Supreme Court judges at $1,200 a year, payable quarterly, and restricted them from holding any other office or position during their service on the court and for one year afterward.[13] Even in that far off day such a salary was much less than the amount that a lawyer of ability could expect to earn in private practice in Chicago, Springfield, Mt. Vernon, Quincy, Jacksonville, or any one of a dozen other towns in the state. Gustave Koerner, the German-born lawyer from Belleville, frankly stated that to remain in judicial office was financially unattractive.[14] His subsequent financial and political success indicated the correctness of his judgment.

Despite the salary limitation, the office of Supreme Court judge attracted men of ability throughout the whole period of the three-judge court. At the elections in September 1848, Treat and Caton of the old court won election for two of the three positions, while the third went to Lyman Trumbull of

Belleville. All three were men of ability whose subsequent careers established that they could have earned far more in private practice than they received as judges of the Supreme Court.

An examination of the list of nine men who held office on the Supreme Court from 1848 to 1870 indicates that public esteem for the court gained tremendously from the court-packing efforts of the legislature and from the Browne affair. In addition to the original three, Judges Breese, Scates, Skinner, Walker, Lawrence, and Beckwith were on the court at various times during the period and all were successful and capable men.

The constitution provided that the judges were to be elected for terms of nine years. For the very first election, the office of one judge was to be vacated at the end of three years, a second was to be vacated at the end of six years, and the third was to serve the full nine-year term. The three first elected decided by lot which term each should have. The best description of the organization of the court under the new constitution was given by Caton, in some ways one of the ablest men ever to hold judicial office in Illinois.

Caton was a New Yorker, born in Monroe County on March 19, 1812. He is reputedly the first lawyer to establish a practice in Chicago, arriving there without funds or friends in 1833. He began his long service on the Supreme Court in 1842, and had the honor of being one of the youngest judges ever to sit on the court.

Early in December 1848, Caton left his home in Ottawa with his wife and child in a double buggy drawn by a team of spirited horses. Their destination was Springfield, where Judge Caton planned to leave his family and to continue the journey to Mt. Vernon with Judge Treat to open the first term of court. Parts of the description of that journey are worth repeating for the picture given of Illinois of 1848.

> We started from Springfield on a dark, cloudy morning, and before we had proceeded half a mile a heavy snow storm set in, which proved to be the most severe that had been known there for many years. I drove a good team and we pressed forward through the blinding storm without stopping until we reached Macoupin Point, twenty-eight or thirty miles, by which time the snow was about ten inches deep, when we were glad to take shelter, though the weather was not cold. The next day we pushed on toward Greenville, in Bond County, which we reached the second night after, and the next day we reached Carlyle, in Clinton County. Here one of my horses was taken ill, when I left him and procured another

John Caton served on the Illinois Supreme Court from 1842 to 1864 and helped to transform the court to an independent branch of government. Randolph Rogers, sculptor, circa 1868; Illinois Supreme Court Historic Preservation Commission.

in his place. The snow was still deep and the roads very heavy. Indeed, for more than three quarters of the way since we left Springfield, not a single track was seen from the road.

The unusual fall of snow seemed to shut everybody up, and we passed many log cabins in the timber which bordered the prairies, and in the forest through which the road passed, where we could see families shivering around large fires in their cabins, with both doors and windows wide open, and pigs squealing around on the outside as if they, too, would be glad to get near the fire.

. . . We got our new horse and made an early start Sunday morning and pushed forward at the best speed we could; but a considerable coat of snow was still on the ground and it was already getting dusk when we reached, in the edge of the timber, the brick farm house of a well-to-do farmer, who, we learned at Carlyle, was in the habit of entertaining travelers, and where we could get excellent quarters unless the good lady of the house should happen to be out of humor, and then we would have to stay out all night, if necessary, in a storm, before she would let us into the house. . . . It was raining hard and a cold wind was blowing, and it was getting dark when we drove up to the fence in front of the house, where the landlord came out and met us, who, upon our application for entertainment with evident embarrassment, frankly told us that his wife was in a tantrum and that he could not afford us shelter. He told us that the nearest house was about two miles ahead, where lived a widow in a log cabin, and that was our only chance for that night.[15]

Although the prestige of the Supreme Court may have improved considerably it was as yet inadequate to impress a woman out of humor.

The judges continued under difficulty and reached the one-room cabin of the widow who took them in. The cabin had but one bed and a trundle bed where "a part of the children slept." Caton and Treat slept in the bed that night while the widow and the "other part" of the children joined their brothers and sisters in the trundle bed.

In due time the travelers reached Mt. Vernon, where Judge Trumbull awaited them. On the first day of the term there was little business of importance and the judges set about the work of organizing the court. To the great disappointment of most of the bar that were present, they determined to draw lots for the three terms in private in their room at Grant's tavern. Accordingly, Trumbull prepared three slips of paper with the figures "3," "6," and "9" written on them, and Caton rolled them up and put them into a hat. Treat drew first and received the long term. On the second draw, Caton received the six year-term.[16]

The constitution provided that the judge having the longest term should be chief justice, and Treat accordingly took over the duties of that position. After the original organization, the judge having the oldest commission was to be chief justice.[17]

Caton's period of service on the Supreme Court lasted until 1864, when he resigned, partly because of ill health. His twenty-two years of service since 1842 covered one of the most eventful periods in the court's history. The opinions he wrote in nearly 1,000 cases molded and shaped the rapidly developing commercial and business law and the law of procedure. Although Caton did much to improve the prestige of the Supreme Court of Illinois and the public opinion of judges generally, it is clear that even he did not regard his position as judge of the Supreme Court as a career in itself.

Hardship and poverty were the companions of his boyhood in New York. When he was nine years old, he left the home of his Quaker mother to work on the farm of another member of the Society of Friends. His tasks there were under the most rigorous of conditions and they proved beyond his physical powers. He returned home to attend school and work on the farms of neighbors until he was fifteen. He was then apprenticed to a harness-maker and later earned his way as a teamster and peddler of woodenware.

When his mother moved to Utica, he saw an opportunity to continue his education at the academy there while earning his way as a hired hand on farms in the neighborhood. He impressed his instructors with his earnestness and ability. An academy recommendation obtained for him a winter job as a school teacher. As soon as he was able, he began the study of law in a Utica law office and finally obtained employment with a lawyer who paid him a small sum for office services.[18]

Such was Caton's equipment when he arrived in Chicago in 1833 with almost no money in his pocket and a stern purpose in his mind to practice law. He obtained his license from Judge Lockwood at Pekin the fall of 1833, the judge saying in his serious way, "Young man, I shall give you a license, but you have a great deal to learn to make you a good lawyer. If you work hard you will attain it, if you do not you will be a failure."[19] Both the white-haired Lockwood and his newly appointed associate must have recalled these words nine years later when the young man took his place on the bench beside his advisor.

Caton may have been lacking in formal legal education, but he brought to the court a sound judgment in business and financial matters and a large capacity for hard work. These were qualities of increasing worth as important cases involving tough questions of commercial law appeared on the court's docket. He was imposing in physical appearance, being over six feet tall and weighing more than two hundred pounds. His dignified manner was enhanced by a high forehead, keen eyes and a straight, sensitive mouth. In his later years he wore a beard, but his upper lip was shaven.

There has been no other career like Caton's among Illinois judges. His great physical vitality enabled him to develop wide interests in the affairs of the work around him. It is reported that while on the circuit in Kendall County in 1844, he became incensed at the neglect of the road supervisors who permitted the roads to become impassable. After being stuck in the mud several times, he went into action, charging the grand jury as to the legal obligations of the supervisors. The grand jury returned indictments, and every road supervisor in the county either pleaded guilty or was found guilty and was fined. Roads in other counties on the judge's circuit were repaired quickly.[20]

The telegraph was a new toy in 1847 and there were few who sensed its future importance during the days when Ezra Cornell was making determined efforts to finance Samuel F. B. Morse's invention.[21] An Irishman from Rochester, New York, named Henry O'Reilly was endeavoring to link Illinois towns like Alton, Springfield, Peoria, Ottawa, and Bloomington to Chicago in the north and Keokuk and Burlington, Iowa, in the west. Interested farmers and merchants and O'Reilly met at Peoria on April 10, 1849, to discuss plans and to organize a corporation. Caton was in Ottawa at the time, and citizens there had pledged money to support the scheme.

A few days before the Peoria meeting the Ottawa subscribers held a meeting of their own in the circuit courtroom to discuss plans. Judge Caton, his senses attuned to the possibilities of the new device, strolled into the room as the meeting was in progress. At the close of the meeting, the subscribers delegated Caton to go to Peoria to represent the others in the negotiations. There he met O'Reilly, became convinced of the future importance of the new means of communication, and subscribed for shares of stock himself. He was elected a director in the newly organized Illinois and Mississippi Telegraph Company with capital of $500,000.

The new company did not prosper in its early years and its original capital was exhausted before the telegraph system was built. By 1852, the situation had become desperate, and Caton again took a hand. This time he secured the enactment of legislation authorizing assessment of the stock and participated in efforts to secure capital through sales of additional shares. He mortgaged his own property heavily in order to increase his investment.

Not content with his efforts in connection with the financing, he also assumed active management of the enterprise. The lines already constructed were in a bad state of repair, and Caton went to the Green Bay region of Wisconsin, where he paddled from place to place in a canoe, purchasing poles with which to rebuild the lines. On his return he contacted the officials of the principal railroads in Illinois and obtained the right to stretch his telegraph lines along the railroad rights-of-way.

Nor did he confine his efforts merely to rescuing the Illinois and Mississippi Telegraph Company from financial ruin. He also secured rights-of-way and erected lines on his own behalf in Illinois and Iowa outside of the territory assigned to the original company. These properties were made part of the capital of two additional corporations that he merged into the revitalized Illinois and Mississippi in 1856. He appreciated the tremendous significance of the telegraph in the operation of railroads and in the same year negotiated one of the first contracts ever made for dispatching trains by this method. Former governor Joel Matteson, then president of the Chicago, Alton, and St. Louis Railroad, concluded the contract.

From the time Caton assumed management of the Illinois and Mississippi Company, its financial success was assured. In 1867, the Western Union Telegraph Company purchased a lease to the company's lines to become a part of that vast system. His telegraph interests were the foundation of Caton's large personal fortune, amounting at his death to more than $2 million.[22]

Be it remembered that these financial and business undertakings were carried out while Caton was one of three judges constituting the court of last resort of a state whose judicial business had attained large volume and was steadily increasing. Nonetheless, Caton carried his full share of the court's work. There is no evidence that he allowed his business activities to interfere with the conscientious performance of his judicial duties. He wrote his fair proportion and more of opinions and was in attendance at every term, save the one immediately preceding his resignation, when illness kept him at home.

In Caton's times, reliance for reform and change in law was still upon the legislatures, and the influence of the courts as architects of the law was only dimly perceived. Therefore, it was consistent with the time that he should not regard his judicial position as satisfying his ambition or as giving sufficient scope to his abilities. It must be noted that there was no voice of criticism for his participation in large business affairs while retaining his place on the Supreme Court; no breath of scandal or suspicion of impartiality ever attached to his work as a judge.

The reasons are not hard to discover. First, the lack of popular understanding of a reviewing court's importance to the political, social, and economic growth of the state recognized no conflict of interest in the activities of the judge and of the business man. In the second place, it was a known fact that the salary of a Supreme Court judge was grossly inadequate to attract men of Caton's ability. In the third place, the enterprises in which he was engaged were in aid of the great economic growth and development that was taking place in the midlands and caught the popular imagination already fired with dreams of greatness.

Indicative of the court's increasing prestige and probably contributing to it were the judge's social activities and those of his family. He built a home on Ottawa's North Bluff in which he entertained many of the important men of affairs. In later years, he built another home at 1900 Calumet Avenue in Chicago, in which he hosted some of the young city's most brilliant social affairs.[23]

Samuel Hubbel Treat, who drew the nine-year term and became the first chief justice under the Constitution of 1848, was destined for one of the longest judicial careers in the history of the state. Like Caton, he was a New Yorker, settling in Springfield in 1834, and became a law partner of George Forquer, half-brother and benefactor of the unfortunate Thomas Ford. He had little money with which to make his way in the world and allegedly walked most of the distance from Richfield, New York, to Springfield. He was a quiet man, dignified in manner with deep-set eyes and a stern mouth. His only available picture shows him to have been clean shaven.

Treat's long service proved that even in Illinois in the formative era, a lawyer could find a satisfactory career in being a judge. In 1839, he was assigned to the eighth judicial circuit, which then included nine counties comprising a territory approximately 120 miles long and 85 miles wide. For the next two years he traveled from county town to county town over what was in time to become the most famous judicial circuit in the Midwestern country. With him on the "horseback circuit" went the circuit rider Lincoln and others to whom these experiences were to mean much in later years and other places.

In March 1855, President Franklin Pierce tendered Treat the appointment as judge of the United States District Court for the newly created Southern District of Illinois. He accepted and resigned from the Supreme Court of Illinois. A judicial career was a satisfactory career but a federal judge held office for life and the salary of a district judge was greater than the $1,200 that the constitution allowed to a judge of the Supreme Court of Illinois. Treat presided over the district court through the troubled days of the Civil War when he had to deal with the problems created by the underground activities of the "copperheads" and the Knights of the Golden Circle. He was continually in service on the district court until a few days before his death in March 1887, a period of more than thirty years.[24]

The newcomer on the court at the December 1848 term was Lyman Trumbull, a Yankee from Colchester, Connecticut. He had studied law in Georgia and was first admitted to the bar there. Trumbull arrived in Illinois on horseback in 1837 and after his admission to the Illinois bar settled at Belleville. He was slight, smooth shaven, and bespectacled with the look of an intelligent school master. He was well suited by temperament and mental ability to the work of the court. Like Sidney Breese, however, he was drawn to politics with an irresistible urge. A lack of human warmth in his personality kept him from achieving all he dreamed of.

Governor Thomas Carlin appointed him secretary of state in 1841, following Douglas, who had started his journey to the Senate by becoming a Supreme Court judge. Thomas Ford, whose program for rescuing the state's finances included liquidation of the state bank, succeeded Carlin. In this fiscal operation, Trumbull opposed him. Ford, who could be steel at times, was angered beyond endurance by Trumbull's needless boasting that the governor's objective would be defeated in the legislature. His removal quickly followed.

Trumbull resigned from the Supreme Court in 1853, assigning insufficiency of the salary as his principal reason. In politics he had been a life-long Democrat but was unable to side with his party after the repeal of the Missouri Compromise. He made a successful campaign for Congress on the basis of opposition to the Nebraska Bill but was elected to the senate by the legislature in 1855 before serving as Congressman. His star for a time thereafter followed that of Lincoln and the Republican Party. But after Lincoln's death he broke with the liberal Republicans over the impeachment of President Andrew Johnson. He was later an unsuccessful candidate for governor on the Democratic ticket.[25]

Trumbull was an able lawyer. As a judge, he was conscientious in the performance of his duties. His opinions are clear and terse, but he lacked the imagination necessary to inspired judicial lawmaking. His eighteen years of service in the United States Senate were filled with hard work and were distinguished by productive effort as chairman of the important Judiciary Committee.

During the life of the Constitution of 1848, nine men served on the three-judge court. When Trumbull resigned in 1853 to resume private practice and seek more remunerative public employment, Walter Bennett Scates succeeded him. Scates had served a prior six years on the Supreme Court beginning in 1841. He should have been of great value to the court since he had been a member of the convention that drafted the Constitution of 1848, serving as chairman of the Committee on Judiciary. Unfortunately, his second period of service ended with his resignation in 1857 after only four years and he resumed private practice in Chicago. No very important questions of constitutional interpretation came before the court during this short period. In 1858, Judge Scates, Judge Treat, and Robert S. Blackwell prepared a compilation of the

Illinois statutes then in force. The book was published by D. B. Cooke & Company but did not receive wide acceptance. Scates apparently did most of the work.[26]

The election of Onias C. Skinner, a New Yorker by birth, who had studied for the bar in Greenville, Ohio, filled the Treat vacancy, which occurred in 1855. Skinner came to Illinois in 1834 and settled in Carthage and later in Quincy. While practicing in Carthage he became aide to Governor Ford during the Mormon trouble. Thereafter he served a term in the legislature and then became a circuit judge. Skinner was a vigorous man, independent in thought and action. He resigned in 1858, likely because of the insufficient salary. Skinner, like Caton, turned businessman, constructing and serving as president of the Carthage and Quincy Railroad, later part of the Burlington system. He remained in the practice of law and was a member of the Constitutional Convention of 1869, and took an active part in the drafting of a third constitution for Illinois, serving as chairman of the Judiciary Committee.[27]

When Scates resigned in 1857, there returned to the court one of its most colorful figures—Sidney Breese. It is difficult to imagine a more appropriate background than his for a Supreme Court judge or one that might be expected to produce more in the way of judicial statesmanship. He was born on July 15, 1800, in New York, like Treat, Caton, and Skinner. He came to Illinois the year the state was admitted to the Union, taking up residence in the old French town of Kaskaskia. There he became the representative of the French-speaking people of the old capital and endeared himself to them through his marriage to a woman of French blood. He was familiar with the ways of the early settlers of Illinois and became an employer of indentured servants, whose status succeeded that of slaves among the *habitants* and frontiersmen of the Prairie State.[28]

Breese practiced law in Kaskaskia under the tutelage of Elias Kent Kane, and as assistant to the secretary of state he participated in the move to Vandalia that left Kaskaskia to dream into oblivion. Who in those days was better prepared to understand the new and the old in the life of the state?

Breese had ambitious dreams—personal dreams. He had a natural aptitude for politics and an affinity for it that was at once a tremendous asset and a great hindrance. He moved through a succession of local offices, postmaster, prosecutor, and United States attorney, finding time somehow to prepare and publish the first volume of Illinois Reports.[29] He was a circuit judge in 1835 and a Supreme Court justice in 1841. Two years later he defeated the Little Giant himself in the latter's first try for the United States Senate.

In the Senate, Breese was chairman of the Committee on Public Lands and dreamed of a transcontinental railway and of another railway that would run the length of Illinois from Galena on the north to Cairo where the Ohio meets the Mississippi.

Back from the Senate in 1849, his hopes for the presidential nomination gone, unsuccessful before the irresistible drive of Stephen A. Douglas in the campaign for reelection, he plunged at once into local politics. After a term as speaker in the lower house of the General Assembly he again became a circuit judge and finally returned to the Supreme Court with a larger experience in public and national affairs than any of his predecessors or associates.

In personal appearance Breese was a big man, weighing well over two hundred pounds. As Lloyd Lewis has said, in his mature years "he went about in a cloud of long white hair and whiskers."[30] In many respects, Breese was a great judge, only lacking the singleness of purpose that is necessary to highest rank among the great state court judges. Had he been less obsessed with the excitement of local politics and a little less self-important, his contributions might have ranked with those of Lemuel Shaw, John Bannister Gibson, Thomas Ruffin, and Chancellor Kent. As it was, Breese remained on the Supreme Court from 1857 until his death in 1878. He contributed opinions in many important cases and lent his knowledge of law, sense of tradition, and broad experience with practical politics to the decisions that were shaping the law of Illinois.

Breese believed that his greatest accomplishment was his sponsorship of the Illinois Central Railroad. He contested with Douglas to the end of his days the honor of having been its real founder. It was a strange expression of human vanity that led him to select the epitaph for his gravestone at Carlyle: "He who sleeps beneath this stone projected the Illinois Central Railroad." So, after all the sound and fury was over, when the great slavery debates in the Senate were merely words in the record, when the strife and contention of the Civil War were ended, when the arguments and decisions in the great cases were part of Prairie State law, Breese wanted to be remembered only for his connection with a great railroad that was also linked to the names of Douglas and Lincoln.

Of the nine men who served from time to time on the three-judge court, Caton, Breese, and Pinkney H. Walker, because of length of service, qualities of mind, and a liking for the work of the court, were more influential than any of the others in shaping the course of the law. Walker was born in Kentucky and came to Illinois in 1834. He was a nephew of Cyrus Walker of Rushville, in his day one of Illinois' most able lawyers. Young Walker studied law with his uncle in Rushville and practiced for a time in Macomb. He was elected circuit judge of the fifth judicial circuit in 1853. In 1858, he resigned this position to accept Governor William H. Bissell's appointment to the Supreme Court in place of Judge Skinner.

It appears that party lines were not as significant in the matter of judicial appointments then as they are now. Caton tells how Skinner asked him one day during the December 1856 term whether he was well acquainted with Governor Bissell, Illinois' first Republican governor. Caton and Skinner were both Democrats, and Skinner indicated to Caton that he wished to resign but would do so only if assured that his friend Walker, also a Democrat, would be appointed. Caton, the man of affairs, held the respect and esteem of men in high places everywhere, regardless of party affiliations. With no hesitation he went to Bissell with a statement of Walker's qualifications.[31]

The governor interviewed Walker personally, signified his intention to make the appointment, and Caton presented Skinner's resignation to the secretary of state who issued Walker's commission just two months before the term was to expire. Walker was then elected in June 1858 and continued as a member of the Supreme Court until his death on February 7, 1885.

From 1858 until November 1863, Caton, Breese, and Walker held terms of the Supreme Court in January, April, and November of each year. The court convened at Mt. Vernon in November 1863 without Judge Caton, who was confined by illness to his home in Ottawa. When the court met in Springfield in January 1864, Caton said that "an imperative domestic duty" compelled him to resign.[32] It is likely that his illness of the preceding term and the increasing demands of his large business interests had most to do with his decision. Like Skinner he resolved to name his successor. Accordingly, he called upon Governor Richard Yates, a Republican, with the request that Corydon Beckwith of Chicago be appointed to fill his place. This time also the suggestion was courteously received. It is likely that the character of the author, whose reputation had grown with the years, was a chief factor in its acceptance.

Corydon Beckwith, in some respects, was a man of mystery. He came to Illinois from Vermont in 1853 when he was thirty years old and entered practice in Chicago. He seems to have become a leading lawyer in a very short time, representing numerous corporate clients and becoming general counsel for the Chicago and Alton Railroad Company. From contemporary accounts it is apparent that he was extremely influential in business and public affairs. He was known as a man who could pull strings when the occasion required.[33]

Judges like Caton, Breese, and others were great lawyers and in most instances were distinguished advocates. Beckwith was the progenitor of the modern counselor. Like all lawyers of his day he appeared frequently in court, but his greatest talents were in formulating the plans of attack or defense that were carried into execution by other and perhaps more fluent advocates. His contemporaries regarded him as one of the most dangerous of adversaries. Although he seems to have been extremely influential in political affairs, Beckwith held only one public office. He filled the five months of Caton's unexpired term and did not run for reelection.

Charles B. Lawrence of Quincy, a close friend of the influential and unimaginative Orville H. Browning succeeded Beckwith on the court. Lawrence was born in Vermont and educated at Middlebury and Union colleges. He studied law in Cincinnati and St. Louis and practiced in the latter place for a short time. In 1845, he moved to Quincy, Illinois, where he soon established a successful practice. In 1856, he left with his family on a two-year trip to Europe in an effort to restore his impaired health. On his return he resumed his practice. Like many successful lawyers of that day, Lawrence decided to seek the distinction of judicial office. After three years on the circuit court bench he won election to the Supreme Court in 1864, in time to participate in some of the difficult cases produced by the Civil War and in the Granger litigation. His turn as chief justice of the court came in 1870.[34]

The legislature in 1871 had passed legislation regulating railroad tariffs and containing a long and short haul clause.[35] This legislature was the product of the Granger Movement and is discussed in connection with the decision in the *Munn* case. In 1873, Lawrence delivered the opinion of the court in a suit against the Chicago and Alton Railroad for violation of the long and short haul statute. His predecessor on the bench, Corydon Beckwith, represented the railroad. Speaking for a unanimous court, Lawrence held the statute unconstitutional.[36]

By 1873, others besides lawyers were reading the Supreme Court reports. Farmers and downstate businessmen were angry at the apparent setback to their program for reform. Even the newspapers had learned that a Supreme Court decision could be news and the *Chicago Tribune* carried a page-one story on February 24, 1873. Judge Lawrence's term was nearly complete, and he was a candidate for reelection in June 1874. He was soundly beaten. This was the first time that a decision of the court was a major issue in a judicial election. The importance of the court to the economic and social development of the state began to be recognized. After his defeat, Lawrence became a leading member of the bar in Chicago and could have been appointed to the Supreme Court of the United States, had he permitted his name to be suggested.

These were the nine men whose combined efforts shaped the course of the Common Law in Illinois from 1848 to 1870. Their work began when the prairie element in law was strongest. But when a third constitution reorganized the court, the era of industrialization was underway, and the decisions of the judges had applied Common Law techniques to new problems created by railroads, banks, and the devices of trade and business.

It was fortunate for the legal growth of the Prairie State that John Dean Caton, the man of business, was for so long a member of the court, that Sidney Breese took his wide experience in public affairs and his vision of the importance of railroads into the conference room, and that Judge Walker was there to contribute his knowledge of community values developed as a lawyer and circuit judge in the agricultural heart of the state. It was also fortunate that the bar of Illinois at this time included so many lawyers of ability who assisted the court through advocacy in the best tradition of the profession. Not only were there "giants of the prairie" in those days, but in the cities that were rising on their edges as well. The phenomenal growth of Chicago from 1833 to 1870 attracted to it some of the finest lawyers that could be found in the country.

For Chicago lawyers, the circuit-riding days were mostly over by 1848. The city's commercial activity was sufficient to require their nearly constant presence, except for such trips as were necessary to represent their clients in Springfield, Washington, and New York. Few lawyers anywhere could be found to surpass Justin Butterfield, who came to Chicago in the fullness of his powers and was counsel in many of the most important Supreme Court cases before his death in 1855. This friend of Daniel Webster was preferred over Lincoln as commissioner of the General Land Office in 1849.[37] Isaac N. Arnold, Grant Goodrich, and Mark Skinner, to mention only a few, were all members of a distinguished Chicago bar before 1860.

Down the state, there were other names and personalities as distinguished as those that were creating a reputation for Chicago. At Jacksonville, there was Murray McConnel, whose name appeared as frequently in the Supreme Court reports as any other. His death at the hands of an unknown assassin on February 9, 1869, caused statewide excitement and memorial notice in the Supreme Court reports.[38] Usher F. Linder, attorney general in the days of Elijah Lovejoy, was practicing at Charleston and there were others like Orville H. Browning, Gustave Koerner, and Orlando B. Ficklin, whose abilities entitled them to first rank among lawyers.

Typical of much that was best in the traditions of the bar and of everything that was romantic was the fabulous eighth judicial circuit. Here the circuit riders continued their journeys from county town to county town, changing with the passage of time from saddle horses to rigs and finally to the little railroad trains that began to puff their ways across the prairies in the 1850s.

Originally, in every circuit in the state at the beginning of the term, the circuit judge would set out with his retinue, the lawyers who practiced on the circuit. Together they traveled on horseback, meeting the hardships of the trail together and lying down together at night, frequently in the most primitive of accommodations. The spirit of cooperation that these conditions engendered has seldom been equaled among persons engaged in a common pursuit, and certainly seldom among professional men.

When the roads improved and saddles gave way to the buggy seat, they traveled in twos and threes, but there was always the meeting together in the inn or tavern of the county town at night, the meals together, and the tall talk when court was over for the day. These things survived even when the trains made possible a return to home and family when court adjourned for the weekend.

It is right to think that many of the prairie bar's finest traditions grew from the life on the circuit that was experienced to some degree by practically every Illinois lawyer before the Civil War. By day they fought to the limit of their physical and mental energies for victory before court and jury, and found time to fight each other for clients with all the means at their disposal.[39] By night they gathered for food and drink, and later, in front of the fire in the common room of a tavern or public house they talked far into the night. Sometimes there were broad jokes and tall stories that went from man to man, with a fair interspersing of practical jests for good measure. Often there was sober talk of points of law and procedure, but more often of freedom and slave, of territorial expansion, or the latest speech of abolitionist or slave-state hothead.

The circuit riders are gone and with them passed much that was picturesque and much that was fine in the practice of the law. The eighth circuit still lives in the tradition of the men who made it famous, lives in the memory of a man whose shadow in those days was long across the prairies, a shadow that would one day extend across the nation. It requires no great imagination to picture Lincoln, the circuit rider, as he is depicted in Torrey's famous statue in Springfield,[40] to see him drive across the prairies in a one-horse rig with a brother lawyer on the seat beside him, or watch him on a Monday morning

Abraham Lincoln, a frequent rider of the Eighth Judicial Circuit, argues the case of *Nolan v. Hunter* in Paris, Illinois, in 1842. Abraham Lincoln Presidential Library and Museum.

in the 1850s anxiously awaiting the return of the judge and lawyers who had taken advantage of the faster pace of the trains to go home for the weekend.

Lincoln, Stuart, Logan, David Davis, Edward D. Baker, Lamon, and Leonard Swett, these are the names that history associates with the eighth circuit. Judge Treat was its first judge, and in time his place was taken by David Davis, able, fat, and lusty. David Davis of Bloomington: his shrewd appraisal of men would send him in 1859 to work unceasingly for Lincoln's nomination for the presidency at Chicago; he would become one of Lincoln's closest friends, yet he seldom volunteered advice or was asked for it in those years of terrible perplexity in the White House; he would one day become his friend's administrator, and his shrewd judgment would increase that friend's modest estate by a considerable amount by the time his stewardship was done. This was David Davis, prairie "justice in eyre," whose path led to the Supreme Court of the United States.[41]

In those earlier days he was the circuit judge to whom Lincoln was a marked man and a favorite—Lincoln, the trial lawyer, the teller of droll stories. Whitney describes it thus:

In the evening all assembled in the Judge's room, where the blazing faggots were piled high, and the yule log was in place, and there were no estrays there, although the door was not locked. Davis' methods were known, and his companions well-defined, and, if a novice came, he soon found out both. For instance, an unsophisticated person might be attracted to the Judge's room by our noise, supposing it to be "free for all." If Davis wanted him, he was warmly welcomed, the fatted calf was killed, and the ring put on his finger; but, if he really was not desired, he was frozen out by the Judge thus: "Ah! Stop a minute, Lincoln! Have you some business, Mr. Dusenberry?" If Dusenberry should venture: "Well, no! came designin'——." Davis would interrupt him. "Swett take Mr. Dusenberry out into the hall, and see what he wants, and come right back yourself, Swett. Shut the door. Now go ahead, Lincoln! You got as far as——. Ha! Ha!! Ha!!! She slid down the hill, and—, but wait for Swett. Swett!! Swett!!!" called he. "Hill," (to Lamon) "call Swett in. Now, Lincoln go ahead," etc. "She slid down the hill, you know. Ho! Ho!! Ho!!!"[42]

Neither Davis nor Lincoln could then know how soon the laughter of those days on the circuit would end, nor how far up the path of fame each would travel. The eighth circuit was good training ground for a president. Lincoln came to know all sorts and conditions of people, their pettiness, and their fineness. He had lessons in give-and-take that left him better equipped to endure the slurs, the insults, and the disappointments that came when he dealt with politicians and amateur statesmen.[43]

Lincoln and Douglas were trained in the same school. As lawyers and on the circuit, each learned that men can engage in bitter contest and yield no quarter yet when the fighting was done and the issue resolved, can resume a friendship based upon mutual respect. Each learned, too, in the best tradition of the bar, that a fight can be just as hard and a cause be better argued when there is no resort to personal insult and backfence invective.

Thus, the "Little Giant" and the "Long Sucker," under these rules could fight out the cause to the end. Rivals almost from the beginning of their careers, they could battle for place and position, taking every technical advantage that appeared to the end of the game.

The Little Giant was ahead in the early years. His brilliant improvising carried him with a rush from the Supreme Court to the Senate. In the later years, great issues became decisive factors. The giants, little and long, went through those later years of controversy each conscious of the other's strengths and weaknesses. There was that wonderful series of debates, when each struck great blows for beliefs he cherished, the most remarkable forensic contest in the history of the midlands or of the country.[44]

The controversy was bitter, the country was nearly aflame, and there were hot words born of deep convictions in the speeches. Yet each was a lawyer pleading, arguing, and striving to the limit of his ability. To each the issues, not the personalities, were important. When the Senate race was over and improvisation had won one last victory, even in defeat it was evident that steady adherence to stated principles was gaining ground. There remained only the final battle for the presidency and the last great victory for the prairie giant—a time when there was nothing more to improvise. The conduct of Stephen A. Douglas in the acute disappointment of his ultimate defeat must always bring the quickening of the pulse and the lump in the throat of those to whom the "good loser" tradition in American life was of real significance.

To every lawyer, in addition to these, must come a sense of pride, for Douglas took defeat in the best spirit of his profession. People remember the hat-holding incident on the inaugural platform, the dramatic incident, the story that will be told as long as there are ears to listen. But there were acts of deeper significance—the slave-state speeches on the eve of election, speeches made with realization that defeat was inevitable, the dramatic invasion of the South with the cry: "I am not here tonight to ask for your votes for the Presidency. . . . I am here to make an appeal to you on behalf of the Union and the peace of the country." And there was the meeting at Willard's Hotel in Washington when defeat was an established fact, "I am with you, Mr. President and God bless you."

Days and weeks of intense effort followed, with Douglas supporting the president in the Senate. Then Beauregard's batteries opened fire on Fort Sumter, and on the night of April 13, 1861, Douglas called at the White House with counsel and advice. The next morning the country at large knew that he had pledged his continued aid to the president, past conflicts and rivalries forgotten or put aside.

9. The Coming of Age

I speak of new cities and new people.
I tell you the past is a bucket of ashes.
I tell you yesterday is a wind gone down,
    a sun dropped in the west.
I tell you there is nothing in the world
only an ocean of tomorrows,
    a sky of tomorrows.

I am a brother of the cornhuskers who say
    at sundown:
        Tomorrow is a day.
        —Carl Sandburg, "Prairie"

THE LITTLE GIANT lay dead in Chicago, his turbulent career ended just as his country's severest ordeal began. The accelerated pace of living that he typified gathered still greater speed in the ensuing years. The remaining four decades of the nineteenth century brought about the rapid maturing of the legal order in Illinois. Before the beginning of a new century, an operating compromise between the agrarian interests of the prairie lands and the new forces of industry and transportation had been achieved. A single system of laws adjusted the conflicts between them, but before such result occurred, there was an ordeal of fire and, after the flames, a trial by battle.

A clear perception of these things requires an examination of the state of the law in the years before 1861 when Lincoln was still the leading circuit lawyer in Illinois with a reputation for ability that became known beyond the limits of the state. The prairie law was still in the ascendancy in those years. Still, a careful observer could have detected the presence of its rivals in the increasing number of cases involving questions of commercial and industrial law appearing in the courts. Yet the prairie law was still the dominant factor in the Illinois legal system. This was the law the circuit lawyers knew and practiced and brought to its highest state of development midway in the first decade after the Constitution of 1848.

Legislation as well as judicial decisions had recognized the great importance of the prairies to the state. In two cases appearing in the Supreme Court in 1849,[1] reference was made to the statute that prohibited setting fire to the prairies between the first of December and the first of March, and during the rest of the year, except when necessary for the preservation of property from accident by fire and then only upon two days' notice to the neighbors.

Even the law of negligence had a distinctly agrarian flavor. The Supreme Court, in a series of cases that began with *Chicago and Mississippi Railroad Co. v. Patchin*,[2] decided at Springfield at the December 1854 term, had established a doctrine of comparative negligence for Illinois, the contours of which remained somewhat vague. Perhaps the best statement of the doctrine is found fifteen years later in the case of *Chicago, Burlington, and Quincy Railroad v. Payne*,[3] in which Judge Walker said:

> It is the established doctrine of this court that, although a plaintiff may be guilty of negligence, still the defendant will be held liable if his negligence is greater than that of the plaintiff. Where the negligence producing the injury is equal or nearly so, or that of plaintiff is greater, then he cannot recover. Although he may be guilty of negligence, yet if that of the defendant is greater, amounting to gross negligence, he would be liable. Negligence resulting in injury is comparative, and it is not required that the plaintiff shall be free from all negligence, or that he shall exercise the highest possible degree of prudence and caution, to entitle him to recover, if the defendant is shown to be guilty of a higher degree of negligence.[4]

The doctrine endured at least until the decision in *Calumet Iron and Steel Co. v. Martin*[5] in 1886. Almost all of the cases in which comparative negligence applied involved railroads and injuries to stock or to persons crossing the track in wagons or rigs. The harshness of the rule, which denied any recovery where plaintiffs' carelessness contributed in any degree to their injuries, was apparent in these cases.

Moreover, in the determination of values implicit in fixing a rule for the decision of such cases, difficulties in the way of fencing railroad rights-of-way through the prairies and irregularity in the train schedules of the day were factors leading to the establishment of the doctrine. It was a doctrine suited to a sparsely settled country with broad stretches of unfenced grazing land. By casting the burden of responsibility for the avoidance of accidents upon the railroad, the court adopted a position logically consistent with the view that required the grain farmers to fence their fields to protect them from animals that ranged at large upon the open prairie.

When changing times indicated the desirability of establishing the stricter Common Law rule, Judge John Scholfield avoided overruling the comparative negligence cases by making the differences appear merely verbal: "It inevitably follows, from the rulings in the numerous cases to which we have referred, that the court has not understood that the rule of comparative negligence changed or modified the general rule requiring that the injured party, in order to recover for the negligence causing his injury, must have observed due or ordinary care for his personal safety, and authorizing him to recover for such injuries where he has observed such care."[6] The gradual turning away from the doctrine of comparative negligence is clearly traceable in the cases that Justice Scholfield cited[7] and, as will be seen, the eventual repudiation of the doctrine accompanied the loss of dominance by the prairie law.

In some of the very cases that announced the doctrine of comparative negligence, the rise of elements that undermined the domination of the prairie law can be observed. In the *Patchin* case, the court was acutely aware of the new problems of safety created by development of railroad transportation. The action was brought to recover for livestock killed by the defendant's trains operating over flat, open prairie. The evidence showed that the engineers sounded no warning whistle although the stock must have been clearly visible. It was shown, too, that the trains did not reduce speed and, in one instance, even increased it.

In response to the argument that failure to reduce speed amounted to negligence, Judge Walter Scates called attention to the fact that there was probable truth in the opinion that in situations where obstructions may be thrown from the track, the higher the speed, the greater safety to the train in collision. Thus, if the engineer saw the cattle on the tracks too late to avoid striking them, then he may have exercised good judgment to maintain the speed of his train or even to increase it. He called attention to the importance of schedules and of speed as the chief advantage in railroad transportation: "Speed in the transit, and punctuality in arrivals and connections, are desirable, are required in this mode of conveyance. They are lawful."[8]

In *Great Western Railroad Co. v. Thompson*,[9] decided the year after the *Patchin* case, the court refused to recognize the view that negligence of the railroad may be inferred from the fact of injury to stock running at large upon the prairies. It required the owner to prove negligence as a condition of recovery. Judge Onias Skinner dissented in an opinion that probably received the approval of every prairie farmer who chanced to read it. These farmers may have been disturbed by the court's decision in reversing a judgment for the plaintiff whose ox had been run down by defendant's train. The engineer had asked the plaintiff "Is this your ox?" The plaintiff had said "Yes, sir," whereupon the engineer had said, "You ought to have another one and go to hell." The decision in this case went on the ground that: "The allegation of negligence in the conduct and management of a train is not supported by proof of making up a train too heavy to be managed and controlled by the engine attached to it for transportation."[10]

Besides railroads, the river steamboat was appearing in the Illinois Reports, attesting to the tremendous importance that this means of transportation was coming to have in the affairs of the state. In 1848 at Illinoistown, across the Mississippi River from St. Louis, the citizens were disturbed by the activities of the city of St. Louis in endeavoring to change the channel of river. For a time the controversy threatened to break out into violence. One channel of the river flowed to the east of Bloody Island south of Alton. St. Louis feared impairment of its harbor facilities through the formation of sandbars along the western shore of the river.

Accordingly, St. Louis conceived a plan to construct a dike and roadway from the Illinois mainland to Bloody Island, which would divert the main channel to the west side of the river. Opposition to the plan developed in Alton, Quincy, and elsewhere along the Illinois side of the river, alleging that the dike would bring about inundation of the American Bottom and the destruction of Illinoistown, now part of East St. Louis. The real basis of the opposition was the fear that commercial advantages in the steamboat trade enjoyed by Illinois cities might be affected. Ever since St. Louis became the gateway to the West and the great trading center of the central Mississippi valley, other cities had dreamed of rivaling its great commercial importance.

Notwithstanding the objections, St. Louis persisted in its plans, undeterred by the prospect of expenditure of large sums of money. The work actually began and the dike partly constructed when Illinois governor Augustus C. French wrote a letter to the St. Louis authorities threatening forcible intervention if there was a continuation of the encroachment upon Illinois sovereignty.

While negotiations proceeded at the executive level, *People v. City of St. Louis et al.*, an injunction suit, began in the Circuit Court of St. Clair County before Judge Gustave Koerner. The City of St. Louis demurred to the bill and raised, among other things, the issue that the construction of the dike was in the public interest and equity ought not to interfere, even though technically the defendants' acts amounted to a public nuisance. Judge Koerner sustained the demurrer as to the City of St. Louis and dismissed the bill as to the other defendants after a hearing. The People took an appeal to the Supreme Court where the case was heard by Justices John Caton and Samuel Treat. Lyman Trumbull had been counsel in the case and took no part in its decision.

In a long opinion by Judge Caton, the court, anticipating the rule established by the Supreme Court of the United States in 1851 in *The Genessee Chief v. Fitzhugh*,[11] held that the Mississippi was a navigable stream, although not so by comprising standards, and ordered a perpetual injunction restraining the defendants from proceeding with the work.[12] Responding to the argument that construction of the dike would be in the public interest, the court held that when a purpresture amounts to a public nuisance, equity cannot refuse injunctive relief. The court took the position that the question of whether construction of the dike was for the public good was for the legislature and not the court to decide.

Notwithstanding the injunction, the work progressed and contempt proceedings were brought against certain of those actually engaged in work on the dike. When it appeared as though the contractor would defy the injunction, the sheriff organized a posse and the governor was prepared to use the state's military force to enforce obedience. Sane counsel prevailed on both sides, however, when it was revealed that the real moving forces behind the scheme were the contractor and a ferry company that owned most of Bloody Island and stood to gain by having its ferry distance cut almost in half by the proposed dike. The legislature settled the matter in 1849, requiring the city of St. Louis to post a bond against injury and to assure the Illinoistown ferry a permanent landing place in the city.[13] The feared disasters did not materialize and the controversy that once inflamed the tempers of many law-abiding citizens in Illinois is now forgotten.[14]

Benefits from the steamboat trade were accompanied by disadvantages. A statute of 1857 made steamboats liable for debts incurred in their operation when contracted by the master, owner, or agent, and for injuries done by the captain, mate, or other officer or by the crew under their direction.[15] Thomas Loy brought an action of trespass against the *F.X. Aubury*, a Mississippi River steamer, for assault and battery committed by the mate. The question in the Supreme Court was whether the action could be maintained since the statute itself specified no form of action and no special procedure. In holding that the action would lie, Judge Sidney Breese commented upon the fact that steamboats plying the water of Illinois were mostly owned by persons residing outside the state, making jurisdiction hard to obtain.

Who would know the character of river men better than Judge Breese from Kaskaskia? Speaking of the owners he said: "[T]hey employed, in responsible positions on their boats, unreliable persons, men of low, rough and brutal character, who, when clothed with 'a little brief authority' would be domineering, tyrannical and cruel towards those temporarily in their power, and withal, wholly irresponsible in every respect, and against whom, should an action be brought for an injury, no matter how flagrant, no redress whatever could be had. These were among the mischiefs that the legislature designed to remedy. The mode by which it was to be accomplished was, by substituting the boat itself in the place of the owners or officers controlling it, and making it liable directly, not only for its contracts, but for its torts; and sell her out, to satisfy the judgment."[16]

The law was developing rapidly in 1855. An important cause was the railroad expansion that would eventually bring Illinois to a position of preeminence in the world of transportation. An impressive network of lines spanned the state from north to south and crisscrossed from east to west. It began with the first small locomotive that was taken off a riverboat at Naples on the Illinois River in the 1840s—a teapot of an engine destined for service on the Northern Cross, the line that connected Jacksonville with the Illinois River at Meredosia.

With the railroads came the telegraph and expansion in the field of communication. The telegraph had a special significance for the Supreme Court of Illinois. In 1856, Judge Caton was asked to incorporate a corporation to operate telegraph lines along the right-of-way of the Illinois Central all the way from Chicago to Cairo.[17]

The railroad and the telegraph made considerable changes in the law. With the development of means of transportation and communication came the establishment of cities, the development of manufacturing, and the beginning

The Illinois Central Railroad was the subject of many lawsuits in Illinois. Abraham Lincoln Presidential Library and Museum.

of the industrial era. It was accompanied by the concentration of industry and population at the northern end of the state. Out of this situation arose the all but insoluble problem of creating a legal system that would give adequate recognition and protection to the rising industrial concentration, yet deal fairly with the prairies, which retained their importance and their independence even in the age of industry.[18]

Although the discovery of oil industrialized large areas of prairie soil and although the tractor, gang plow, and combine established the machine age in farming, the prairies retained much of their distinctive character. The men and women who lived there maintained a point of view that cannot be wholly assimilated to that of Chicago.

The rapidly changing economy and social order in Illinois created new problems for the legal system. As each year went by, the amazing fertility of the deep prairie soil attracted more and more people whose efforts would center in the production of the grains that ultimately made the midlands the breadbasket of the nation. Along with the developments in agriculture, there came into existence, in Illinois as elsewhere, the great numbers of little towns that became a pleasant aspect of American life. With the towns came the merchants, and with the merchants came the greater need for certainty in the system of credit and of definiteness in the law of commercial paper.

With the rise of manufacturing in the north, there began the legal problems of labor, already present in the Supreme Court Reports before 1870. Most of the cases dealt with the duties of employers in furnishing safe places to work and safe tools and appliances. With the development of transportation and communication, there came also changes in the law of carriers and a tremendous expansion in the law of public callings. The discovery of the use of electricity for power was just a few years ahead, and the invention that would turn coal into electric energy was already on the way.[19] The increase in productivity of the prairies led to the establishment of the world's greatest grain exchange and opened up an entirely new field for the application of established legal principles and the development of new ones.

Another great change was taking place in the method by which the law was being adjusted to meet the conditions of a shifting world. Academic training in the Common Law was so far advanced that the Harvard Law School advertised in the *Illinois Journal* published in Springfield:

Law School of the University of Cambridge, Massachusetts.

The Instructors in this school are:
Honorable Joel Parker, LLD, Royal Professor
Honorable Theophilus Parsons, LLD, Dana Professor
Honorable Emory Washburne, LLD, University Professor.

The course of instruction embraces the various branches of the common law and of equity, admiralty, commercial and constitutional law and the jurisprudence of the United States. The law library consists of about 14,000 volumes and as new works appear they are added and effort is made to render it complete.

Instruction is given by oral lectures and expositions (and by recitations and examination in connection with them) of which there are ten each week, two moot courts are also holden in each week at each of which a cause previously given out is argued by four students and opinion delivered by the presiding instructor. Rooms and other facilities are also provided for the club courts and an assembly is held weekly for practice in debate in acquiring a knowledge of parliamentary law and proceedings.

Students may enter the school in any status of their professional studies or mercantile pursuits, and at the commencement of either term or in the middle or other part of the term. They are at liberty to select what studies they will pursue according to their view of their own wants and attainments.

The academical year which commences on Thursday, six weeks
after the 3d Wednesday in July, is divided into two terms of 20 weeks
each with a vacation of six weeks at the end of each term.

During the winter vacation the library is opened, warmed and
lighted for use of members of the school. Applications for admission or
for catalogues or any further information may be made to either of the
professors at Cambridge. Cambridge, Massachusetts, December 1856.

With the rise of formal legal education, and partly because of it, came
increased respect for courts and the legal profession.[20] In many states, including
Illinois, a contest between the courts and the legislature took place, the results
of which for a time elevated the judiciary to a position of popular regard that it
had never before occupied.[21] During the decade from 1850 to 1860, cases began
to appear in the courts in which legislative supremacy was seriously challenged
and the Common Law doctrine that the legislature itself was subject to the
law began to be relied upon. In Illinois, as elsewhere in the United States, this
doctrine took the form that the legislature was subject to the constitution as
interpreted and applied by the courts in the course of ordinary litigation.

Besides the establishment of schools for formal training in the law, there
were other causes for the increase of respect for courts. Not the least of these
was legislative conduct, which tended to impair confidence in the legislatures.
Roscoe Pound pointed out that one of the principal legislative abuses was to
be found in special legislation which was indulged in by all state legislatures.
"[T]he volume of it and abuses to which it gave rise, for we can scarcely credit,
as we know state legislation today, what the session laws of an older time
disclosed, led to provisions in state constitutions prohibiting it or limiting it,
either generally or to certain subjects or classes of subjects."[22] He referred also
to abuses leading to confusion in amending and supplementing legislation and
the attaching of riders to bills. Moreover, the legislatures tended to interfere
with the discharge of executive and judicial functions to a very serious degree.

All of these things induced the courts to shake off their developed
restraints against interference with the legislative will. The leading causes
were the inclusion of specific restraints in state constitutions with the obvious intention that they be judicially enforced, and the necessity for judicial
interpretation of statutes to ameliorate confusion.

The factors just enumerated were all operative in Illinois, and the language
of the Supreme Court opinions dealing with constitutional questions was
firm in discussing the court's power and duty with respect to constitutional

limitations on legislative authority. At the June 1851 term, the court held unconstitutional a statute abolishing the counties of Gallatin and Saline and creating a new Gallatin County from them, which included removal of the county seat from Shawneetown to Equality.[23] The court's rationale was that it was in violation of the spirit of the Constitution of 1848 forbidding the striking of territory from a county without the consent of the majority of the people of the county eligible to vote.[24] Judge Caton argued that the "design of the constitution is to prevent things, not names. It is to forbid results and effects, and not the form of expression to be used in accomplishing them. A substance was sought after, and not a shadow. A real power was designed to be reserved to the people, and not to their hope of right."[25]

The court had a clear idea of the purpose behind constitutional provisions affecting the drafting of statutes, such as the provision requiring private and local laws to embrace no more than one subject, which should be expressed in the title. In upholding a provision in the Northwestern University charter prohibiting the sale of liquor within four miles of the University, Judge Breese said:

> It is well known a system of legislation had grown up in this State, anterior to the adoption of our present constitution, by which much injury was inflicted upon community and individuals. Laws were found to be snares for the unwary, having injected into the body of them important provisions, affecting public and private interests, of which, no indication whatever was afforded by their titles. Various objects, having no necessary or material connection, were united in the same bill, for the purpose of combining various interests in support of the whole, which could not be combined in favor of either standing by itself. Separate and independent subjects were united in the same bill, so as to embarrass the legislature in understanding and voting intelligently upon them, or so as to compel the members to vote for one measure of which they disapproved, to carry the other of which they did approve.[26]

The Constitution of 1848, as part of the effort to rescue the state from its desperate financial plight, provided for a tax of two mills upon each dollar's worth of taxable property to be applied against state indebtedness. In 1861, the legislature provided for the transfer of the balance in the fund derived from the tax to the general revenue fund with the goal to make the proceeds generally available for such purpose as the legislature should decide.[27] In *People ex rel. Merchants' Savings, Loan and Trust Co. of Chicago v. Auditor,*[28] decided at the January 1863 term, the court held the legislative effort void and administered a sharp reproof that received favorable public comment. "That article is the foundation stone of the State credit. It is on that rock, it has been built up to such magnificent dimensions, and if removed, it must totter to its fall, and be, once more, a ruin. When any authority attempts to suspend any portion of the organic law, without provision for such purpose, in the law itself, that moment a blow is struck at the very being of the government, and its existence seriously endangered."[29]

The opinions of the court from 1850 to 1860 demonstrate that the court was conscious of the gains it had made in public respect since the adoption of the new constitution. The gains that the court made at the expense of the legislature enhanced the opinion held by ordinary citizens of judges such as Caton, Breese, Treat, and Lawrence. The men who carried on the work of the court, without exception, were a credit to the bench.

Although praise for the court was general, there could be criticism too. Most of it was criticism the public generally had of the law and its administrators. Most of the time the criticism was as good natured as this letter printed in the *Illinois State Journal*, April 3, 1857, indicates:

Beauties of going to Law

Editor of Journal:

I noticed in your paper on Wednesday morning an item entitled "The Beauties of going to Law." There is a case reported in the 16th Illinois Reports, page 63, just issued from the pages of D. B. Cook and Company of this city called in the Ninth District, the Hommony case which beats the case you refer to. The case is that of *W. W. Richie v. William M'Bean* where plaintiff sued defendant to recover two and one-half dollars overpaid M'Bean for ferriage on Hommony. M'Bean became a witness and swore there was no contract. Richie made complaint before a justice [of the peace] charging M'Bean with perjury and M'Bean was discharged. M'Bean then brought suit for damage for malicious prosecution. Damages $10,000. Richie proved that M'Bean stated that he had agreed to ferry at five cents per barrel but that now he would not do it less than ten cents per barrel. Judgment $500. Judgment reversed.

The above suit and those arising from it have already cost Richie $1,000 lawyer's fees and it is still pending for $10,000 damages. It is nearly four years since it first commenced.

As the influence of the court upon the development of the law grew rapidly in the years following the adoption of the Constitution of 1848, the nation moved rapidly toward the catastrophe of civil war. The Kansas-Nebraska Bill, repeal of the Missouri Compromise, and the Wilmot Proviso split the Democratic Party despite all the efforts of Douglas to close the breaks. These same issues brought an end to the old Whig conservatism and brought the Republican Party into being.[30]

Illinois was for a time the center of national interest as Douglas rallied his followers for the Senate contest of 1858, opposed by Lincoln, the tall circuit lawyer from Springfield. This was the last battle but one for the Little Giant and was the victory that cost him the presidency. The great debates caught the attention and the imagination of all who heard and many who read them. Few could fail to be stirred when at Alton Lincoln disregarded opportunities for technical advantage, and struck to the heart of the slavery issue that was dividing the country:

> That is the real issue. That is the issue that will continue in this country when these poor tongues of Judge Douglas and myself shall be silent. It is the eternal struggle between these two principles—right and wrong—throughout the world. They are the two principles that have stood face to face from the beginning of time, and will ever continue to struggle. The one is the common right of humanity, and the other the "divine right of kings." It is the same principle in whatever shape it develops itself. It is the same spirit that says, "You work and toil and earn bread, and I'll eat it." No matter in what shape it comes, whether from the mouth of a king who seeks to bestride the people of his own nation and live by the fruit of their labor, or from one race of men as an apology for enslaving another race, it is the same tyrannical principle.[31]

Before the contest for the presidency came in 1860, Lincoln summoned all of his old courtroom skill and his stump speech ability to aid the campaign, but these skills were sublimated by the fierce heat of the issues they were used upon. The practice of law had developed in him a sense of justice that was almost intuitive, and he brought it to bear on the problems government had to solve. Thought and feeling were made articulate by his developed skill in persuasion acquired in prairie courtrooms across the state. His great power shone at Cooper Union and in the portentous warning of the "house divided" speech on the eve of his Senate nomination.[32]

In the last great contest between them, Douglas, caught at last by inconsistencies bred of improvisation, could not match that skill. Yet his last acts demand respect and admiration. In the profound disappointment of defeat realized before it happened, he turned from personal ambition to prevent disunion if he could, and died in the last great endeavor.

Lincoln's victory in 1860 carried the Republican state ticket into office. Richard Yates, Lincoln's spokesman during the days between his election and inauguration, won election as governor and served during the principal war years. His actions became the subject matter of one of the great cases in the Supreme Court during those years.

No change in the Supreme Court, composed of Judges Caton, Breese, and Walker, occurred until the resignation of Caton in 1864. These three were Democrats although party lines meant little in judicial elections. Corydon Beckwith finished Caton's unexpired term, and Judge Charles B. Lawrence succeeded him. The effects of the Civil War on the development of the law were powerful but most of them were not manifested until after a new constitution had once again reconstituted the Supreme Court. However, there were a few cases that dealt directly with issues involved in the conflict.

A line drawn east from the southern tip of Illinois would cross Virginia south of Richmond, and the implications of the geographical position of the state are obvious. To the south, across the Ohio, was Kentucky, a border state held in the Union by the slenderest of ties; to the east was Indiana, scene of the events of *Ex Parte Milligan*[33] in the Supreme Court of the United States; and west was Missouri, where only the force of arms sustained federal supremacy. Southern sympathy ran strong in Illinois. Even when the efforts of Douglas and a change of attitude on the part of leaders from the territory south of Springfield had assured support for the national government, there were many whose hopes were fired by the Confederate cause.

The early years of the Lincoln administration created intense dissatisfaction among loyal men in both the Republican and Democratic parties. His perceived temporizing with the issue of slavery caused the disaffection of zealous free soilers while efforts at firmness in dealing with secession alienated the Union Democrats.

In 1857 and 1859, the General Assembly made an effort to maintain democratic control of the state by gerrymander, but Governor William H. Bissell, a Republican, had vetoed the bill both times, and the Republican members had walked out to prevent passage over his veto.[34] In 1861, the state had been redistricted along lines favoring the Republicans, and the legislature passed an act calling a constitutional convention.[35] When delegates to the convention were elected in 1861, control of the state had passed temporarily to the Democrats due to dissatisfaction with the Lincoln administration.

Democrats largely comprised the constitutional convention, but the proposed constitution was an unworthy document and was beaten at the popular election. The Democrats regained control of the General Assembly in 1862 and succeeded in passing through the house resolutions calling for a cessation of hostilities and a peace conference at Louisville. Senate Republicans prevented passage by absenting themselves to break a quorum. Governor Yates vetoed a reapportionment bill passed along Democratic lines and adjourned the General Assembly before it could pass the measure over his veto. This action came before the Supreme Court for review at the November 1863 term.[36]

The problem was presented to the court in a manner reminiscent of *Marbury v. Madison*.[37] In each of two cases, the court heard applications for alternative writs of mandamus. In the first of these, *The People ex rel. Harliss v. Hatch*,[38] one of the persons named in a bill to incorporate the Wabash Railroad Company introduced in the senate in 1863, sought to compel Secretary of State Ozias M. Hatch to issue a copy of the bill certifying, under the great seal of the state, that it was a law.

In the other case, *The People ex rel. Keyes v. Dubois*,[39] a member of the house of representatives sought to compel the auditor of public accounts, Jesse K. Dubois, to issue his warrant for the sum of two dollars in payment of the per diem of the legislator for June 23 and 24, 1863. The facts as revealed by the applications were that the senate on June 8, 1863 passed and sent to the house a joint resolution providing for adjournment sine die at 6 P.M. on that day. The house took up the resolution at its afternoon session and amended it by changing the time and date for adjournment to 10 A.M., June 22, 1863. The resolution returned to the senate, which refused to concur in the amendment.

The house learned of the senate action apparently before official notification and passed a resolution stating that it desired to recede from its action in amending the joint resolution and so advised the senate, requesting its return. Following the activities of the General Assembly closely, Governor Yates awaited any misstep. At the close of its session on June 8, the senate adjourned until the next morning, while the house recessed at 9:35 P.M. that night until the morning of June 10. The senate met on June 9, and transacted business, adjourning on the afternoon of that day until the morning of June 10.

On June 10, after the transaction of routine business, the speaker of the senate read a message from Governor Yates that cited section 13, article IV of the Constitution of 1848 which provided: "In case of disagreement between the two houses with respect to the time of adjournment, the governor shall have the power to adjourn the general assembly to such time as he thinks proper, provided it be not a period beyond the next constitutional meeting of the same." Purporting to exercise the power vested in him by this language the governor stated that he adjourned the General Assembly until "the Saturday next preceding the first Monday in January, A.D. 1865." The message contained language that left undisguised the contempt that Yates felt for what he considered the craven conduct of the Democratic members of the legislature. "Whereas, I fully believe that the interests of the State will be best subserved by a speedy adjournment, the past history of the present assembly holding out no reasonable hope of beneficent results to the citizens of the State, or the army in the field, from its further continuance."

Yates's support of the national administration merited the support it received from the people, but his words and actions were sometimes intemperate and ill-advised.[40] On the other hand, the Democrats in Illinois, Indiana, and elsewhere in the midlands did not act wisely or prudently in their opposition to the war. By their conduct they impaired the influence of their party for many years to come.

Active in Democratic leadership in the house at this troubled session was the Maine-born Chicago lawyer, Melville Weston Fuller, who would one day be Chief Justice of the United States Supreme Court. Fuller presented the indignant protest of the legislature, which formally accused the governor of dealing a death blow to legislation vital to the welfare of the state. The somewhat tumid language of the following paragraph gives the spirit of the document: "Even partisanship affords no palliation for the pursuit of such a course, since no political measure has been pressed upon either branch of the assembly during the recent period of its session. Which is the more guilty, the individual who proposes, or the wretched agents who carry into effect, an act so utterly indefensible, it is not for us to determine. It is sufficient that all the actors, aiders and abettors of this scheme to block the wheels of government, will receive the condemnation they deserve from an outraged people."[41] Fuller appeared as counsel for the relator in the case involving the Wabash Railroad Company.

The political significance of the cases made the Supreme Court's task a difficult one. Although the alternative writs issued over the signature of Caton as chief justice, he did not sit with the court during the November 1863 term at Mt. Vernon. Caton, Breese, and Walker were all three Democrats, although Caton's influence with men of affairs in both major parties reduced his party affiliation to insignificance at this time. Breese, on the other hand, was active in Democratic affairs, even on the local level, almost to the day of his death. For him the cases presented implications that he must have disliked. Walker had fewer active ties to politics but these were enough to make the decision between a Republican governor and a Democratic General Assembly a difficult one.

The bill to incorporate the Wabash Railroad Company passed the senate on January 22, 1863, and passed the house on June 8, 1863, and the governor received it four days later. Yates did not sign the bill nor did he return it to the senate with any objections that he might have had. He did, however, on June 19, prepare a message stating his objections to the bill, which he forwarded privately to the lieutenant governor. The lieutenant governor did not deliver the bill or the message to the secretary of state.

Judge Walker wrote separate opinions in each case. He avoided the dilemma presented by the issue of the validity of Governor Yates's action by deciding that the ten days allowed the governor by the constitution for consideration of the bill had not expired when the legislature finally quit on June 24. He decided that "days" in the constitutional provision meant whole days, not parts of days.[42] As was held by the Supreme Court of the United States in the Pocket Veto[43] case, it was necessary for the legislative body to have been in session in order that the bill might have been returned with objections. Not "legislative days," but "natural days" was meant.

In the *Hatch* case, Walker decided that the legislature had acquiesced in the adjournment by taking no steps from June 11 to June 23 to remain in session and to compel the return of a quorum. There was, he thought, a de facto adjournment.

Breese treated both cases in a single opinion. In language suggestive of that of Chief Justice John Marshall in *Marbury v. Madison*, he raised the question of whether mandamus was the proper remedy. With respect to the meager $2 per diem, he thought the facts indicated sufficient uncertainty in the right of the relator that the writ of mandamus should not be used. In the case of the Wabash charter, he thought the secretary of state could not issue a certified copy of any law that had not come into his possession in the regular constitutional manner. Curiously, he went on to consider other issues in the cases after a tribute to the counsel who presented them: "The respect, however, which I sincerely entertain for the counsel who have managed the case, and who have presented arguments in its support, not only in the most plausible and persuasive form, but with a force and power seldom exhibited in any form, impels me to a further examination of it, although it be supererogation, upon the facts presented by the returns, and admitted by the demurrer."[44] This further consideration gave him the opportunity to imply the possible illegality of the governor's conduct while deciding that the issue as to the proper exercise of his power was a legislative and not a judicial question.

The great majority of the Democrats who opposed continuation of the war after the discouraging losses in the field during 1861 and 1862 and who regarded the Emancipation Proclamation as an act of tyranny were, like Fuller, sincere and loyal men. There were, however, on the fringes of their ranks, those whose activities took on a more sinister caste.[45] There were members of the legislature who were affiliated with the Knights of the Golden Circle and similar pro-Southern organizations. Their activities were directed toward actually impeding the efforts of the national government to wage war successfully. The federal authorities retaliated with measures calculated to drive the opposition underground. There were arbitrary arrests and many instances of imprisonment without charge and without trial. Some of these cases eventually found their way into the courts, and the possibilities of successful legal action were strengthened by the decision of the Supreme Court of the United States in the *Milligan* case in 1866.[46]

The Supreme Court of Illinois considered two such cases at the April 1867 term. Madison Y. Johnson and David Sheean were lawyers practicing in Galena in Jo Daviess County, and both were allegedly members of the Knights of the Golden Circle. They were arrested, taken secretly to Chicago and New York, and imprisoned first in Fort Lafayette and later at Fort Delaware for a total of four months. They were released without any formal charge ever having been filed against them. Both sued the United States marshal for the Northern District of Illinois and other federal officers for damages for false arrest and false imprisonment. The defendants justified under the terms of an executive order pursuant to which most of such arrests were made. Both Johnson and Sheean were averred to be engaged in impeding the effort of the national government to secure volunteers for the army.[47] Caton was no longer on the court, and Judges Breese, Walker, and Lawrence considered the appeals, with Judge Lawrence writing the opinion of the court in the *Johnson* case.[48] No separate opinion was necessary for the *Sheean* case.

The court relied principally on the *Milligan* decision in holding that the existence of a state of war does not authorize a state of martial law or the arbitrary arrest and imprisonment of citizens without a formal charge and without a hearing. The order of the president was said to be unlawful under the conditions prevailing in Illinois and available only in mitigation of exemplary damages. Judge Breese filed a separate opinion on this latter point in which he stated that the marshal, knowing that the president's order was unlawful and arbitrary, should take all the consequences of his obedience.[49]

The ordinary law, of course, was slow in showing the effects of the great ordeal of fire through which the country passed in the years 1861 to 1865. The immediate effects were felt in public and constitutional law, in which the great amendments to the federal Constitution solved some problems but created others. Still other problems raised during the ordeal were settled through trial by battle and some were solved in court.[50]

In Illinois, a new constitution reorganized the state government in 1870, resulting in part from problems growing out of the war, but more immediately from the rapid growth of industry and the shift from a predominately agricultural state to one in which other great interests competed with those of the prairies. There had been widespread dissatisfaction with the Constitution of 1848 for many years, particularly with the special legislation its provisions permitted. In other respects the state had simply grown too big to be governed adequately by the provisions of the existing constitution.

The machinery provided by the Constitution of 1848 for the administration of justice had become inadequate to meet the needs of the enlarging population. Complaints from Chicago were particularly severe, to the effect that overcrowded court dockets threatened a breakdown in the administration of justice if the legislature did not provide relief.[51] This situation was an interesting illustration of what had happened in Illinois since the last constitutional revision. The heavy concentration of population in Chicago produced a disproportionate increase in the volume of litigation. In other words, the densely populated industrialized north produced legal problems differing both in quality and in quantity from those that arose in the rest of the state.

Pursuant to the legislative action of 1869, eighty-five delegates convened in the statehouse at Springfield in December 1869 with authority to draft proposals "to revise, alter, or amend the Constitution of the State of Illinois." Of the eighty-five delegates, fifty-six were lawyers. The convention finished the work of writing a new constitution in May 1870, and voters approved it on July 2 of that year.

The new constitution had many and important changes from the Constitution of 1848. It borrowed some new provisions from the federal Constitution and reflected the issues involved in the Civil War. It had other provisions constructed to meet the special problems that had developed in Illinois. Article II, the "Bill of Rights," of the new document replaced Article XIII of the old constitution, the "Declaration of Rights." Section 2 of Article II added a "due process" clause, the first time the famous phrase appeared in the basic law of Illinois.

Article VI completely reorganized the judicial system beginning with the Supreme Court. In language modeled after that of the federal Constitution, the judicial power of the state was vested in a supreme court, circuit court, county courts, justices of the peace, police, and magistrates, "and such courts as may be created by law in and for cities and incorporated towns."

The three-judge Supreme Court was replaced by a court of seven judges elected from seven districts described in section 5. The legislature had the power to change the boundaries of the districts at the session next preceding the election for judges, but it was required to act upon the rule of equality of population as nearly as county boundaries would allow. Judges had terms of nine years, and four judges were to be elected at the time of voting on the new constitution. The three sitting judges were to finish out their terms.

The constitution fixed the salaries of the judges at $4,000 per year with power in the legislature to change the amount. No judge's salary was to be increased nor decreased during the term for which he was elected. The judges themselves were to have power to select the chief justice after the expiration of the existing chief justice's term. Places of holding court were to continue at Springfield, Mt. Vernon, and Ottawa until the legislature provided otherwise. Chicago could have a term of the Supreme Court if it or Cook County "shall provide appropriate rooms therefor," and the use of a suitable library without expense to the state.[52]

A provision of special significance authorized the legislature to create inferior appellate courts after 1874 to review decisions from the circuit and other courts. These intermediate courts were to be held by judges of the circuit courts, but no judge was to be permitted to review cases decided by him. Decisions of such appellate courts were to be final except in criminal cases and cases involving a freehold, a franchise, and the validity of a statute.

The circuit courts continued as the principal courts of first instance, and the legislature had the power to form the circuits to be composed of contiguous counties. Cook County was designated as a single circuit and the Superior Court of Cook County was continued. Other provisions created the Criminal Court of Cook County and probate courts in counties of more than 50,000 in population.

The 1870 Illinois Constitution set the number of justices at seven to represent seven geographic districts for the Illinois Supreme Court. Map prepared by Matt Burns.

The convention recognized that increase and concentration of population did more than increase the volume of litigation. Chicago's representatives clamored for nearly twice as many judges in proportion to population than were thought necessary for other areas in the state. The reasons were clear. Considering the criminal law alone, concentration of population in smaller space resulted in a tremendous increase in burglary cases, robbery, and all other crimes of violence. On the civil side of law administration, concentration of commercial activity brought about a vast increase in the volume of civil litigation. Add to these factors the great grain exchange and the railroads with termini in Chicago, and it is not difficult to understand why Chicago would need additional courts and additional judges.

The new constitution became effective August 8, 1870. Thereafter in Ottawa, seven judges met to hold the September term of the Supreme Court as reorganized. Judge Breese, in his "cloud of white hair and whiskers," presided as chief justice and with him were Judges Walker and Lawrence of the old court. Among the newcomers was Anthony Thornton of Shelbyville, a Kentucky-born ex-congressman destined to be the first president of the Illinois State Bar Association. He would serve only three years. He was fifty-five years old and would live to be ninety.[53]

From Bloomington came John M. Scott who had succeeded David Davis as judge of the eighth circuit after Abraham Lincoln appointed his old friend Davis to the Supreme Court of the United States. Scott was forty-six. He was a Republican and had campaigned from the same platform with Lincoln in the circuit-riding days. He served on the court for eighteen years and published a volume on the history of the court that deserved wider recognition than it received.[54]

Benjamin R. Sheldon of Rockford represented the sixth district. He had graduated from Williams College and studied law at Yale. Sheldon was fifty-seven in 1870 and like Scott would serve on the court for eighteen years.[55]

William K. McAllister came to the court from Chicago, where he had been judge of the recorder's court. He was fifty-two and served only five years of his nine-year term, resigning to return to Chicago as circuit judge.[56]

This was the court that began a new era in the judicial history of Illinois. By 1870, the lines of future development could be clearly perceived. Chicago was becoming the railroad center of the nation. Douglas had insisted that the Illinois Central have a Chicago terminal even though the "main line" went to Galena. By 1870, the "branch line" carried the principal traffic of the system.[57] By rail, river, and lake the goods of the nation came to Chicago for distribution, needing warehouses and elevators to store the grain the railroads brought, and another important industry grew up in the city on the lake.

Prior to 1870 many conditions had contributed to a feeling of unrest among farmers throughout the country from western New York and Pennsylvania to the area across the Mississippi. A system of farm financing based upon crop mortgages had been inherited from the years before the Civil War. The panic of 1857 had ruined many farmers and left others in difficult financial straits. In the era of railroad building, many invested life savings in the new means of transportation on the promise of high returns and the belief that they were contributing to the development of highways to take their crops to the great population centers and the high prices that prevailed there.

These expectations did not materialize. Improper financing, high construction costs, and other less legitimate factors made railroad profits elusive. High freight tariffs prevented farmers from realizing expected advantages in marketing their products. In short, the railroads had been a serious disappointment to the farmers. Most farmers were ready to believe the worst about those engaged in railroad management.

Public regulation of railroads was practically unheard of and price regulation in general would not have been favored, but the cause of the farmers was becoming desperate. Gradually the idea of organization began to take hold after the Civil War. This sentiment culminated in the creation in 1867 of the Patrons of Husbandry, or the Grange, as the organization came to be called. Originally a social organization, the Grange took up the cause of the farmers against the railroads as an active crusade. All of the important farming areas of the midlands organized local Granges. With the cry of "Down with the monopolies," they soon began actively seeking relief through legislation. The Granger movement was especially strong in Illinois, where farmers had been the chief sufferers from the extravagant internal improvement program of the 1830s.[58]

The active campaign of the Illinois Granges led to the passage by the legislature in 1871 of the statute commonly called "the Warehouse Law."[59] The statute required public warehouse owners, including operators of grain elevators, to procure licenses from the circuit court before transacting business. It also provided maximum rates that public warehouse owners could charge for services.

In 1872, the state's attorney of Cook County filed an information against Ira Y. Munn and George L. Scott, warehouse owners in Chicago, for violation of the statute. The criminal court of Cook County found the defendants guilty and fined them $100 and costs. This was the beginning of the famous case of *Munn v. Illinois*.[60] Munn and Scott sued out a writ of error in the Illinois Supreme Court to reverse the judgment of Judge William W. Farwell. The issue was the constitutionality of the Warehouse Law under the new due process clause of the Fourteenth Amendment to the Constitution of the United States.

Munn and Scott obtained distinguished counsel to represent them. In first place was John N. Jewett, former partner in the firm to which Judges Scates and McAllister had belonged. Jewett had a wide reputation as a constitutional lawyer, and his familiarity with interpretations of federal constitutional limitations was doubtless a factor in his selection. With him on the brief in the

Grain warehouses, similar to those lining the Chicago River in this 1868 representation, were the subject of the public regulation case of *Munn v. Illinois*. Library of Congress, Geography and Map Division.

Supreme Court was William C. Goudy and the firm of McCagg, Fuller & Culver. Goudy was a man of wide experience in the law whose acquaintance and influence reached into high places. He became a partner of Melville W. Fuller, who was associated with him in the case. McCagg and Culver likewise were men of wide experience and influence.

Against this formidable group the state sent its newly elected attorney general, James K. Edsall, with whom were associated Charles H. Reed, the state's attorney for Cook County, and Reuben M. Benjamin and the firm of Hitchcock, Dupee & Evarts. Ablest of these was Benjamin, drafter of the Bill of Rights Article in the Constitution of 1870. His argument in the convention against special privileges to railroads was widely commented upon outside of Illinois. His argument and that of Charles Hitchcock, who had been president of the constitutional convention, were regarded as particularly forceful by those who heard them.[61]

This case came up for decision before the Supreme Court at the September 1873 term. Two changes had occurred in the court. John Scholfield of Marshall, in Clark County, succeeded Judge Thornton. Alfred M. Craig of Knox County defeated Judge Lawrence at the polls because of an unpopular decision by Lawrence.

Chief Justice Breese wrote the opinion of the court in the *Munn* case. He summarily dismissed the contention of unconstitutionality based upon the Fourteenth Amendment of the federal Constitution by saying that the amendment was intended to protect blacks:

> It was well known the amendment in question was incorporated into the federal constitution to shield a certain class, who had been born and reared in slavery, from pernicious legislation, by which their newly acquired rights by their emancipation might be so crippled as to render them wholly worthless.
>
> In the discussions upon the effect of this amendment, in the slaughter house cases[62] from New Orleans, and the case of Myra Bradwell, plaintiff in error,[63] taken up from this court, it was not intimated by the Supreme Court of the United States that a regulation by a State legislature of a pursuit or profession, or a regulation of the use of property, abridged in any manner the liberty of the citizen, white or black.[64]

Judge Breese considered the question under the due process clause of the state constitution more fundamental. He rejected the argument, however, that the regulation contemplated by the statute was a taking of property through appropriation of its use. The legislature, he said, is the guardian of the public welfare:

> [A]nd if, in their examination of it, they find the owners and managers of these warehouses are an organized body of monopolists, possessing sufficient strength in their combination, and by their connection with the railroads of the State, to impose their own terms upon the producers and shippers of these cereals, to the great detriment of the latter, who are under a kind of moral duress in resorting to them, can it be said to be an usurpation of power on the part of the legislature to bring them in subjection to law, so to regulate their conduct and charges by law, as to prevent oppression and extortion? Can there be a more legitimate subject for the action of a legislative body? We think not. Shall it be said an interest so vast as this is does not deserve governmental care, and is not a proper subject of some kind of governmental control? And if, in the means provided by the legislature to that end, some reduction in their monthly or annual receipts may be the result, can it be said the owners are thereby deprived of their property?[65]

Judge Walker concurred in a separate but unpublished opinion.

Judge McAllister filed a strong dissenting opinion, and Judge Scott concurred with it.[66] The dissenting judges thought that not only were the due process clauses of the state and federal constitutions violated, but also that the statute conflicted with the power of Congress to regulate interstate commerce.

There was popular approval throughout the state regarding the decision as it was regarded as a blow against the railroads whose charges were considered excessive and discriminatory. Judge Breese and the majority saw nothing extraordinary in legislation that regulated prices. The opinion stressed the monopolistic character of the defendants' business along with the connection of the business with the railroads. The answer to the argument based upon the due process clause of the state constitution was a legalistic one. It rested in large part upon the premise that future profits are not property within the meaning of the term as used in the constitution.

The opinion also foreshadowed the beginnings of the public utility concept. Judge Breese had in mind analogies to public ferries, public mills, hackmen, draymen, and statutes regulating the weight and price of bread. He placed strong reliance upon statutes fixing compensation for the use of money.[67] The distrust of banks and eastern capitalists, so strong among midland farmers of that day, found a place in the opinion: "The interest on money loaned is, by law, six per cent, with the right to contract for ten per cent, and such has been the law for a long series of years. Under the cover of that law, capitalists have engaged in loaning money at those rates. Some, on the strength of it, have erected costly buildings of granite and marble in which to transact their vast business, surrounded by a corps of clerks and other officials, to whom high salaries are paid."[68] It is significant that he chose to avoid positive reliance on Article XIII of the constitution, which dealt with warehouses, and might have been used as a basis for a determination of the public character of the operation of Munn and Scott. The majority sought a decision with a broader base, one that would confirm the power of the legislature to regulate fees of those from whom essential services must be obtained and who have no competitors. This was the concept of governmental regulation of public utilities in its infancy.

Munn and Scott were convinced their cause was just. They lost no time in suing out a writ of error in the Supreme Court of the United States. Again it was Jewett and Goudy who advanced to do battle against the advocates of price regulation. They placed their reliance principally upon the due process clause of the Fourteenth Amendment, but they argued also that the Warehouse

Law was a regulation of commerce in conflict with Congressional power and a preference to the ports of one state in violation of Article I, section 9, clause 6. Edsall, the attorney general, presented the argument for the state of Illinois.

The *Munn* case was one of six cases that the Supreme Court of the United States decided at the October 1876 term, commonly known as the "Granger" cases.[69] The other five cases involved railroads and came up from Iowa, Wisconsin, and Minnesota. The railroads drew heavily on Illinois lawyers to defend them against the steadily advancing forces of regulation. Orville H. Browning represented the Burlington against the state of Iowa. In the Wisconsin cases, William M. Evarts and Burton C. Cook were associated with ex-Justice Lawrence, who was apparently gaining in private practice from his unpopular decision in another railroad case that cost him his seat on the court.

The United States Supreme Court selected the *Munn* case to set the pattern of decision in all of the Granger cases and adopted the basic view of the Supreme Court of Illinois. A consciousness of a broader problem than regulation of railroads was inherent in this selection.

The doctrine of *Munn v. Illinois*—that rates or prices charged in a business affected with a public interest are subject to legislative (or administrative) regulation—is familiar to every lawyer. Points of difference in the opinion of Chief Justice Waite, himself a former railroad lawyer,[70] and the views expressed for the majority in the state court by ex-senator and railroad builder Sidney Breese should be noted. How far these points of difference were real and not merely verbal is a question for debate. Waite was a judge of ability whose powers of perception were impaired by an inability to give his ideas the crystal clear expression they deserved. A phrase borrowed out of context in an almost forgotten book was made to express the whole justification for state regulation of prices. "Business affected with a public interest" was Waite's way of summarizing the position of Munn and Scott and the other grain men whose elevators lined the Chicago River.

Breese's prose was frequently labored and flamboyant, but in the *Munn* case he set forth the factors that Waite had expressed by a sort of legal shorthand. The ideas of each were familiar, but monopoly meant more to Breese than the concept of public calling. In the Waite opinion there was the basis for a result he probably did not intend—the development of a closed category.[71] The phrase intended to justify state regulation of prices was turned into an instrument to fix limits to state regulation. Thus, the public utility concept was born, a nearly closed-end concept for more than half a century, until the decision in the *Nebbia* case.[72]

Breese's opinion had less apparent concreteness but laid more emphasis on factual consideration of the problem with which the legislature was concerned. Although Breese could not foresee the course the due process clause would take in the decisions of the Supreme Court of the United States, his technique was consistent with what would be done in cases that were fifty years in the future.[73]

The importance of the state court decision in the *Munn* case has been obscured by the years of comment and controversy over "business affected with a public interest." But the *Munn* case, alone of all the Granger cases, was not a railroad case. The opinion of Judge Breese stood for the power of the legislature to regulate a business in which the operation of the business and its characteristics, apart from legal concepts, created a reasonable need for regulation in the legislature's considered opinion. Only the addition of the word "reasonable" somewhere in the opinion was needed to express the doctrine of substantive due process as it is understood today.

Judge Breese cited few cases in his opinion but he did refer to the decision of the Supreme Court of the United States in the case of *Bradwell v. Illinois*.[74] The appearance of this case in court was a sign of the changing times.

Myra Colby Bradwell is chiefly remembered for two things: her success as publisher of the *Chicago Legal News* and her efforts to become admitted to the bar. She was the wife of James B. Bradwell, at one time county judge of Cook County. After the Civil War, Mrs. Bradwell determined to study law and went about the venture with the same vigor she displayed in all her other activities. After successful completion of her studies, she applied in 1869 for a license to practice. The Supreme Court of Illinois denied her admission on the ground that she was a married woman under Common Law disabilities. Not daunted, Mrs. Bradwell filed a printed brief that brought from Judge Lawrence a long opinion, the substance of which was that whatever Mrs. Bradwell's other qualifications, she was after all a woman, and women simply did not practice law.[75]

As though regretful of lack of gallantry, Judge Lawrence sought to avoid blame by saying that the Creator was responsible for the difference in the sexes and the legislature for not having removed the barriers that sex imposed, adding that if the legislature should choose to act, the court would cheerfully obey, "trusting to the good sense and sound judgment of women themselves, to seek those departments of the practice in which they can labor without reasonable objection."[76]

Myra Bradwell attempted to become the first woman licensed to practice law in Illinois, but the Illinois Supreme Court denied her application, and the U.S. Supreme Court upheld the denial. Abraham Lincoln Presidential Library and Museum.

Mrs. Bradwell promptly sued out a writ of error in the Supreme Court of the United States. Her attorney, U.S. Senator from Wisconsin Matthew H. Carpenter, presented a learned argument, and the attorney general of the state of Illinois did not appear as opposing counsel. The federal Supreme Court was even less gallant than the Supreme Court of Illinois. A terse opinion by Justice Samuel F. Miller stated that Mrs. Bradwell had no claim by virtue of the privileges and immunities clause of Article IV of the federal Constitution and no claim by virtue of the similar language of the Fourteenth Amendment. The privilege of practicing law was not one of those privileges of citizens of the United States that a state was forbidden to abridge.[77]

Justice Joseph P. Bradley concurred, but in a separate opinion he said, "The paramount destiny and mission of woman are to fulfill the noble and benign offices of wife and mother."[78] Justices Noah H. Swayne and Stephen J. Field concurred with Bradley, while Chief Justice Salmon P. Chase "dissented from the judgment of the court, and from all the opinions."[79]

Ultimately, however, Mrs. Bradwell was successful, securing admission to the bar in 1890 and becoming the first woman member of the Illinois State Bar Association. Her efforts were indicative that the old order was passing, that men and women were living then in a society undergoing profound changes.

The emergence of the law of Illinois into maturity was guided by the court of seven judges created by the Constitution of 1870. The period from the decision in the *Munn* case to the beginning of the twentieth century was a period when the law passed through an ordeal by battle between the strongly fortified interests of agriculture and the new forces of industry. The latter forces made northern Illinois and the lake region a stronghold from which to contest with the rest of the midlands for supremacy. The period began with the dominance of agriculture symbolized by the success of the Granger movement. It ended with industry achieving its proper sphere of influence through an operating compromise with the areas that produced the food without which industry could not live.

A considerable amount of credit is due the Supreme Court of Illinois for its part in making such a compromise possible. In no state in the midlands was there such a contrast of agriculture and industry. Nowhere else ran the continental arteries of transportation by land and water, tying the two together and increasing the intricacies of the problems of government.

At the time of the decision of the *Munn* case, only Breese and Walker had served on the court more than three years. The newcomers, Scholfield, Scott, Craig, Sheldon, and McAllister, were competent judges, but only one among them was destined to be regarded as a great judge.

John Scholfield was born in Illinois, one of the few native sons of his day to have risen to position of eminence as a lawyer and judge. He studied law in Louisville, Kentucky, and practiced at Marshall, Illinois, where he achieved some political success as state's attorney and legislator. His interest was primarily in active practice rather than in politics, and he soon achieved first rank as a lawyer. Scholfield was apparently equally good either as a trial lawyer or as a counselor. He formed in practice the habits of sound research that carried him to a top ranking position among Illinois judges. He served on the Supreme Court from 1873 until his death in 1893, participating in almost all of the important cases that came before the court in that period. The vigor of his personality was carried into the opinions he wrote for the court. They were plain in language but clear in thought and expression. His directness and independence were illustrated by countless stories told for decades wherever lawyers gathered.

In one example, in his days as a practicing lawyer, Scholfield had a reputation for having no patience with judges who were not members of the legal profession. While trying a case before a county judge who was not a lawyer, he made a motion to dismiss the proceeding. The judge overruled the motion and learnedly delivered an opinion that established that he knew nothing whatever about the law of the case before him. Scholfield was said to have remarked to Judge Jacob Wilkin, who was associated with him: "Call a jury, Jake, let's take the case from one damned fool to twelve!"[80]

Scholfield received the greatest professional honor that can be conferred upon an American lawyer. After the quality of his work upon the Supreme Court had established him as a great state court judge, President Grover Cleveland offered him the appointment as Chief Justice of the United States Supreme Court, the appointment that ultimately went to Melville W. Fuller.[81] Already near the end of his career, Scholfield declined the honor, stating that the happiness of his wife and family would be jeopardized by a move to Washington. His health was also a matter of concern at the time of the offer.[82]

The court grew in stature with the developing system of law in the quarter century between the *Munn* case and the beginning of a new century. There were other able judges to sit with Scholfield to deal with new problems that the changing world presented. There was T. Lyle Dickey, the corporation lawyer from Ottawa and Chicago, with a gift for analysis of commercial problems and a distinguished record as a soldier.[83] There was Scholfield's own former law partner, Jacob Wilkin, companion of many escapades when they were young lawyers together, trying cases in the circuit courts in the eastern part of the state. Wilkin settled at Danville and built an important law practice with his young partner, Francis Rearick. Wilkin was probably as able a judge as Scholfield but lacked some of the latter's impressive personality.[84]

Joseph Meade Bailey, from Freeport and Chicago, served with these men for seven years. He brought to the court an interest in legal education and training for the bar that benefited many a struggling young student. He gave generously of his time as a teacher and extended the respect for the court, which had steadily increased since the decision in the *Munn* case.[85]

At the end of the period, two men joined the court whose service extended into the years after 1900. They maintained the position of influence that the court had attained. One of these approached Scholfield in judicial stature. He was James H. Cartwright of Oregon in the Rock River Valley. Cartwright served until 1924 and many of his opinions have been cited and followed in the courts of other states.[86]

The other judge was Jesse J. Phillips of Hillsboro, a capable lawyer who brought the practical viewpoint of the central Illinois farming communities to the council room. It is of Phillips that lawyers like to repeat the story of his pride in a horse he drove hitched to a racing sulky. One day when driving the horse near the courthouse in Hillsboro, he met another citizen in a similar rig. Neither wished the other to pass him and soon they were driving down the main street at a rapid pace. Both were arrested by the city marshal and charged with exceeding the speed limit of ten miles per hour. Phillips's opponent pleaded guilty and paid his fine, but the judge was outraged and requested a hearing at a later date.

Just after having arranged to have his case heard, he met Dr. Samuel H. McLean, mayor of Hillsboro. The judge expressed himself vigorously. Dr. McLean, with grave face said: "I agree with you, Judge. The fact is I don't believe that old plug of yours could go over ten miles an hour if he tried." Judge Phillips indignantly replied: "Damn you, Sir, damn you, Sir, he was going twenty if he was going one." And with the retort he stalked back to the magistrate's office, entered a plea of guilty, and paid his fine.[87]

Midway in this maturing period of the law occurred another of those cases which sorely try the effectiveness of courts as institutions for the administration of justice according to law. The year 1873 saw more significance than merely the year in which the Granger cases were decided. It was a year of business collapse and financial panic.

The year 1873 saw the labor movement gather momentum. Organized labor began its campaign for shorter hours and better working conditions. This was a period when far-sighted management might have averted much of the conflict that came in 1877 and beyond. Both sides lacked sound leadership between 1873 and 1877, and government did not or could not take the initiative. Whatever the faults on both sides, the extremists of both were in control. Moreover, the economic maladjustment favored the cause of the Socialist party whose ranks began an astonishing increase.

The extremists among the socialist leaders fomented discontent by rash advocacy of anarchism. Those who were influential in shaping public opinion matched this attitude with a complete lack of sympathy and understanding of the causes of unrest. The result was a situation of public tension that steadily mounted until it reached the breaking point.

In Chicago, the influence of socialism with the large foreign-born population and the incendiary activities of fanatical leaders were matched by the uncompromising attitude of business leaders and the public press. They believed that Socialists and labor leaders were scum that should be driven from the city by police action.

Among the agitators were August Spies, editor of the extremist German language paper, *Arbeiter-Zeitung*; Albert R. Parsons, editor of the anarchist *Alarm*; Samuel Fielden, a well-known agitator with considerable gifts of oratory; and several others. They continued their train of abuse of business and political leaders. With inflammatory and ill-considered language, they urged their followers to direct action.

The public tension fostered by lack of clear thinking on both sides mounted steadily until the breaking point on Tuesday evening, May 4, 1886. On that evening the tragedy at Haymarket Square took the lives of eight policemen and resulted in injuries to scores of other persons.[88] Amid public clamor for revenge on all anarchists, a grand jury indicted thirty-one known anarchists. Of these thirty-one, eight went to trial, including Spies, Parsons, and Fielden. The others were Michael Schwab, George Engel, Adolph Fischer, Louis Lingg, and Oscar Neebe.

The trial began before Judge Joseph E. Gary on July 15, 1886.[89] On August 20, the jury's verdict resulted in a sentence of death by hanging for all but Neebe, who was sentenced to fifteen years in prison for conspiracy.

A year later, on September 14, 1887, at Ottawa, the Supreme Court of Illinois filed its longest opinion. The report of the case occupies 267 pages of the Illinois Reports.[90] The opinion written by Justice Magruder, reviewed the mostly circumstantial evidence and sustained the court below. All efforts at relief from the Supreme Court of the United States proved unavailing. Patently, the case was one of executive clemency rather than judicial action.

The atmosphere of prejudice, the public excitement, the unpopular political views of the defendants were all against them. Many people doubted the justness of the jury's verdict. Governor Richard Oglesby offered to commute the sentences if the influential Chicago businessmen would request it.[91] Lyman J. Gage, then president of the First National Bank, allegedly endeavored at a secret meeting to get the city's business leaders to request action by the governor. But Marshall Field was outspoken against it and the action was not taken.

After great agitation during which Judge Gary and the prosecutor, Julius S. Grinnell, intervened on behalf of Fielden and Schwab, the governor commuted the sentences of these two to life imprisonment. A few hours before, Louis Lingg had committed suicide in the Cook County jail. On November 11, 1887, the sentence of death by hanging was carried out on Spies, Parsons, Engel, and Fischer. Fielden and Schwab lived on to create a problem for Governor John P. Altgeld, who pardoned them in 1893 amid a storm of criticism.[92]

The Supreme Court had justification for sustaining the trial court. However, a new trial after a cessation of some of the public excitement might have had a different result for some of the defendants. Whether certain errors of the trial judge were or were not prejudicial was a question on which the atmosphere of public hostility had a direct bearing. Such cases tax the capacity of judges as well as jurors to be objective and are evidence that human institutions, however conceived, are less than perfect.

When the year 1900 began, the Supreme Court of Illinois had existed for more than eighty years. Law in the mid-continent area of which Illinois was a part was at least a hundred years older than the court. The midlands had evolved from a wilderness threatening to engulf the tiny settlements that clung to favored locations into a vast agricultural and industrial area that produced mightily for the country at large. Most of this development had taken place within the eighty years of the Supreme Court's existence.

As the growth of Illinois is now viewed, the pace of development was terrific. The very speed with which the prairies and woodlands became prosperous farms, pleasant villages, and great cities intensified every problem that could confront a developing legal system. That the Supreme Court was able to bring about an orderly development of the law that regulated and adjusted the conflicting interests in the state is in itself a major accomplishment. Adding to the problems of rapid development in Illinois was the fact that nowhere else in the country was the dichotomy between industrialization and agriculture so great. In this context, the work of the court in adjusting and developing the legal system assumes tremendous significance. A great tribute is due the individual judges who throughout the court's history guided the course of the law with a vision before them of future greatness of state and nation.[93]

Epilogue

THE LEGAL HISTORY of Illinois is of special significance in the development of law in the United States. Settlement of the Illinois country began early and proceeded at an extremely rapid pace because of its position on the Great Lakes and the Mississippi and Ohio Rivers. This rapid growth intensified the problems attending the expansion of population into a new territory. The resources of the legal system were taxed to find solutions that would satisfy the need for certainty in the law but not impede the course of social and economic development. This, of course, was the common task of the law in all the great Midwest. In Illinois, however, the task was larger because development, once started, moved faster than in most of the other states of the old Northwest.

In addition to the problems created by the compression of development from frontier to settled community in a relatively short time, the geographical and physical characteristics of the Illinois country made special demands on the legal system. The prairie lands of the central section established the importance of Illinois as an agricultural state. The accessibility of Chicago and the northern part of the state to all means of transportation made possible the industrial development that was without parallel in the United States. The interests of agriculture and industry were in some important respects conflicting interests. Their adjustment presented complex legal questions.

The legal system that grew up in the Illinois country was in many respects typical of legal systems throughout the Midwest. However, the history of this system has many unique features. The concentration and intensification of forces in the state enabled its law to exert considerable influence on parts of the United States still largely undeveloped when the Illinois law entered its period of maturity.

The French law made a strong start under circumstances that favored its development. Its passing has left almost no traces of its once vigorous existence. Although the reasons for the failure of French law to survive are complex, one conclusion stands out with greatest clarity. No system survives for long the debilitating effects of lack of knowledge and the will to care about the mechanics of its administration. The visible traces of these factors in the records of the French era are a lesson in themselves to a later and more sophisticated age.

The law in Illinois contributed greatly to the solution of legal problems facing the entire country, and its influence spanned the period beginning with the building of the first railroad in the Middle West and ending with the decision of the Supreme Court of the United States in the *Munn* case. A close examination of the story of the slavery issue in Illinois reflects credit on the manner in which the courts met the problem as it was presented. It should be remembered that the institution of slavery was established in Illinois by the French in their villages along the Mississippi. Further, the southern tier of counties is in the same latitude as other parts of the country where slaveholding was an established way of life. Yet the Supreme Court of Illinois kept its attention fixed on the basic antipathy toward slavery that was voiced in the Ordinance of 1787. The court's decisions correctly estimated the spirit of the whole people of the state while avoiding imprudent pronouncements that have kindled local fires long before the country became involved in a general conflagration.

While the Supreme Court of Illinois did not always maintain the position of leadership its importance to the Union would seem to require, it some-times pointed the way for the entire country. In drainage matters, before the legislature complicated the law with conflicting statutes, the court saw the necessity for the adaptation of legal rules to permit development of the vast agricultural resources of the prairie lands. The statesmanship of the court was again evident in the cases involving the legal problems of the railroads and the communities they served.

Although the decision of the court in Illinois in the *Munn* case has been overshadowed by the importance attached to the opinion of the Supreme Court in Washington, the opinions of the Illinois judges nevertheless evidenced an understanding of the factors that made inevitable the special treatment of public utilities. The opinions of the Illinois judges reflected a more effective understanding of the necessity for the free exercise of legislative judgment than did that of Chief Justice Morrison Waite of the United States Supreme Court. The course taken in Illinois served to influence the course of legislative action not only in Illinois but throughout the country.

The purpose of this book is meant to sketch the broad outlines of legal development in a particular and important state of the United States. When the story of law in other sections of the country has been examined, the real task of the legal historian will be apparent. The preparation of the legal history of the United States and an appraisal of the place of the law and its servants, the judges, and lawyers, in the work of building a great nation, will be a revealing and rewarding achievement.

Notes

Foreword

Dennis A. Rendleman, A.B. 1978, University of Illinois, Urbana-Champaign; J.D. 1981, University of Illinois College of Law; Ethics Counsel, Center for Professional Responsibility, American Bar Association; president, Illinois Supreme Court Legal Historical Society. Special thanks to Illinois Bar Foundation, Karen Davidson, Donna Schechter, Isolde Davidson (especially for her first round of manuscript edits), Ralph Brill, Michael Kramer, David Anderson, Bridget Burke, Mark Mathewson, John Lupton, William Wheeler, Sandy Macfarland, Gary Stockton, and others too numerous to mention.

1. *Chicago Daily Law Bulletin*, 29 April 1959, p. 1.

2. ISBA Bar News, 15 March 1996.

3. Supreme Court Historic Preservation Act, 705 ILCS 17/1 et seq.

4. Ralph M. Snyder, "An Introduction," *Chicago Daily Law Bulletin*, 30 April 1959, p. 1.

5. Editor's Note, "Prairie Justice," *Chicago Daily Law Bulletin*, 30 April 1959, p. 1.

6. Letter, William L. Severns to Dennis Rendleman, 2 February 2000.

7. Laurin A. Wollan Jr., ed., "Law in Illinois under France," *Illinois Bar Journal* 56 (January 1968): pp. 384–91; William F. Zacharias, ed., "Illinois Courts Prior to Statehood," *Illinois Bar Journal* 56 (March 1968): pp. 556–68.

8. "Equity and 'Fusion' in Illinois," *Chicago-Kent Law Review* 18 (September 1940): pp. 333–70.

9. Letter, William L. Severns to Dennis Rendleman, 2 February 2000.

Editor's Introduction

1. See, for example, Robert P. Howard, *Illinois: A History of the Prairie State* (Grand Rapids, MI: William B. Eerdman's Publishing, 1972), which largely notes Constitutional changes in the judiciary and the Haymarket and Pullman cases.

2. Michael Les Benedict and John F. Winkler, eds., *The History of Ohio Law*, 2 vols. (Athens: Ohio University Press, 2004); David J. Bodenhamer and Hon. Randall T. Shepard, eds., *The History of Indiana Law* (Athens: Ohio University Press, 2006); Paul Finkelman and Martin J. Hershock, eds., *The History of Michigan Law* (Athens: Ohio University Press, 2006); Alan G. Gless, *The History of Nebraska Law* (Athens: Ohio University Press, 2008). Other books on state supreme courts include Gerald T. Dunne, *The Missouri Supreme Court: From Dred Scott to Nancy Cruzan* (Columbia: University of Missouri Press, 1993) and James W. Ely Jr. and others, eds., *The History of the Tennessee Supreme Court* (Knoxville: University of Tennessee Press, 2002); James L. Haley, *The Texas Supreme Court: A Narrative History, 1836–1986* (Austin: University of Texas Press, 2013); James M. Murphy, *Laws, Courts, and Lawyers: Through the Years in Arizona* (Tucson: University of Arizona Press, 1970).

3. George Fiedler's little-known and little-used documentary history is the exception. George Fiedler, *The Illinois Law Courts in Three Centuries, 1673–1973: A Documentary History* (Berwyn, IL: Physicians' Record Company, 1973).

4. John M. Palmer, ed., *The Bench and Bar of Illinois: Historical and Reminiscent*, 2 vols. (Chicago: Lewis Publishing, 1899). For an example of a specific county, see *The Combined History of Shelby and Moultrie Counties, Illinois* (Philadelphia: Brink, McDonough & Co., 1881), pp. 75–82.

5. There were several school segregation cases in which the Illinois Supreme Court consistently ruled that separate schools for African American children were an unnecessary burden on taxpayers. In 1873, the Illinois Supreme Court established that doctrine in *Chase et al. v. Stephenson et al.* In a series of cases originating in Alton beginning in 1897, Scott Bibb repeatedly attempted, and was repeatedly supported by the Illinois Supreme Court, to send his children to a white-only school. He was, however, repeatedly defeated by the local Alton leaders, and Alton remained a segregated school community until the 1950s. *Chase v. Stephenson*, 71 Ill. 383 (1874). *Bibb v. Mayor and Council of Alton*, 179 Ill. 615 (1899); August Meier and Elliott M. Rudwick, "Early Boycotts of Segregated Schools: The Alton, Illinois Case, 1897—1908," *The Journal of Negro Education* 36 (Autumn 1967): pp. 394–402; Shirley J. Portwood, "The Alton

School Case and African American Community Consciousness, 1897–1908," *Illinois Historical Journal* 91 (Spring 1998): pp. 2–20. For a general treatment of African Americans and Illinois schools, see Robert L. McCaul, *The Black Struggle for Public Schooling in Nineteenth-Century Illinois* (Carbondale: Southern Illinois University Press, 1987).

In *Blake v. People*, the Supreme Court found an 1879 act of the legislature that provided for the organization of sanitary districts to be constitutional. Another case at the same term, *Peck v. Herrington*, ruled that land owners could tile drain their land. The symbiotic relationship between agriculture and industry are demonstrated in these two cases as the *Peck* case allowed farmers to convert low-lying lands to increase significantly agricultural production, while the *Blake* case provided oversight for a growing sanitation industry for an exploding population. *Blake v. People*, 109 Ill. 504 (1884) and *Peck v. Herrington*, 109 Ill. 611 (1884).

At the end of the nineteenth century in one of the last cases decided before 1900, the Supreme Court of Illinois summed up its independence as a branch of Illinois government in *In re Day*. It asserted the right of the Court to prescribe the qualifications for admission to the bar of Illinois and declared unconstitutional a law passed by the legislature to fix those qualifications. *In Re Day*, 181 Ill. 73 (1899).

6. James Willard Hurst, *The Growth of the American Law: The Law Makers* (Boston: Little, Brown and Co., 1950).

7. James Willard Hurst, *Law and the Conditions of Freedom in the Nineteenth-Century United States* (Madison: University of Wisconsin Press, 1956).

8. James Willard Hurst, "The State of Legal History," *Reviews in American History* 10 (December 1982): p. 292. John R. Wunder also makes this argument in John R. Wunder, *Law and the Great Plains: Essays on the Legal History of the Heartland* (Westport, CT: Greenwood Press, 1996), pp. 4–6.

9. See particularly the works of John Phillip Reid on the movement of law on the Overland Trail. John Phillip Reid, *Law for the Elephant: Property and Social Behavior on the Overland Trail* (San Marino, CA: Huntington Library, 1997) and John Phillip Reid, *Policing the Elephant: Crime, Punishment, and Social Behavior on the Overland Trail* (San Marino, CA: Huntington Library, 1997).

10. Morton J. Horwitz, *The Transformation of American Law, 1780–1860* (Cambridge: Harvard University Press, 1977); Kermit L. Hall, *The Magic Mirror: Law in American History* (New York: Oxford University Press, 1989); Peter Karsten, *Heart versus Head: Judge-Made Law in Nineteenth-Century America* (Chapel Hill: University of North Carolina Press, 1997), p. 26.

11. Martha L. Benner and Cullom Davis, eds., *The Law Practice of Abraham Lincoln: Complete Documentary Edition* (Urbana: University of Illinois Press, 2000); Daniel W. Stowell et al., eds., *The Papers of Abraham Lincoln: Legal Documents and Cases,* 4 vols. (Charlottesville: University of Virginia Press, 2008).

12. Daniel W. Stowell, ed., *In Tender Consideration: Women, Families, and the Law in Abraham Lincoln's Illinois* (Urbana: University of Illinois Press, 2002).

13. See particularly John Phillip Reid, cited earlier, as well Michael Grossberg's work on family law, William Novak's work on regulation, Norma Basch's work on divorce, and James Ely's work on railroads. Michael Grossberg, *Governing the Hearth: Law and the Family in Nineteenth-Century America* (Chapel Hill: University of North Carolina Press, 1985); Michael Grossberg *A Judgment for Solomon: The D'Hauteville Case and Legal Experience in Antebellum America* (New York: Cambridge University Press, 1996); William J. Novak, *The People's Welfare: Law and Regulation in Nineteenth-Century America* (Chapel Hill: University of North Carolina Press, 1996); Norma Basch, *Framing American Divorce: From the Revolutionary Generation to the Victorians* (Berkeley: University of California Press, 1999); James W. Ely Jr., *Railroads and American Law* (Lawrence: University Press of Kansas, 2001).

1. "Whose Home Is in the Wilderness"

1. The office of *greffier* combined many of the functions of court clerks, recorders, and notaries public. The word means "scribe," and the official status of the office in France dates from 1521. Jean Brissaud, *A History of French Public Law* (Boston: Little, Brown and Company, 1915), p. 471. In the Illinois country the greffier kept several important public records such as the *Registre des Donations* and the *Registre des Audiences,* referred to hereafter.

2. The original Fort de Chartres was a structure of earth and logs, and was located approximately a quarter of a mile west of the site of the stone structure begun about 1750. The State of Illinois has restored the main gate and certain of the buildings of the stone fort. It is located approximately twenty miles northwest of Chester, Illinois.

3. To the French, the Mississippi was always *La Grande Riviere,* and the Ohio was *La Belle Riviere.*

4. Quoted by Natalia Maree Belting, *Kaskaskia under the French Regime* (Urbana: University of Illinois Press, 1948), p. 19. The author used the version in Francis Parkman, *A Half-Century of Conflict,* 2 vols. (Boston: Little, Brown and Company, 1902), Vol. 1, pp. 317–18.

5. Law is here used in the sense of a body of rules applied by judges in the determination of controversies.

6. Clarence Walworth Alvord, *The Illinois Country, 1673–1818* (Springfield: Illinois Centennial Commission, 1920), pp. 117, 132. After a review of the Kaskaskia manuscript records, Belting concluded that the village of Kaskaskia began in 1703 with the settlement there of a number of *coureurs du bois* who had married into the Kaskaskia Indian tribe. Belting, *Kaskaskia under the French Regime*, p. 10. Alexander Davidson and Bernard Stuve, *A Complete History of Illinois from 1673 to 1873* (Springfield: Illinois Journal Company, 1874, p. 110; John Moses, *Illinois, Historical and Statistical* (Chicago: Fergus Printing Company, 1895), pp. 81–85. See Sidney Breese, *The Early History of Illinois* (Chicago: S. B. Meyers & Co., 1884), pp. 141–53. Also see Carl J. Eckberg, *French Roots in the Illinois Country: The Mississippi Frontier in Colonial Times* (Urbana: University of Illinois Press, 1998), and Stephen Aron, *American Confluence: The Missouri Frontier from Border Land to Border State* (Bloomington: University of Indiana Press, 2006).

7. See the discussion and annotations in John Francis McDermott and others, eds., *Old Cahokia: A Narrative and Documents Illustrating the First Century of Its History* (St. Louis: St. Louis Historical Documents Foundation, 1949), pp. 4–10. See also Joseph H. L. Schlarman, *From Quebec to New Orleans: The Story of the French in America* (Belleville, IL: Buechler Publishing Company, 1929), pp. 130–59. Henry Brown stated that Kaskaskia and Cahokia were both established by followers of La Salle who were left there by him in 1682. Henry Brown, *The History of Illinois from its First Discovery and Settlement to the Present Time* (New York: J. Winchester, New World Press, 1844), p. 124.

8. In 1949, the 250th anniversary of the founding of Cahokia was celebrated and efforts were made to obtain funds for the rebuilding of the old church. The State of Illinois reconstructed the courthouse, after removal of part of its materials from Wooded Island in Chicago's Jackson Park, where the material had been taken at the time of Chicago's first World's Fair. One or two of the houses still standing on the site of the village common were constructed in French days and have been remodeled and covered with modern siding. Cahokia Court House is currently a historic site owned and operated by the Illinois Historic Preservation Agency.

9. See Charles J. Balesi, *The Time of the French in the Heart of North America, 1673–1818* (Chicago: Alliance Francaise, 1992).

10. Belting, *Kaskaskia under the French Regime*, p. 21; Clarence Walworth Alvord, ed., *Cahokia Records, 1778–1790* (Springfield: Illinois State Historical Library, 1907), pp. xxiv, xxv.

11. Alvord, *The Illinois Country, 1673–1818*, p. 154.

12. The Kaskaskia Manuscripts include fragments of proceedings before the Provincial Council (Court) in the 1720s. For a history of the Kaskaskia Manuscripts, see Margaret Kimball Brown, "The Kaskaskia Manuscripts," *Illinois Libraries* 62 (April 1980): pp. 312–24.

13. Alvord, *The Illinois Country, 1673–1818*, p. 151.

14. Professor Charles C. Pickett, one of the original three members of the faculty of the law school of the University of Illinois, and until his death, a member of the faculty of Chicago-Kent College of Law, has told the author that he was advised by the then circuit judge of Randolph County that there were several boxes of manuscripts in the French language standing in various rooms of the courthouse at Chester that were used to light fires and as waste paper. These facts were communicated by him to the history department of the university, and Professor Alvord was delegated to go to Chester in 1905 or 1906 and examine this material. See Alvord's introduction to *Cahokia Records, 1778–1790*. See also, Marguerite Jenison Pease, "Archives in Randolph County: A Revised Inventory," *Illinois Libraries* 43 (June 1961): pp. 433–48, and Marguerite Jenison Pease, "Early Illinois Records in Randolph County," *Illinois Libraries* 46 (June 1964): pp. 364–66.

15. Chiefly useful on the period covered by this chapter are the Cahokia manuscripts in the Illinois State Archives and particularly those in the Perrin collection. Some other records of interest are in the St. Clair County Court House at Belleville. The documents edited by McDermott in *Old Cahokia* are of special interest.

A considerable collection of French documents and records from Cahokia were assembled by J. Nick Perrin and were eventually transferred to the Illinois State Archives in Springfield where they have been properly preserved. Many of these have been calendared and translated. Chance has preserved some of the French records from the destruction of early records that occurred elsewhere in Illinois, notably at Shawneetown.

16. The record of this case, a *Suitte de L'interogattoire*, or Proceeding of Inquiry, before Michel Chassin and Perillau, the *greffier*, is found in a box of miscellaneous documents in the office of the Randolph County Circuit Clerk at Chester, to which place the Kaskaskia records were removed. The case involved one Pierre Perico, who was accused and convicted of stealing from

the *magasin* or warehouse at Fort Chartres. He was sentenced to be hanged. See Belting, *Kaskaskia under the French Regime*, p. 60.

17. Alvord, *The Illinois Country*, p. 154.

18. The author examined numerous Council records in the office of the Circuit Clerk of Randolph County in Chester, Illinois.

19. Fragments of this record are among the Kaskaskia manuscripts.

20. Norman Ward Caldwell, *The French in the Mississippi Valley, 1740–1750* (Urbana: University of Illinois Press, 1941), pp. 9–34.

21. Caldwell, *The French in the Mississippi Valley, 1740–1750*, pp. 16–17.

22. Perhaps the best proof is in the *Registre des Donations*, discussed hereafter, which is preserved in the Illinois State Archives at Springfield. Vaudreuil, Governor of Louisianne, on August 8, 1751, issued an "Order of Command" to Macarty (Makarty) who was in command at Fort Chartres. In it were included instructions as to legal matters (the translation is that of Pease): "Although M. Buchet, chief clerk of the marine, is especially charged with judging law suits which may arise among the French, the said Sieur de Macarty on his side will end them so far as he can by the method of accommodation and will entertain them for such disposal, it being of definite consequence to prevent the spirit of chicanery being introduced in new settlements. For that reason he will oppose as far as he can the inhabitants' employing proctors [*gels d'affaires*], whose subtleties would become of dangerous consequence." Theodore Calvin Pease, ed., *Illinois, On the Eve of the Seven Years War, 1747–1755* (Springfield: Illinois State Historical Library, 1940), pp. 295–96. This is the only reference noted to professional advocates in the French records. If lawyers ever appeared in Kaskaskia or Cahokia in the French period, they did not practice as professional advocates.

23. The document of sixty-five pages is in a good state of preservation.

24. Kaskaskia Manuscripts.

25. See Alvord, *The Illinois Country*, p. 151.

26. See Alvord, *The Illinois Country*, p. 151.

27. The administration of the law in transactions such as the voluntary gifts and transfers recorded in the *Registre* was entirely in the hands of the *greffier*. Throughout the French period from 1722 to 1764, there is no evidence that professional advocates appeared for the parties in any legal matters. The performance of formalities required for the validity of various kinds of transactions seems to have depended upon the knowledge and skill of the *greffier* and the Judge, or *Ecrivain Principal*.

2. Law and Anarchy, Virginia County, Federal Territory

1. See Gregory Evans Dowd, *War under Heaven: Pontiac, the Indian Nations, and the British Empire* (Baltimore: Johns Hopkins University, 2002); Norman A. Graebner, "The Illinois Country and the Treaty of Paris of 1783," *Illinois Historical Journal* 78 (Spring 1985): pp. 2–16; and Clarence E. Carter, *Great Britain and the Illinois Country* (Port Washington, NY: Kennikat Press, 1970).

2. See Richard White, *The Middle Ground: Indians, Empires, and Republics in the Great Lakes Region, 1650–1815* (New York: Cambridge University Press, 1991), pp. 269–315.

3. Solon J. Buck, *Illinois in 1818* (Springfield: Illinois Centennial Commission, 1917), p. 88; Clarence Walworth Alvord and Clarence Edward Carter, eds., *The Critical Period, 1763–1765* (Springfield: Illinois State Historical Library, 1915), p. xxxv; Joseph Wallace, *The History of Illinois and Louisiana under the French Rule* (Cincinnati: Robert Clarke & Co., 1893), pp. 387–89; Reuben Gold Thwaites, *France in America, 1497–1763* (New York: Harper Brothers, 1905), p. 285.

4. Just prior to this time difficulties for the Jesuit Order had occurred in France and the Order was banished from Louisianne by an order that became effective in Illinois in 1763. Father Forget Duberger, a priest of the Seminary, left his post at Cahokia after selling the property of the parish to Jean Baptiste Lagrange. See Alvord, *The Illinois Country, 1673–1818*, pp. 268–69. For a discussion of the banishment of the Jesuits, see Alvord and Carter, *The Critical Period, 1763–1765*, pp. 62–133.

5. Alvord, *The Illinois Country, 1673–1818*, p. 264.

6. See Robert Livingston Schuyler, *The Transition in Illinois from British to American Government* (New York: AMS Press, 1966), pp. 1–33.

7. Alvord, *The Illinois Country, 1673–1818*, pp. 265–66. See generally, Clarence Walworth Alvord and Clarence Edwin Carter, eds., *The New Regime, 1765–1767* (Springfield: Illinois State Historical Library, 1916).

8. Letter of Thomas Stirling to General Thomas Gage, 15 December 1765, Alvord and Carter, *The New Regime*, p. 124–27.

9. Robert R. Rea, *Major Robert Farmar of Mobile* (Tuscaloosa: University of Alabama Press, 1990).

10. Alvord, *The Illinois Country*, p. 267; Kaskaskia Manuscripts.

11. Theodore Calvin Pease, *The Story of Illinois* (Chicago: A. C. McClurg & Co., 1925), p. 38.

12. Kaskaskia Manuscripts; Alvord, *The Illinois Country, 1673–1818*, p. 266.

13. Alvord, *The Illinois Country, 1673–1818*, pp. 267–68.

14. Alvord, *The Illinois Country, 1673–1818*, p. 266; several examples of arbitrators' decisions appear among the Kaskaskia Manuscripts.

15. See Edward G. Mason, "British Illinois—Philippe de Rocheblave," and John Moses, "The Rocheblave Papers," in Edward G. Mason, ed., *Early Chicago and Illinois* (Chicago: Fergus Printing Company, 1890).

16. The text here given is that contained in Milo Milton Quaife, ed., *The Conquest of the Illinois by George Rogers Clark* (Chicago: Lakeside Press, 1920), pp. 54–55. The editor Quaife eliminated the difficulties with spelling, punctuation, and style that appeared in the original. See James Alton James, ed., *George Rogers Clark Papers* (Springfield: Illinois State Historical Library, 1912); See William Hayden English, *Conquest of the Country Northwest of the River Ohio, 1778–1783 and Life of George Rogers Clark* (Indianapolis: Bowen-Merrill Company, 1896), in which important Clark papers are reproduced.

17. William Waller Hening, *Statutes at Large: Being a Collection of All the Laws of Virginia*, 13 vols. (Richmond, VA: J. & G. Cochran, 1821), Vol. 9, p. 553; Alvord, *Cahokia Records, 1778–1790*, p. 9.

18. Mason, *Early Chicago and Illinois*, pp. 289–94.

19. See Livingston, *The Transition in Illinois from British to American Government*, pp. 34–140; Carl Evans Boyd, "The County of Illinois," *The American Historical Review* 4 (July 1899): pp. 623–35.

20. Alvord, *Cahokia Records, 1778–1790*, p. 10.

21. Alvord, *The Illinois Country*, pp. 336–37; Mason, *Early Chicago and Illinois*, p. 295.

22. Alvord, *Cahokia Records, 1778–1790*, p. cxviii-cxix; Alvord, *The Illinois Country*, p. 358.

23. The history of these courts is best examined through the remaining records of their official acts. Many of the Cahokia records are in the Illinois State Archives, others are in the St. Clair County Court House at Belleville. Many important records are in Alvord, ed., *Cahokia Records, 1778–1790*; most of the important Kaskaskia records are in the office of the Circuit Clerk of Randolph County in the Court House at Chester, Illinois, although some records from Kaskaskia have turned up among the Cahokia Manuscripts. Many of the Kaskaskia records have been microfilmed and are available in the Illinois State Archives in Springfield.

24. Alvord, *The Illinois Country*, p. 376; see generally, Alvord, *Cahokia Records, 1778–1790*, pp. ix–clvi; see also McDermott, *Old Cahokia*.

25. Kaskaskia Manuscripts.

26. Alvord, *Cahokia Records, 1778–1790*, p. 167; Cahokia Manuscripts, Perrin Collection, Illinois State Archives, Springfield, Illinois.

27. Kaskaskia Manuscripts, Miscellaneous Box.

28. Cahokia Manuscripts, Perrin Collection, Illinois State Archives.

29. Alvord, *The Illinois Country*, pp. 363–69.

30. Alvord, *The Illinois Country*, pp. 374–75; Alvord, *Cahokia Records, 1778–1790*, pp. cxlv–cli.

31. Alvord, *Cahokia Records, 1778–1790*, p. 605; Cahokia Manuscripts.

32. Theodore Calvin Pease, ed., *The Laws of the Northwest Territory 1788–1800* (Springfield: Illinois State Historical Library, 1925), p. 522.

33. Pease, *The Laws of the Northwest Territory 1788–1800*, p. 521.

34. Pease, *The Laws of the Northwest Territory 1788–1800*, pp. xvii–xviii.

3. The Coming of the Common Law

1. See Peter S. Onuf, *Statehood and Union: A History of the Northwest Ordinance* (Bloomington: Indiana University Press, 1987); and Robert M. Taylor Jr., ed., *The Northwest Ordinance 1787: A Bicentennial Handbook* (Indianapolis: Indiana Historical Society, 1987).

2. Pease, *The Laws of the Northwest Territory, 1788–1800*, p. xvii; see chapters I through IX in William Henry Smith, *The St. Clair Papers: Life and Public Services of Arthur St. Clair*, 2 vols. (Cincinnati: Robert Clarke & Co., 1882).

3. Pease, *The Laws of the Northwest Territory*, p. xvii.

4. Pease, *The Laws of the Northwest Territory*, pp. xvii–xviii.

5. Pease, *The Laws of the Northwest Territory*, pp. 1–8.

6. Clarence Edwin Carter, ed., *The Territorial Papers of the United States: Vol. II, The Territory Northwest of the River Ohio 1787–1803* (Washington, DC: Government Printing Office, 1934), pp. 39–40.

7. Smith, *St. Clair Papers*, Vol. II, p. 72.

8. Smith, *St. Clair Papers*, Vol. II, p. 72.

9. The judicial records of the General Court have not been found. Inquiries of the National Archives, and at Marietta, Cincinnati, Columbus, and Chillicothe, Ohio, as well as at Vincennes, Indiana, failed to produce results. It is possible that they have been destroyed, although the record of the General Courts of Indiana and Illinois Territories are available.

10. Alvord, *The Illinois Country*, p. 378.

11. Alvord, *Cahokia Records, 1778–1790*, p. lxiii.

12. Alvord, *The Illinois Country*, pp. 378, 404.

13. May Allison, "The Government of Illinois, 1790–1799," *Transactions of The Illinois State Historical Society for the year 1907* (Springfield: Illinois State Historical Library, 1907), pp. 282–83.

14. Pease, *The Laws of the Northwest Territory*, pp. 156–57, see discussion by Francis S. Philbrick in *Laws of The Illinois Territory, 1809–1818* (Springfield: Illinois State Historical Library, 1950), pp. xxi–xxxix.

15. Alvord, *The Illinois Country*, pp. 404–5.

16. Carter, *The Territorial Papers of the United States*, Vol. II, p. 46.

17. Smith, *St. Clair Papers*, Vol. II, p. 71.

18. The Perrin Collection, Illinois State Archives, Springfield, Illinois.

19. W. A. Burt Jones, "John Rice Jones," in Mason, *Early Chicago and Illinois*, pp. 230–70; Francis S. Philbrick, ed. *The Laws of the Indiana Territory, 1801–1809* (Springfield: Illinois State Historical Library, 1930), p. xviii; Charles E. Burgess, "John Rice Jones, Citizen of Many Territories," *Journal of the Illinois State Historical Society* 61 (Spring 1968): pp. 58–82.

20. No record of an official order that the records be kept in English has been found.

21. See James R. Cameron, *Frederick William Maitland and the History of English Law* (Norman: University of Oklahoma Press, 1961).

22. Carter, *The Territorial Papers of the United States*, Vol. II, p. 329.

23. The Cahokia Records, Illinois State Archives, Springfield, Illinois.

24. Kaskaskia and Cahokia Records.

25. Cahokia Court Records, Illinois State Archives Building, Springfield, Illinois.

26. Cahokia Court Records.

27. Alvord, *The Illinois Country*, p. 407.

28. Allison, "The Government of Illinois, 1790–1799," p. 290.

29. Allison, "The Government of Illinois, 1790–1799," pp. 287–88.

30. Alvord, *The Illinois Country*, p. 405.

31. Carter, *Territorial Papers of the United States*, Vol. II, pp. 542–43.

32. See Darrel E. Bigham, ed., *Indiana Territory: A Bicentennial Perspective* (Indianapolis: Indiana Historical Society, 2001).

33. Philbrick, *The Laws of Indiana Territory*, p. xvi.

34. Philbrick, *The Laws of Indiana Territory*, pp. xv–xvi.

35. Philbrick, *The Laws of Indiana Territory*, pp. clxiii–clxviii.

36. George Bullitt, William C. Carr, Isaac Darnielle, Benjamin H. Doyle, Rufus Easton, James Haggin, Robert Hamilton, William Hamilton, Edward Hempstead, Henry Jones, John Rice Jones, William Mears, Nathaniel Pope,

John Rector, Robert Robinson, John Scott, and John Taylor. Philbrick, *The Laws of Indiana Territory*, p. ccxxxiv.

37. For an examination of non-English colonization on the North American continent, see Alan Taylor, *American Colonies: The Settling of North America* (New York: Penguin Books, 2001).

38. Philbrick, *The Laws of Indiana Territory*, pp. cxcv–cxcvi.

4. A Frontier Court

1. For a general picture of Illinois during this period, see Robert E. Hartley, *Lewis and Clark in the Illinois Country: The Little-Told Story* (Westminster, CT: Sniktau Publications, 2002).

2. W. A. Burt Jones, "Rice Jones," in Mason, *Early Chicago and Illinois*, pp. 271–84.

3. For more information about violence on the Illinois frontier in general, see James E. Davis, *Frontier Illinois* (Bloomington: Indiana University Press, 1998).

4. Alvord, *The Illinois Country*, p. 425.

5. Nathaniel Pope, *Laws of the Territory of Illinois Revised and Digested under the Authority of the Legislature* (Kaskaskia, IL: Matthew Duncan, 1815).

6. Alvord, *The Illinois Country*, p. 430.

7. Francis S. Philbrick, ed., *Pope's Digest 1815* (Springfield: Illinois State Historical Library, 1938), p. xii.

8. Jesse B. Thomas was well-known by historians in the 1940s and 1950s as the U.S. Senator from Illinois who proposed the Missouri Compromise in 1820 to resolve the largest slavery crisis that the new country had faced.

9. Jones appears never to have served as a judge and has no biographical information. Alvord, *The Illinois Country*, p. 430.

10. Clarence E. Carter, ed., *The Territorial Papers of the United States: Vol. V. The Territory of Mississippi* (Washington, DC: Government Printing Office, 1937), p. 385.

11. John Reynolds, *The Pioneer History of Illinois*, 2nd ed. (Chicago: Fergus Printing Company, 1887), p. 401.

12. Thomas Ford, *A History of Illinois* (Chicago: S. C. Griggs, 1854) p. 30.

13. See David Kenney and Robert E. Hartley, *An Uncertain Tradition: U.S. Senators from Illinois, 1818–2003* (Carbondale: Southern Illinois University Press, 2003), pp. 4–8.

14. Francis S. Philbrick, ed., *The Laws of Illinois Territory, 1809–1818* (Springfield: Illinois State Historical Library, 1950), pp. 5–18.

15. Philbrick, *The Laws of Illinois Territory*, pp. 14–16.

16. Philbrick, *The Laws of Illinois Territory*, p. 5.

17. Reynolds, *Pioneer History of Illinois*, p. 402.

18. Philbrick,, *The Laws of Indiana Territory*, pp. lxxvii–lxxix.

19. For more information on land titles in general, see James W. Oberly, *Sixty Million Acres: American Veterans and the Public Lands before the Civil War* (Kent, OH: Kent State University Press, 1990).

20. Philbrick, *The Laws of Indiana Territory*, pp. lxxx–c.

21. Philbrick, *The Laws of Indiana Territory*, pp. lxxxvii–lxxxviii.

22. Philbrick, *The Laws of Indiana Territory*, p. xc.

23. Philbrick, *The Laws of Indiana Territory*, p. cclxv.

24. Philbrick, *The Laws of Indiana Territory*, p. xcv.

25. Alvord, *The Illinois Country*, p. 427.

26. Reynolds, *The Pioneer History of Illinois*, p. 402.

27. Philbrick, *The Laws of Illinois Territory*, pp. 8–10.

28. Order Book of the General Court, Randolph County Circuit Clerk, Chester, Illinois.

29. See the thorough discussion of this and related problems in Philbrick's introduction to *The Laws of Illinois Territory*.

30. "An Act regulating and defining the duties of the United States' Judges for the territory of Illinois," 3 March 1815, *U.S. Stat. at Large*, 3:237–39.

31. "An Act supplemental to the act, entitled 'An Act regulating and defining the duties of the United States' Judges for the territory of Illinois and for vesting in the courts of the territory of Indiana, a jurisdiction in chancery cases, arising in the said territory,'" 29 April 1816, *U.S. Stat. at Large*, 3:327–28.

5. Lawyers and Law Courts

1. See Ernest R. May, *The Making of the Monroe Doctrine* (Cambridge, MA: Belknap Press, 1975).

2. Biographies of Clark, even the most recent by John Bakeless, *Background to Glory: The Life of George Rogers Clark* (Philadelphia: J. B. Lippincott Company, 1957) leave many questions about him unanswered. He possessed a keen intelligence and superb qualities of leadership. For more recent biographies of Clark, see Lowell H. Harrison, *George Rogers Clark and the War in the West* (Lexington: University Press of Kentucky, 2001); William R. Nester, *George Rogers Clark: "I Glory in War"* (Norman: University of Oklahoma Press, 2012).

3. See Nicole Etcheson, *The Emerging Midwest: Upland Southerners and the Political Culture of the Old Northwest, 1787–1861* (Bloomington: Indiana University Press, 1996.

4. See Douglas K. Meyer, *Making the Heartland Quilt: A Geographical History of Settlement and Migration in Early-Nineteenth-Century Illinois* (Carbondale: Southern Illinois University Press, 2000).

5. The United States salines were salt springs, one of which was located not far from Shawneetown.

6. The decline of Shawneetown followed the decline in river boat traffic on the Ohio in the age of railroads. A return to some part of its prior importance was made unlikely by the periodic flooding of the Ohio and the breaking of the great levees that protected the old town. Most of the business activity of Shawneetown (including that of the county offices and courts) has been transferred to a new town built several miles back from the river.

7. Records in the offices of the Circuit Court Clerks of St. Clair County (Belleville) and Randolph County (Chester) contain ample proof.

8. See chapter 1 in Mark DeWolfe Howe, *Readings in American Legal History* (Cambridge, MA: Harvard University Press, 1949).

9. See chapter 3.

10. Pease, *Laws of the Northwest Territory*, p. 253.

11. This record is in the Illinois State Archives Building in Springfield, Illinois.

12. See Introduction in Philbrick, *Pope's Digest, 1815*.

13. Theodore Calvin Pease, *The Frontier State* (Chicago: A. C. McClurg & Co., 1919), pp. 94–95. See also, Kenney and Hartley, *An Uncertain Tradition*, pp. 16–19.

14. Frederic B. Crossley, *Courts and Lawyers of Illinois*, 3 vols. (Chicago: The American Historical Society, 1918), Vol. 1, p. 211. See also Kenney and Hartley, *An Uncertain Tradition*, pp. 15–16. Not to be confused with John McLean, the U.S. Supreme Court Justice from 1829 to 1861, who frequently presided in the federal circuit court in Illinois.

15. Philbrick, *Laws of Indiana Territory*, pp. cclxxvi–cclxxvii.

16. See chapter 4 in James Willard Hurst, *The Growth of American Law* (Boston: Little, Brown and Company, 1950).

17. Pease, *Laws of the Northwest Territory*, pp. 88–89.

18. Pease, *Laws of the Northwest Territory*, pp. 340–47.

19. Pease, *Laws of the Northwest Territory*, pp. 170–80.

20. Philbrick, *Laws of Indiana Territory*, p. 2.

21. Philbrick, *Laws of Indiana Territory*, p. 86.

22. Philbrick, *Laws of Indiana Territory*, p. 141–42.

23. Philbrick, *Laws of Indiana Territory*, pp. 340–44.

24. Philbrick, *Laws of Indiana Territory*, pp. 47, 561.

25. Philbrick, *Laws of Illinois Territory*, pp. 238–39.

26. Reynolds, *Pioneer History of Illinois*, pp. 395–97; John M. Scott, *Supreme Court of Illinois, 1818: Its First Judges and Lawyers* (Bloomington, IL: John M. Scott, 1896), pp. 308–12.

27. Alvord, *The Illinois Country*, pp. 461–64; R. Carlyle Buley, *The Old Northwest* (Indianapolis: Indiana Historical Society, 1950) pp. 78–93.

28. See Richard V. Carpenter, "The Illinois Constitutional Convention of 1818," *Journal of the Illinois State Historical Society* 6 (October 1913): 327–424.

29. Illinois Constitution (1818), Art. III, Sec. 19.

30. Scott, *Supreme Court of Illinois, 1818*, pp. 60–74; "Joel Childress and Joseph Philips Families," *Rutherford County [Tennessee] Historical Society Publication No. 9* (Summer 1977), 23; Court Minutes Book C (1808–1810), 3 July 1809, 142, Rutherford County Archives, Murfreesboro, Tennessee. The editor located much of the information on Joseph Philips and replaced text in the manuscript in which the author stated that nothing much was known of Philips after 1822.

31. Scott, *Supreme Court of Illinois, 1818*, pp. 75–99.

32. Ford, *A History of Illinois*, p. 29; Scott, *Supreme Court of Illinois, 1818*, pp. 14–34.

33. Ford, *A History of Illinois*, pp. 105–6; John Reynolds, *My Own Times: Embracing Also the History of My Life* (Chicago: Fergus Printing Company, 1879), pp. 1–383; Scott, *Supreme Court of Illinois, 1818*, pp. 100–258.

34. John Dean Caton, *Early Bench and Bar of Illinois* (Chicago: Chicago Legal News Company, 1893), pp. 173–77.

35. See chapter 7.

36. *Cornelius v. Boucher*, 1 Ill. (Breese) 32 (1820).

37. Crossley, *Courts and Lawyers of Illinois*, Vol. 1, p. 221.

38. *Mason v. Wash*, 1 Ill. (Breese) 39 (1822).

39. *Ackless v. Seekright ex dem. Lunceford*, 1 Ill. (Breese) 76 (1823).

6. Law and Politics

1. Ford, *A History of Illinois*, p. 24; Reynolds, *The Pioneer History of Illinois*, p. 410.

2. Glover Moore, *The Missouri Controversy, 1819–1821* (Lexington: University of Kentucky Press, 1953); Robert Pierce Forbes, *The Missouri Compromise and Its Aftermath: Slavery and the Meaning of America* (Chapel Hill: University of North Carolina Press, 2007).

3. "An Act Constituting and Regulating the Supreme Court and Circuit Courts of This State," 29 December 1824, *Laws of Illinois* (1825), pp. 36–48.

4. Reynolds, *My Own Times*, p. 160.

5. Ford, *A History of Illinois*, p. 49.

6. Michael J. Howlett, *Keepers of the Seal: A History of the Secretaries of State of Illinois and How Their Office Grew* (Springfield: State of Illinois, 1977), pp. 29–31.

7. Thomas J. McCormack, ed., *Memoirs of Gustave Koerner, 1809–1896*, 2 vols. (Cedar Rapids, IA: The Torch Press, 1909), Vol. 1, p. 374.

8. Ford, *A History of Illinois*, p. 220.

9. Usher F. Linder, *Reminiscences of the Early Bench and Bar of Illinois*, 2nd ed. (Chicago: Chicago Legal News Company, 1879), pp. 73–74.

10. McCormack, *Memoirs of Gustave Koerner, 1809–1896*, Vol. 1, p. 374.

11. Caton, *Early Bench and Bar of Illinois*, pp. 170–71.

12. McCormack, *Memoirs of Gustave Koerner, 1809–1896*, Vol. 1, p. 373.

13. Philbrick, *Pope's Digest*, p. lxix.

14. *The Revised Code of Laws of Illinois* (Vandalia, IL: Robert Blackwell, 1827); *The Revised Code of Laws of Illinois* (Shawneetown, IL: Alexander F. Grant & Co., 1829).

15. Reynolds, *My Own Times*, p. 174.

16. *Chandler v. Gay*, 1 Ill. (Breese) 88 (1825).

17. *People ex rel. Ewing v. Forquer*, 1 Ill. (Breese) 104 (1825).

18. *Marbury v. Madison*, 5 U.S. (1 Cranch) 137 (1803).

19. 1 Ill. (Breese) 104 at 112.

20. *Coles v. County of Madison*, 1 Ill. (Breese) 154 (1826).

21. *Snyder v. State Bank of Illinois*, 1 Ill. (Breese) 161 (1826).

22. *Phoebe, a woman of color v. Jay*, 1 Ill. (Breese) 268 (1828).

23. *Fanny, a woman of color v. Montgomery et al.*, 1 Ill. (Breese) 247 (1828).

24. *Nance, a girl of color v. Howard*, 1 Ill. (Breese) 242 (1828).

25. *Boon v. Juliet*, 2 Ill. (1 Scam.) 258 (1836).

26. *Choisser v. Hargrave*, 2 Ill. (1 Scam.) 317 (1836).

27. *Jackson ex dem. McConnell v. Wilcox*, 2 Ill. (1 Scam.) 344 (1837).

28. *People ex rel. Wright v. Lamborn*, 2 Ill. (1 Scam.) 123 (1834).

29. *Stone v. People*, 3 Ill. (2 Scam.) 326 (1840).

30. *Linn v. President and Directors of the State Bank of Illinois*, 2 Ill. (1 Scam.) 87 (1833).

31. *Craig v. State of Missouri*, 29 U.S. (4 Pet.) 410 (1830).

32. 1 Ill. (Breese) 161.

33. 2 Ill. (1 Scam.) 123 at 125–26.

34. Ford, *A History of Illinois*, p. 166–67.

35. Ford, *A History of Illinois*, p. 168.

36. *People ex rel. Matheny v. Mobley*, 2 Ill. (1 Scam.) 215.

37. *Field v. People ex rel. McClernand*, 3 Ill (2 Scam.) 79 (1839).

38. Ford, *A History of Illinois*, p. 215.

39. *Spragins v. Houghton*, 3 Ill. (2 Scam.) 377 (1840).

40. Ford, *A History of Illinois*, p. 220. See also Robert W. Johanssen, *Stephen A. Douglas* (Urbana: University of Illinois Press, 1997), pp. 93–95.

7. Giants in the Prairie

1. For more information on the Black Hawk War, see Patrick J. Jung, *The Black Hawk War of 1832* (Norman: University of Oklahoma Press, 2007).

2. See Paul Simon, *Lincoln's Preparation for Greatness: The Illinois Legislative Years* (Urbana: University of Illinois Press, 1971), pp. 76–106. For further information about Vandalia's years as Illinois' capital city, see Paul E. Stroble, *High on the Okaw's Western Bank: Vandalia, Illinois 1819–39* (Urbana: University of Illinois Press, 1992).

3. The National Road or Cumberland Road, as it was also known, was not actually opened as an improved road to Vandalia until 1852 but was in use prior to the date. See Philip D. Jordan, *The National Road* (Indianapolis: Bobbs-Merrill Company, 1948); James Truslow Adams, ed., *Dictionary of American History*, 6 Vols. (New York: Charles Scribner's Sons, 1946), Vol. 4, p. 63; Buley, *The Old Northwest*, Vol. 1, pp. 446–49.

4. The author refers to the story, never proven true, that Lincoln jumped out of a window in Vandalia's new statehouse. He actually jumped out of the Methodist Church, which was serving as the House of Representatives, in Springfield in 1840. Sunderine Temple and Wayne Temple, *Illinois' Fifth Capitol* (Springfield, IL: Phillips Brothers, 1988), pp. 41–44.

5. See Frederick Gerhard, *Illinois as It Is* (Chicago: Keen and Lee, 1857), pp. 271–88; *Illinois in 1837* (Philadelphia: S. Augustus Mitchell, 1837), pp. 11–15.

6. Joliet was originally named Juliet. See *Illinois In 1837*, p. 123.

7. This attitude was characteristic of all pioneer communities and would become familiar in the later fiction stories of the West. Ford, *A History of Illinois*, p. 86.

8. See Merton L. Dillon, *Elijah P. Lovejoy, Abolitionist Editor* (Urbana: University of Illinois Press, 1961).

9. Ford, *A History of Illinois*, pp. 234–35.

10. Theodore Calvin Pease, *The Frontier State* (Chicago, A. C. McClurg & Co., 1919), p. 367.

11. Pease, *The Frontier State*, p. 368.

12. Pease, *The Frontier State*, p. 367. The "red badge of courage" refers to the 1895 Stephen Crane novel *The Red Badge of Courage* in which the protagonist wishes for a battle wound during the Civil War.

13. *People ex rel. Peair v. Board of Education*, 127 Ill. 613 (1889); *People ex rel. Bibb v. Mayor and Common Council of Alton*, 179 Ill. 615 (1899); *People ex rel. Bibb v. Mayor and Common Council of Alton*, 193 Ill. 309 (1901); *People ex rel. Bibb v. Mayor and Common Council of Alton*, 209 Ill. 461 (1904); *People ex rel. Bibb v. Mayor and Common Council of Alton*, 221 Ill. 275 (1906); *People ex rel. Bibb v. Mayor and Common Council of Alton*, 233 Ill. 542 (1908).

14. See William J. Novak, *The People's Welfare: Law & Regulation in Nineteenth Century America* (Chapel Hill: University of North Carolina Press, 1996).

15. "An Act to Establish Circuit Courts," 23 February 1841, *Laws of Illinois* (1841), p. 105; "An Act Reorganizing the Judiciary of the State of Illinois," 10 February 1841, *Laws of Illinois* (1841), pp. 173–74.

16. "An Act to Establish Circuit Courts," *Laws of Illinois*, p. 105.

17. "An Act to Establish Circuit Courts," *Laws of Illinois*, p. 105.

18. *Duncan v. McAffee*, 3 Ill. (2 Scam.) 559 (1840).

19. See generally George Fort Milton, *The Eve of Conflict: Stephen A. Douglas and the Needless War* (Boston: Houghton Mifflin Company, 1934), pp. 15–35; Frank E. Stevens, *Life of Stephen Arnold Douglas* (Springfield: Illinois State Historical Society, 1924), pp. 247–363. For a more modern biography of Douglas, see Johannsen, *Stephen A. Douglas*.

20. Stevens, *Life of Stephen Arnold Douglas*, p. 273.

21. Stevens, *Life of Stephen Arnold Douglas*, pp. 288–89.

22. *Field v. People ex rel. McClernand*, 3 Ill. 79.

23. These names appear in the reports of cases, but other equally prominent lawyers undoubtedly appeared, for names of counsel were frequently omitted in reporting cases.

24. See for example *Warren v. Nexsen*, 4 Ill. (3 Scam.) 38 (1841).

25. Milo Milton Quaife, ed., Thomas Ford, *A History of Illinois*, 2 vols. (Chicago: Lakeside Press, 1945), Vol. 1, pp. xv–xxxiii.

26. Ford himself does not mention this incident in his *History*.

27. Quaife, ed., Ford, *A History of Illinois*, Vol. 1, pp. xxxv–xliii.

28. Quaife, ed., Ford, *A History of Illinois*, Vol. 1, p. xxxii.

29. See the biographical sketch by Melville W. Fuller in Breese, *The Early History of Illinois*, pp. 3–60. Hartley and Kenney, *An Uncertain Tradition*, pp. 27–30.

30. Scates resigned in 1847 but returned to the court in 1853. In the interim, he practiced law in Mt. Vernon.

31. Linder's contemporary appraisal is of interest, *Reminiscences of the Early Bench and Bar of Illinois*, pp. 388–89. See also Daniel W. Stowell, *Samuel H. Treat: Prairie Justice* (Springfield: Illinois Historic Preservation Agency, 2005).

32. Robert P. Howard, *Mostly Good and Competent Men*, 2nd ed. (Springfield: University of Illinois Springfield), pp. 58–67.

33. Ford, *A History of Illinois*, p. 258–61.

34. For a contemporary biography of Joseph Smith, see Richard Lyman Bushman, *Joseph Smith: Rough Stone Rolling* (New York: Alfred A. Knopf, 2005).

35. "An Act to Incorporate the City of Nauvoo," 1 February 1841, *Laws of Illinois* (1841), pp. 52–57.

36. Ford, *A History of Illinois*, pp. 325–28.

37. Ford, *A History of Illinois*, pp. 326–28.

38. Ford, *A History of Illinois*, p. 321.

39. See Jeffrey N. Walker, "Habeas Corpus in Early Nineteenth-Century Mormonism: Joseph Smith's Legal Bulwark for Personal Freedom," *BYU Studies Quarterly* 52 (2013) 1: pp. 5–97 for a more modern treatment of Joseph Smith's use of the writ of habeas corpus.

40. Ford, *A History of Illinois*, pp. 336–37.

41. For an account of the murder and the trial of the conspirators, see Dallin H. Oaks and Marvin S. Hill, *Carthage Conspiracy: The Trial of the Accused Assassins of Joseph Smith* (Urbana: University of Illinois Press, 1975).

42. Ford, *A History of Illinois*, pp. 403–36; Pease, *The Frontier State*, pp. 356–62.

43. Ford, *A History of Illinois*, p. 436.

44. Lack of accurate information and the refusal of the Mormon leaders to make any information available contributed greatly to their difficulties.

45. Social and religious barriers maintained by the French in territorial days created difficulties for them with the incoming Yankees, Virginians, and others, and contributed greatly to their decline in influence.

46. Restrictions against the crimes of extreme violence, such as murder and rape, had become fairly effective, but outbreaks of mob rule and vigilante activities were common.

47. There was one other vacancy. Lockwood actually resigned in November 1848, a month before the new court sat. David M. Woodson replaced Lockwood on the court but he never sat on the supreme bench, nor heard any cases. *Daily Illinois State Journal* (Springfield), 28 August 1877, p. 2.

48. The salaries of the justices were fixed at $1,500 a year. "An Act to Establish Circuit Courts," *Laws of Illinois*, p. 104.

49. *Andrews, et al. v. Sullivan*, 7 Ill. (2 Gilm.) 327 (1845).

50. *Jackson, ex dem. McConnell v. Wilcox*, 2 Ill. (1 Scam.) 344 (1837).

51. *Wilcox v. Jackson, ex dem. McConnell*, 38 U.S. (13 Pet.) 498 (1839).

52. 38 U.S. 498 at 508.

53. *Mills et al. v. Brown et al.*, 41 U.S. (16 Pet.) 525 (1842); *Moore v. People*, 55 U.S. (14 How.) 13 (1852); *Mills et al. v. The County of St. Clair*, 49 U.S. (8 How.) 569 (1850); *Udell, et al. v. Davidson*, 48 U.S. (7 How.) 769 (1849).

54. *Seeley v. Peters*, 10 Ill. (5 Gilm.) 130 (1848).

55. *Jarrot v. Jarrot*, 7 Ill. (2 Gilm.) 1 (1845).

56. 7 Ill. (2 Gilm.) 1 at 30–33 (Opinion of Young, J.).

57. Linder says he was "the Falstaff of the Bench." *Reminiscences*, p. 73. Caton's appraisal was that "he was a man of very considerable ability and a much better judge than he usually has the credit of being." *Early Bench and Bar of Illinois*, p. 177.

58. Davidson and Stuve, *History of Illinois*, p. 460 note.

59. For a modern treatment of the impeachment episode, see Bryon C. Andreasen, *Defending Judge Browne: A Case Study in the Legal, Legislative, and Political Workings of Abraham Lincoln's Illinois* (Springfield: Illinois Supreme Court Historic Preservation Commission, 2013).

60. Caton said that he had "reason to believe that he [Browne] never wrote an opinion." *Early Bench and Bar of Illinois*, p. 173: However, the evidence indicates that Browne wrote some opinions, although some unquestionably were prepared for him by other judges. See Scott, *Supreme Court of Illinois*, pp. 75–97.

8. Trails of the Circuit Riders

1. *Munn v. People*, 69 Ill. 80 (1873).

2. See the appraisal of Douglas by Allan Nevins in *The Emergence of Lincoln*, 2 vols. (New York, Charles Scribner's Sons, 1950), Vol. 1, pp. 24–26.

3. For primary source material, see *Seeley v. Peters* (L01728) in Martha L. Benner and Cullom Davis and others, eds., *The Law Practice of Abraham*

Lincoln: Complete Documentary Edition, 2nd ed. (Springfield: Illinois Historic Preservation Agency, 2009), www.lawpracticeofabrahamlincoln.org.

4. *Seeley v. Peters*, 10 Ill. 130 at 141.

5. Caton discussed the case in his book *Early Bench and Bar of Illinois*, pp. 181–84.

6. *Misner v. Lighthall*, 13 Ill. 609 (1852).

7. Illinois Constitution (1848), Art. V, Sec. 2.

8. Illinois Constitution (1848), Art. V, Sec. 12.

9. Illinois Constitution (1848), Art. V, Sec. 11.

10. Illinois Constitution (1848), Art. V, Sec. 5.

11. Illinois Constitution (1848), Art. V, Sec. 7.

12. See "A Tour of Two Circuits with Lincoln (Spring 1842)" in Daniel W. Stowell, et al., eds., *The Papers of Abraham Lincoln: Legal Documents and Cases*, 4 vols. (Charlottesville: University of Virginia, 2008), Vol. 1, pp. 191–238; and "A Tour of the Circuit with Lincoln (Spring 1852)" in Stowell, *The Papers of Abraham Lincoln*, Vol. 2, pp. 211–304.

13. Illinois Constitution (1848), Art. V, Sec. 10.

14. McCormack, *Memoirs of Gustave Koerner, 1809–1896*, Vol. 1, p. 524.

15. Caton, *Early Bench and Bar of Illinois*, pp. 154–55.

16. Caton, *Early Bench and Bar of Illinois*, p. 157.

17. Illinois Constitution (1848), Art. V, Sec. 4.

18. "John D. Caton," in Allen Johnson, ed., *Dictionary of American Biography*, 20 vols. (New York: Charles Scribner's Sons, 1929), Vol. 3, pp. 575–76; Palmer, *The Bench and Bar of Illinois*, Vol. 1, pp. 39–41.

19. Caton, *Early Bench and Bar of Illinois*, pp. 170–71.

20. Wayne C. Townley, *Two Judges of Ottawa* (Carbondale, IL: Egypt Book House, 1948), p. 38.

21. Samuel Finley Breese Morse was a cousin of Sidney Breese. Breese, *The Early History of Illinois*, p. 25.

22. Townley, *Two Judges of Ottawa*, pp. 38–41.

23. Townley, *Two Judges of Ottawa*, pp. 34–35.

24. Palmer, *The Bench and Bar of Illinois*, Vol. 1 pp. 34–35.

25. Palmer, *The Bench and Bar of Illinois*, Vol. 1, pp. 51–54.

26. Palmer, *The Bench and Bar of Illinois*, Vol. 1, pp. 35–36.

27. Palmer, *The Bench and Bar of Illinois*, Vol. 1, pp. 54–55.

28. The records in the office of the Circuit Clerk of Randolph County contain two interesting documents that are reproduced verbatim:

To William C. Greenup, Esq., a Justice of Peace for Randolph County, State of Illinois

Sir—a negro man named William Indentured by Ninian Edwards and by him sold to John Edgar and by said Edgar to me is obstinate and refuses to work or render me any service. I claim his time by virtue of his said Indenture and Sale, and wish an order pursuant to the 12th Section of the act of 1819 to have him punished for such his disobedience and refusal; or a warrant to compel him to appear before you to give his reasons for his disobedience, and to hear his case—

Sidney Breese

Kaskaskia
March 31st 1829
Indorsement:

The People	)	89–
vs.	)	Compl. of
William	)	Breese"

"State of Illinois)
) SS.
Randolph County)
The people of the State of Illinois
To Samuel Walker constable of said County

Greeting

Whereas complaint has been made to me by Sidney Breese that William a negro man an Indentured Servant to said Breese is disobedient and refuses to work, and he having been brought before me and declares he will not serve nor obey the said Breese and it appearing satisfactory to me that the said William owes service and labour to said Breese. Therefore you are hereby commanded to take the said William now in your custody and inflict on him fifteen Stripes with a cowhide on his bare back and then deliver him to the said Sidney Breese. Given under my hand and Seal this 31st day of March A.D. 1829.

Wm. C. Greenup, J. P. (Seal)

Indorsement:

> Not Executed by
> Request of the Complainant
> March 31st, 1829
> Sam. Walker Const.

29. For an interesting account of the exchange of letters between Breese and Chief Justice John Marshall of the United States Supreme Court concerning Breese's Reports, see William F. Zacharias, "John Marshall, Sidney Breese, and Illinois' First Law Book," *Chicago Kent Law Review* 33 (September 1955): pp. 291–312.

30. Lewis's observation was based on the portrait of Breese in Northwestern University Law School. See Crossley, *Courts and Lawyers of Illinois*, Vol. 1, p. 181; and see Caton, *Early Bench and Bar of Illinois*, p. 64.

31. Caton, *Early Bench and Bar of Illinois*, pp. 191–94.

32. Caton, *Early Bench and Bar of Illinois*, p. 194.

33. Crossley, *Courts and Lawyers of Illinois*, Vol. 1, pp. 253–54.

34. Newton Bateman and Paul Selby, eds., *Historical Encyclopedia of Illinois* (Chicago: Munsell Publishing Company, 1902), p. 331.

35. "An Act to Prevent Unjust Discriminations and Extortions in the Rate to be Charged by the Different Railroads in this State for the Transportation of Freight on Said Roads," 1 July 1871, *Laws of Illinois* (1871), pp. 635–36.

36. *Chicago and Alton Railroad v. People, ex. rel. Koerner et al.*, 67 Ill. 10 (1873).

37. See Thomas F. Schwartz, "An Egregious Political Blunder: Justin Butterfield, Lincoln, and Illinois Whiggery," *Journal of the Abraham Lincoln Association* 8 (1986): pp. 9–19.

38. 50 Ill. xvii–xviii.

39. For information on juries in general in Illinois, see Stacy Pratt McDermott, *The Jury in Lincoln's America* (Athens: Ohio University Press, 2012).

40. Fred M. Torrey sculpted "Lincoln the Circuit Rider," which is displayed in the Lincoln Tomb in Springfield, Illinois.

41. See Willard L. King, *Lincoln's Manager, David Davis* (Cambridge: Harvard University Press, 1960).

42. Henry Clay Whitney, *Life on the Circuit with Lincoln* (Caldwell, ID: Caxton Printers, 1940), p. 66. Whitney's limitations as an observer are carefully pointed out in the introduction written by Paul M. Angle.

43. For recent treatments on Lincoln's law practice, see John J. Duff, *A. Lincoln: Prairie Lawyer* (New York: Rinehart & Company, 1960); John P. Frank, *Lincoln as a Lawyer* (Chicago: Americana House, 1991); Mark E. Steiner, *An Honest Calling: The Law Practice of Abraham Lincoln* (DeKalb: Northern Illinois University Press, 2006); Brian Dirck, *Lincoln the Lawyer* (Urbana: University of Illinois Press, 2007); Roger Billings and Frank J. Williams, eds., *Abraham Lincoln, Esq.: The Legal Career of America's Greatest President* (Lexington: University Press of Kentucky, 2010); Guy C. Fraker, *Lincoln's Ladder to the Presidency: The Eighth Judicial Circuit* (Carbondale: Southern Illinois University Press, 2012). See particularly, Stowell, *The Papers of Abraham Lincoln: Legal Documents and Cases.*

44. See David Zarefsky, *Lincoln, Douglas, and Slavery: In the Crucible of Public Debate* (Chicago: University of Chicago Press, 1990).

9. The Coming of Age

1. *Johnson v. Barber*, 10 Ill. (5 Gilm.) 425 (1849); *Armstrong v. Cooley*, 10 Ill. (5 Gilm.) 509 (1849).

2. *Chicago and Mississippi Railroad v. Patchin*, 16 Ill. 198 (1854).

3. *Chicago, Burlington, and Quincy Railroad v. Payne*, 49 Ill. 499 (1869).

4. 49 Ill. 499 at 503.

5. *Calumet Iron and Steel Co. v. Martin*, 115 Ill. 358 (1886).

6. 115 Ill. 358 at 370.

7. See the very informative discussion by Ernest A. Turk, "Comparative Negligence on the March," *Chicago-Kent Law Review* 28 (1949–1950): pp. 189–245, 305–46.

8. 16 Ill. 198 at 204.

9. *Great Western Railroad v. Thompson*, 17 Ill. 131 (1855).

10. *Central Military Tract Railroad v. Rockafellow*, 17 Ill. 541 (1856).

11. *Genessee Chief et al. v. Fitzhugh et al.*, 53 U.S. (12 How.) 443 (1851).

12. *People v. City of St. Louis*, 10 Ill. (5 Gilm.) 351 (1848).

13. "Joint Resolution Relative to the Construction of a Dyke in the Mississippi River opposite the City of St. Louis," *Laws of Illinois* (1849), pp. 238–29.

14. See Davidson and Stuve, *History of Illinois*, pp. 558–61. Today, Bloody Island is part of East St. Louis. Illinoistown, too, is now part of East St. Louis.

15. "An Act to Amend Chapter 102, Revised Statutes, entitled 'Steamboats,'" 16 February 1857, *Laws of Illinois* (1857), pp. 105–7.

16. *Loy v. Steamboat F. X. Aubury*, 28 Ill. 412 (1862) at 415.

17. Carlton J. Corliss, *Main Line of Mid-America: The Story of the Illinois Central* (New York: Creative Age Press, 1950), p. 63.

18. See generally, James W. Ely Jr., *Railroads and American Law* (Lawrence: University of Kansas Press, 2001).

19. The first practical steam turbine was built in 1884 by Charles A. Parsons.

20. See James D. Heiple, "Legal Education and Admission to the Bar: The Illinois Experience," *Southern Illinois University Law Journal* 12 (Fall 1987): pp. 123–51.

21. See Roscoe Pound, *The Formative Era of American Law* (Boston: Little, Brown and Company, 1938), pp. 81–137; James Willard Hurst, *The Growth of American Law* (Boston: Little, Brown and Company, 1950), pp. 85–89.

22. Pound, *The Formative Era of American Law*, p. 53.

23. "An Act to Create the County of Gallatin out of the Counties of Gallatin and Saline," 11 February 1851, *Laws of Illinois*, (1851): pp. 28–29. See also *People ex rel. Stephenson v. Marshall* (L00933), Benner and Davis, eds., *Law Practice of Abraham Lincoln: Complete Documentary Edition*.

24. Illinois Constitution (1848), Art. VII, Sec. 2.

25. *People ex rel. Stephenson v. Marshall*, 12 Ill. 391 (1851) at 394.

26. *O'Leary v. County of Cook*, 28 Ill. 534 (1862) at 541–42. The quotation is from Justice Sidney Breese's dissenting opinion.

27. "An Act to Relieve the People of this State from the Payment of Exorbitant and Unnecessary Taxes," 24 April 1861, *Laws of Illinois* (1861), pp. 208–9.

28. *People ex rel. Merchants' Savings, Loan & Trust of Chicago v. Auditor of Public Accounts*, 30 Ill. 434 (1863).

29. 30 Ill. 434 at 444.

30. See Michael F. Holt, *The Rise and Fall of the American Whig Party: Jacksonian Politics and the Onset of the Civil War* (New York: Oxford University Press, 1999); and William E. Gienapp, *The Origins of the Republican Party 1852–1856* (New York: Oxford University Press, 1987).

31. Paul M. Angle, ed., *Created Equal?: The Complete Lincoln Douglas Debates of 1858* (Chicago: University of Chicago Press, 1958), p. 393.

32. See Harold Holzer, *Lincoln at Cooper Union: The Speech That Made Abraham Lincoln President* (New York: Simon & Schuster, 2004).

33. *Ex Parte Milligan*, 71 U.S. (4 Wall.) 2 (1866).

34. Arthur Charles Cole, *The Era of the Civil War, 1848–1870* (Springfield: Illinois Centennial Commission, 1919), p. 181. See also "People ex rel. Lanphier and Walker v. Hatch," in Stowell, eds., *The Papers of Abraham Lincoln: Legal Documents and Cases*, Vol. 4, pp. 64–91.

35. "An Act to Provide for Calling a Convention to Amend the Constitution of the State of Illinois," 24 April 1861, *Laws of Illinois* (1861), pp. 84–87.

36. Cole, *The Era of the Civil War*, p. 299.

37. *Marbury v. Madison*, 5 U.S. 137.

38. *People ex rel. Harliss v. Hatch* and *People ex rel. Keyes v. Dubois*, 33 Ill. 9 (1863).

39. 33 Ill. 9. (The two cases are reported together.)

40. See Howard, *Mostly Good and Competent Men*, pp. 100–110.

41. 33 Ill. 9 at 27. The full-length biography of Fuller ably presents the picture of an Illinois lawyer of this period in practice and in local and national politics. Willard L. King, *Melville Weston Fuller: Chief Justice of the United States, 1888–1901* (New York: The Macmillan Company, 1950).

42. 33 Ill. 9 at 138.

43. *Okanogan et al. v. United States*, 279 U.S. 655 (1929).

44. 33 Ill. 9 at 150.

45. See Cole, *The Era of the Civil War*, pp. 290–311.

46. Cole, *The Era of the Civil War*, pp. 302–3. See also Mark E. Neely Jr., *The Fate of Liberty: Abraham Lincoln and Civil Liberties* (New York: Oxford University Press, 1991), and Frank L. Klement, *The Copperheads in the Middle West* (Chicago: University of Chicago Press, 1960); Jonathan W. White, *Abraham Lincoln and Treason in the Civil War: The Trials of John Merryman* (Baton Rouge: Louisiana State University Press, 2011).

47. See Gene Edwin Arnold, "Without Due Process: Madison Y. Johnson and the Civil War," master's thesis, DePaul University, 1967.

48. *Johnson v. Jones, et al.*, 44 Ill. 142 (1867).

49. 44 Ill. 142 at 165–66.

50. The best discussion of these problems is that of James G. Randall, *Constitutional Problems under Lincoln* (Urbana: University of Illinois Press, 1951). Also see Daniel Farber, *Lincoln's Constitution* (Chicago: University of Chicago Press, 2003).

51. Ernest Ludlow Bogart and Charles Manfred Thompson, *The Industrial State, 1870–1893* (Springfield: Illinois Centennial Commission, 1920), pp. 22–23.

52. Illinois Constitution (1870), Art. VI, Sec. 4.

53. Palmer, *The Bench and Bar of Illinois*, Vol. 1, pp. 458–59.

54. Palmer, *The Bench and Bar of Illinois*, Vol. 1, pp. 55–60.

55. Palmer, *The Bench and Bar of Illinois*, Vol. 2, pp. 969–70.

56. Palmer, *The Bench and Bar of Illinois*, Vol. 1, p. 60.

57. The story of the development of the Illinois Central is well told in Corliss, *Main Line of Mid-America*.

58. See generally Solon Justus Buck, *The Granger Movement: A Study of Agricultural Organization and its Political, Economic, and Social Manifestations, 1870–1880* (Lincoln: University of Nebraska Press, 1963); and Thomas R. Pegram, *Partisans and Progressives: Private Interest and Public Policy in Illinois, 1870–1922* (Urbana: University of Illinois Press, 1992), pp. 25–40.

59. "An Act to Regulate Public Warehouses, and the Warehousing and Inspection of Grain, and to Give Effect to Article Thirteen of the Constitution of this State," 1 July 1871, *Laws of Illinois* (1871): pp. 762–73.

60. *Munn v. People*, 94 U.S. 113 (1876).

61. Palmer, *The Bench and Bar of Illinois*, Vol. 2, p. 728.

62. *Slaughterhouse Cases*, 83 U.S. (16 Wall.) 36 (1872); see also Kermit L. Hall, ed., *The Oxford Companion to the Supreme Court of the United States* (New York: Oxford University Press, 1992), pp. 789–91.

63. *Bradwell v. Illinois*, 83 U.S. (16 Wall.) 130 (1872).

64. *Munn, et al. v. People*, 69 Ill. 80 (1873) at 85.

65. 69 Ill. 80 at 89.

66. 69 Ill. 80 at 94–103.

67. 69 Ill. 80 at 92.

68. 69 Ill. 80 at 92.

69. 94 U.S. 113; *Chicago, Burlington and Quincy Railroad v. Iowa*, 94 U.S. 155 (1876); *Peik v. Chicago and Northwestern Railroad*, 94 U.S. 164 (1876); *Chicago, Milwaukee, and St. Paul Railroad v. Ackley*, 94 U.S. 179 (1876); *Winona and St. Peter Railroad v. Blake*, 94 U.S. 180 (1876); *Stone v. Wisconsin*, 94 U.S. 181 (1876).

70. See Bruce R. Trimble, *Chief Justice Waite, Defender of the Public Interest* (Princeton, NJ: Princeton University Press, 1938).

71. See Gustavus H. Robinson, "The Public Utility Concept in American Law," 41 *Harvard Law Review* (January 1928): p. 277.

72. *Nebbia v. People of the State of New York*, 291 U.S. 502 (1934).

73. Breese's approach may be compared to the ad hoc treatment of problems of substantive due process by the Supreme Court of the United States after 1925.

74. 83 U.S. 130.

75. See Jane Friedman, *America's First Woman Lawyer: The Biography of Myra Bradwell* (Buffalo, NY: Prometheus Books, 1993), pp. 17–33; John A. Lupton, "Myra Bradwell and the Profession of Law: Case Documents," *Journal of Supreme Court History* 36 (No. 3, 2011): pp. 236–63.

76. *In re Bradwell*, 55 Ill. 535 (1869) at 542.

77. 83 U.S. 130 at 139.

78. 83 U.S. 130 at 141.

79. 83 U.S. 130 at 142.

80. Palmer, *The Bench and Bar of Illinois*, Vol. 1, p. 139.

81. Palmer, *The Bench and Bar of Illinois*, Vol. 1, p. 140.

82. Scholfield told some of his intimates that "he would give his good right arm to be Chief Justice of the United States, but that he couldn't take his wife to Washington. She was a woman of sterling worth but of frontier habits; she went barefoot in the summer." King, *Melville Weston Fuller*, p. 107.

83. Palmer, *The Bench and Bar of Illinois*, Vol. 1, p. 61–63.

84. Palmer, *The Bench and Bar of Illinois*, Vol. 1, pp. 68–69.

85. Palmer, *The Bench and Bar of Illinois*, Vol. 2, p. 1196.

86. Palmer, *The Bench and Bar of Illinois*, Vol. 1. p. 71.

87. See the biographical sketch of Judge Phillips in Newton Bateman and Paul Selby, eds., *Historical Encyclopedia of Illinois* (Chicago: Munsell, 1900), p. 423.

88. See Harry Barnard, *Eagle Forgotten: The Life of John Peter Altgeld* (Indianapolis, IN: Bobbs-Merrill Company, 1938), pp. 96–114. See also James Green, *Death in the Haymarket: A Story of Chicago, the First Labor Movement and the Bombing that Divided Gilded Age America* (New York: Anchor Books, 2007).

89. Palmer, *The Bench and Bar of Illinois*, Vol. 2, pp. 650–51.

90. *Spies, et al. v. The People*, 122 Ill. 1 (1887).

91. See Mark A. Plummer, *Lincoln's Rail Splitter: Governor Richard J. Oglesby* (Urbana: University of Illinois Press, 2001), pp. 190–201.

92. Barnard, *Eagle Forgotten*, pp. 183–259.

93. Breese, Caton, Scholfield, and Cartwright, in particular, possessed judicial insight entitling them to first rank among state court judges.

Index

Italicized page numbers indicate figures.

Clay, Henry, 78
Clement, Catherine, 10
Cleveland, Grover, 203
codification movement, 107–8. *See also*
Revised Code of Laws of 1827 and 1829
Coles, Edward, 90, 97, 113, 115, 133
Coles v. County of Madison, 115
Common Law: adapted to frontier, 68, 69,
74–75, 129, 149–52; as basic system of
law, 38, 40, 43, 45, 48, 56, 99, 154, 169,
182, 200; beginning of, 25; differences
from Custom of Paris, 16–17, 40; lawyers
trained in, 49, 83, 154, 181; reception
statutes, 75, 93, 151–52; reluctance in
accepting, 38, 75, 80–81, 88, 144; similarities to Custom of Paris, 8, 13–14
constitution. *See* Illinois Constitution
(1818); Illinois Constitution (1848);
Illinois Constitution (1870)
constitutional convention: of 1818, 86–87,
88, 110; of 1823, 103, 104; of 1847, 154; of
1862, 187; of 1869, 165, 196
Cook, Burton C., 97, 199
Cook, Daniel Pope, 76, 80, 94, 102, 119;
biography, 86
Cook, John, 94
Cornelius v. Boucher, 98
Cornell, David, 161
Council of Revision, 89–90, 99, 100, 108, 153
coureurs de bois, 2, 4, 5, 51, 73
court as theater, 76, 127
Court of Appeals for Illinois Territory,
52, 66–67
Court of Common Pleas (Northwest
Territory), 37, 38, 45, 59, 80, 83
Cowles, Alfred, 76
Cox, Thomas, 54, 55, 56
Craig, Alfred M., 196, 202
Craig et al. v. State of Missouri, 118
criminal justice: in British period, 20–21;
in French period, 8, 9, 10, 43; in Illinois,
108, 193; in Illinois Territory period,
51, 57, 69; murder cases, 46, 51, 55, 6,
103–4, 118; in Northwest Territory
period, 37, 44, 45
Cumberland Road, 124, 229n3
Curry, Sarah, 68–69

Custom of Paris: as basic law, xvi, 6, 10, 13,
14–15; differences from Common Law,
16–17, 40; end of, 49; similarities to Common Law, 8, 13–14; vestiges of, 25, 41, 74

Danville, Illinois, 126, 203
Darneille, Isaac, 48, 80, 223n36
Davidson, Karen, ix
Davis, David, 156, 171–72, 194
Davis, Levi, 121
Davis, Thomas Terry, 47, 85
Decatur, Illinois, 126
Denning, William, 142, 156
Detroit, Michigan, 4, 21
Dickey, T. Lyle, 203
disbarment, 118–19
divorce, 68
Dodge, John, 38
Douglas, Stephen A., 134, 136, 173; as an
attorney, 122, 172; biography, 131–33;
embodiment of Illinois, 148–49; Illinois
Central Railroad, 166, 194; opinions
written by, 132, 144; political activity,
137, 142, 165, 166, 172–73, 185–86; on
Supreme Court, 123
Doyle, Benjamin H., 223n36
Duberger, Forget (priest), 220n4
Dubuque, Julian, 91
Ducharme, Charles, 36
Dudevoir, Anne, 14
dueling, 61, 104
Dumoulin, Jean 37, 45
Duncan, James M., 95
Duncan, Joseph, 121
Dunlap, James, 50–51, 57, 61

Easton, Rufus, 48, 55–56, 85, 223n36; in
assault suit, 69; leader of Illinois bar,
77, 80; in libel suit, 68
East St. Louis, Illinois, 4, 177–78
Edgar, John: biography, 59; home in Kaskaskia, 50, 101; as judge, 37, 45; land fraud
claims, 58–59, 126; in libel case, 62, 68;
merchant, 28, 38; owned indentured
servant, 233–35n28
Edgar-Morrison faction, 59–60, 61, 78,
92, 101, 102, 119

ROGER L. SEVERNS (1906–61) earned degrees from Beloit College and Chicago Kent College of Law and earned his juris doctor degree in 1938 from the University of Chicago Law School. Severns taught law at Chicago Kent College of Law and practiced law at the firm of Isham, Lincoln, and Beale before leaving that firm to form Parkhill, Severns, and Stansell.

JOHN A. LUPTON is the director of history programs at the Illinois Supreme Court Historic Preservation Commission. He was an assistant editor of *The Papers of Abraham Lincoln: Legal Documents and Cases* and has written articles and chapters about legal history and Abraham Lincoln.